By MAURICE SAMUEL

LEVEL SUNLIGHT

(*1953*)

THE DEVIL THAT FAILED

(*1952*)

THE GENTLEMAN AND THE JEW

(*1950*)

PRINCE OF THE GHETTO

(*1948*)

WEB OF LUCIFER

(*1947*)

HARVEST IN THE DESERT

(*1944, 1945*)

THE WORLD OF SHOLOM ALEICHEM

(*1943*)

THE GREAT HATRED

(*1940*)

THESE ARE *Borzoi Books,*
PUBLISHED BY *Alfred A. Knopf* IN NEW YORK

Level Sunlight

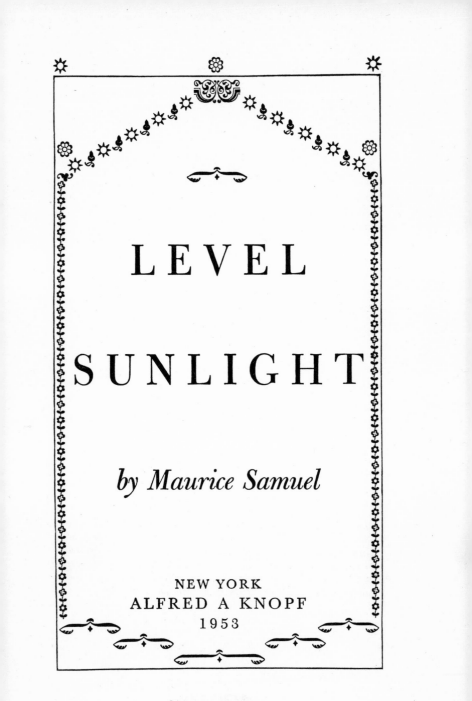

LEVEL

SUNLIGHT

by Maurice Samuel

NEW YORK
ALFRED A KNOPF
1953

956.9
S 193 l

L. C. catalog card number: 53–9475

THIS IS A BORZOI BOOK,
PUBLISHED BY ALFRED A. KNOPF, INC.

FIRST EDITION

42010

T O

Meyer W. Weisgal

WITH FORTY YEARS OF FRIENDSHIP

Advice to the Reader

THE STRUCTURE of this book is somewhat irregular, and the reader is entitled to a word of guidance before he enters on it. My themes, in order of importance—though not of treatment—are: the State of Israel, its evolution, present condition, and promise; the relation between Israel and world Jewry—therefore principally American Jewry; the role that Chaim Weizmann played in Zionism and Jewish history generally. The personal element in the writing is, I hope, something more than an emotional necessity; my philosophy of Jewish life, my contacts with Weizmann and other Zionist leaders, my experiences in Israel and America, my views on America, on communism, on science, on anti-Semitism, are also intended as a frame of reference. If they interfere with the formal objectivity of the book, they should also provide their own corrective. Nor do I pretend to be wholly objective except as to facts; for this book is, as much as anything else, a universal study in Ideal and Realization, and in such a study interpretation is everything.

MAURICE SAMUEL

✤ ix ✤

Contents

✤

CHAPTER		PAGE
I	Morning and Evening	3
II	Refuge or Renaissance?	15
III	The Chalutzim	35
IV	We Didn't Plan It This Way	51
V	Winds of Change	78
VI	In Process of Time	94
VII	After the Stampede	108
VIII	The World Division	121
IX	The Future of the Kibbutz	133
X	Multitude	148
XI	Histadrut	166
XII	"I Choose to Believe"	187
XIII	The Sundering	197
XIV	Tug of War	214
XV	The Generations Between	229
XVI	A New Perspective	242
XVII	America and Anti-Semitism	253
XVIII	If Thou Forget Me, O Jerusalem	264
XIX	The Democracy of Science	275
XX	The Summing Up	292
	Index	follows page 303

Level Sunlight

CHAPTER I

Morning and Evening

I

THE room in which I have been ordering my thoughts during the last month has three windows to the north and one to the east. The northern windows look out on an undulating plain of field and orchard, a panorama of fruitfulness and peace. At my feet begins the village of Ness Zionah; beyond it, red clusters on a green background, stretches the townlet of Rishon-le-Zion. Before the single eastern window the garden dips sharply to a little valley, the further side of which, heavily mantled with orange groves, ascends to a rounded hilltop and a palisade of cypresses. Toward the middle of the skyline arc, in a break of the trees half a mile away, rises a white house dominated by a massive, fluted cylinder, which forms its centerpiece. The flag of the State of Israel floats over the house, and within, in a room of whispering anxieties, lies the first President of the State of Israel, an old man mortally sick these many months.

I wake up regularly in the second half of the night and wait for the signal of the birds. As soon as I hear it I slip out of bed and stand at the eastern window. The hill, the cypresses, the house, the flag, are a solid black silhouette against the first pallor of morning. I think of an enormous mausoleum, of generations in defile across the landscape, and of the profit of a man's labor under the sun. After a while I turn round to the northern windows. There, in a bluish, dewy glimmer, the fields and orchards north and west are awakening. The jackals that lamented in the vineyards through the night are silent; the first thin twitter of the birds gathers into a joyous mass salutation; the cool dawn wind carries the fragrance of the waiting harvests across the plain. I look alternately right and left—at the silhouette of death in the east, the panorama of awakening life in the west: the mausoleum and the harvest.

All day long, with shutters rolled down against the blinding sunlight, I work on my notes, the accumulation of many years, and on my memories, recent and remote. It is a kind of retreat. Sometimes, deep-sunk in pursuit of a far-off incident, I forget to go down for my meals. Sometimes I evoke the past so vividly that I cannot keep pace with the impressions. I want everything to come out at once, because everything deserves first place; and I start away from my desk in a burst of impatience. And sometimes I give up with a sigh; I shall never finish.

Toward evening I roll up the shutters. Now the sunlight pours tumultuously from the west over field and grove and orchard. Rishon-le-Zion and Ness Zionah, the plain as far as the invisible Sharon in the north and the wilderness in the east, are flooded with radiance; and now the house among the cypresses, seen from the eastern window, is a white splendor on a green-gold hill. It is level sunlight again, but evening instead of morning, and the landscape is illumined from the opposite quarter of the heavens.

II

I was very young when Chaim Weizmann came into my life, to assume by degrees a role that I could not then anticipate and of which he was never quite aware. I stood then in the level sunlight of morning, and he was in the noon of his superb manhood. I am now about to enter on my seventh decade, and he is dying on the threshold of his ninth. I stand in the level sunlight of evening and glance back along the foreshortened years.

An era—my era—is dying with Weizmann, and he was the symbol of one of its most remarkable episodes. He was, no less, the central figure in my dominant life interest. Except for a brief aberrant period the entire interval between my boyhood and my imminent old age has unrolled in the movement that he represented, and though I shall perhaps survive him by a few years, my usefulness, such as it is, will continue to derive from the days of my discipleship. It was not a formal discipleship, for he was not a formal teacher; his wisdom, though often unforgettably phrased, was the wisdom of being and action. What he said, and what he did, and what he was all went together, and all of it is inseparable from his age and his role in it. His spiritual craftsmanship is written into many lives, of which mine is one; and I cannot write about my relationship to Zionism without writing more about him, or about his relationship to the movement without writing more about it.

His personality was not to be understood as a thing in itself. Beyond his conscious and self-conscious leadership, beyond his patient and farsighted self-preparation, beyond his ambitious understanding of his place in Jewish history, there was a congruence not of his devising between him and his mission. He would have been a conspicuous figure in any age and any society; but in his time and place he achieved that perfection of fulfillment which is impossible without the co-operation of Destiny. I shall refer often to particular gifts, or to special insights which he displayed. When they are added up, they fall short of what he was because I cannot include the coefficient of history. It is misleading to say of Weizmann that he was a Zionist. He was Zionism.

Something more than the verbal identification "Weizmann-Zionism" must be understood here, and something more than the sublimation of the man in the movement. In an extraordinary sense the movement became sublimated in him. Zionism used him for some of its most striking effects. I pondered on this the last time I visited him: the soaring house on the hill, the flag flying above it, the gardens surrounding it, the sentinels at his gate, the uniformed armed men that guarded it, the honor that rested on it—all declared to be real, palpable, and undeniable the folk fable of the little Jewish boy of the east European ghetto who dreamed of the resurrection of the Jewish State after an interlude of two thousand years—dreamed of it, determined to bring it into being, and lived long enough to become its first President. And lest "dreamed" be taken here as a figure of speech, albeit a permissible one, let it be recorded that a letter still exists which the boy Chaim Weizmann, of Pinsk, Russia, aged eleven, wrote to his Hebrew teacher in the Hebrew tongue, to foretell—this in the year 1885—that the Jewish State would come in his, the boy's, lifetime, and that England would have much to do with the event.

True, given a Jewish State, who should be its first President but the man whose name had become synonymous with Zionism? But we are taking too much for granted. The man who was the foremost representative of Zionism to the world—first, without a second—was born in the Pale of Settlement, the compulsory ghetto of Czaristic Russia, and did not leave it until his nineteenth year. He was par excellence the east European Jew, the product of the classic traditions of the ghetto. It was he, and not a Louis D. Brandeis, or an Israel Zangwill, or a Baron Edmond de Rothschild, or a Stephen S. Wise, products of the West, who placed on Western statesmanship the stamp of Zionism. The language Weizmann spoke best till the end was Yiddish; his wit was Yiddish, of Sholom Aleichem's world; his mental idiom was Yiddish. In a mystic way, Zionism chose a ghetto Jew, a child of the oppressed areas, through whom to demonstrate its transforming powers. For Zionism made of Weizmann the most magnificent Jew of his time.

The perfect co-operation between this individual and Destiny is illustrated by his preparation for the role of President of the reborn state. Destiny prepared him and he prepared himself, and we cannot tell where the work of one ends and the work of the other begins. Certainly we must say that Destiny gave him his personality and pres- ence—both obviously pointed at a high purpose. But we are tempted to add that it was the man himself who con- sciously built this house on the hill, so obviously meant to be the residence of the head of a state. I doubt whether it was as self-conscious as that. But even if it was, we would have to ask: where did he get the sense of form, this ghetto boy, the feeling of congruence between the substance and the meaning?

I shall have much to say about Weizmann's sense of form, which manifested itself subtly and persistently throughout his life. It was part of his mastery of the West. He was, in fact, much more Western than I, who grew up in the use and love of the English language. If English literature had a more organic place in my life than his, he had mastered the scientific mode of the Western world in a way quite beyond my capacities. He was all Western, while I was only English-Western. Yet nothing had been lost or denatured of the folk-Jewishness that was his invet- erate self. He was the assimilating Jew in reverse action:

he had assimilated the best of the Western discipline, remaining himself. Until I learned to know Weizmann, I had never considered the possibility of such a phenomenon.

III

I first met him in 1911 when, at the age of sixteen, I entered Manchester University. It was a fleeting contact, and tén years passed before a personal bond was created between us. In the interim I became a Zionist, finding my way back to my people after sojourning briefly with rationalism, Marxism, atheism, mechanism, positivism, and nihilism. My first teacher after the transition was Shmarya Levin, remembered by the older generation of Zionists as a man of dazzling oratorical gifts and profound Jewish feeling. But Levin, for all his superior equipment, was too much like me, with a bias toward speculation for its own sake. He helped me greatly in three ways. His brilliant Yiddish provoked me to a systematic study of the language. Like Weizmann and many other Zionists of pre-Herzlian origin, Levin was a disciple and friend of the philosopher Achad Ha-Am; and so, in studying Achad Ha-Amism (a special interpretation of Jewish history and Zionism) I had the benefit of the oral tradition, which was already flourishing during Achad Ha-Am's lifetime. Finally, Levin introduced me to something altogether new—something I had not even heard of—the intellectual life of the Jewish masses of eastern Europe. My first professional Jewish work was translating Levin's articles from Yiddish into English; and my Zionist speeches of the time were, I think, largely restatements of his.

Chaim Nachman Bialik, the greatest Hebrew poet of a thousand years, was a second influence preceding Weizmann's. Bialik, the friend of Shmarya Levin and of Weizmann, was like them a disciple of Achad Ha-Am; and my first translations from the Hebrew were of Bialik's poems. But while, by a piece of good luck, I was able to cultivate a friendship with Levin when I came to America in 1914, I did not meet Bialik until ten years later, at the time of my first visit to Palestine. Thus, when Weizmann came strongly into my life, I was already set in my permanent practical interests: I wanted to have some part in the creating of the Jewish homeland; I had discovered the treasuries of modern Yiddish and Hebrew literature, and I planned to make part of them available to English readers. It seems, then, that my life would have been much the same if I had never known Weizmann. The truth is quite otherwise.

I cannot imagine that without Weizmann I would have drifted out of Zionism, but I can imagine my Zionism becoming either chauvinistic (the lesser likelihood) or else passive and theoretical. Shmarya Levin, Chaim Nachman Bialik, and Achad Ha-Am helped me to relate Zionism to the whole course of Jewish history; Weizmann confirmed this relationship and added something vital: he showed me Jewish history working in the Jewry I knew. He converted the words "the Jewish people" from an idea into my parents, my uncles and aunts, my childhood memories.

Not that my childhood environment had been actively Zionist. There were, indeed, active Zionist circles in Manchester, and Weizmann was there from 1906 until 1917, teaching chemistry at the local university and playing a leading role in world Zionism. But our section of the ghetto—the Rumanian—was probably its most primitive and medieval. When I left it for America in 1914, it knew of the movement, but stood off in awe. Its unformulated, half-unconscious response was: "What have we to do with these high things?" I myself was not a Zionist at the time. I was—as I thought—not interested in remaining Jewish.

9

But when I had become a Zionist, and met Weizmann again, the impression he made on me was peculiarly intimate, as well as massive. I would have put it thus: "He speaks as my people would speak if it were articulate; he acts as it would act if it were awakened; he is what I want my people to become!"

He was drenched in Jewishness or, to use a homelier word, in *Yiddishkeit*. He knew the ghetto through and through—its weaknesses, sufferings, tricks of the mind, longings, stigmata; he also knew at first hand the everlasting sources from which ghetto life drew its nourishment —the Biblical memory and the dream of the restoration. Now in these respects he was not different in kind from many other men I have known; he differed in the perfection with which he had absorbed what was best in the non-Jewish world. A great many east European Zionist leaders had received a Western education, and could have made distinguished places for themselves in the West. With Weizmann it was more than education; it was organic absorption of form. And it is not enough to say that he could have risen to prominence in the Western world: he would in fact have been one of its foremost figures. This combination nevertheless presented itself as a perfect Jewish identity.

IV

It is almost a year since I have seen him, and it is not likely that I shall see him again among the living. Last summer I spent many evenings with him on the massive stone veranda of his house—more a rampart than a veranda. We sat looking across the fields of southern Judea at the mountains of Moab, ablaze and barren in the setting sun, he in his wheel chair, I at his side. He was already much too weak and tired to talk as he would have liked to. He listened eagerly, throwing in now and again a few half-inaudible words. He conserved his failing energies for occasional interviews with ministers of state and foreign representatives. But his mind was unimpaired, and he could be as incisive as in the old days. It was an awesome thing to reflect that in this exhausted suffering old man was embodied the most triumphant personal career of the twentieth century, and one of the strangest in history. In one sense the distinction of his career had only a common-place rarity. He belonged to a not unfamiliar type—libera-tors, statebuilders, "men of destiny." But in the range of his background, the vastness of the area from which he drew his purpose, he was unique. His beginnings were with Abraham in Ur of the Chaldees, and his political program could not be understood without reference to the plans of Moses and Isaiah; the communications with these origins, however, led hitherward through sixty generations of Jewish exile, so that Maimonides of North Africa, and the Baal Shem of the Carpathian Hills, the martyrs of the Crusades and of Chmelnitzky, were likewise a conscious part of him. His first contacts were with Russian Jewry; his later connections and experiences covered most of the Western world. He was by nature, and not with any special effort, at home with the Yiddish-speaking masses; he was equally at home negotiating with Arab princes; he was held in honor by the most honored statesmen, and he was a distinguished figure among scientists.

He was as timeless as the Bible, as topical as Winston Churchill. What personal fulfillment, in this or any other century, could compare with his? What triumphant career ranged so widely in time and space?

You were tempted to moralize, when you had seen him led off to bed, reluctant as a child: "This is Chaim Weiz-mann! Let envy look its fill!" You remonstrated with fate:

"Why could not this unparalleled life have been crowned fittingly with a hale old age? There's so-and-so, no younger than he, and certainly not as deserving, still vigorous and combative. There was this one and that one." He fought every step of the retreat; even now, bedfast many months, seeing no one but members of the family, conscious only a few hours a day, and even then not always himself, he will not accept the oncoming end. And the moralizing takes another turn: "He had every greatness except the greatness of resignation! What is he struggling for? Since he must go, let him go in peace."

These are trivial reflections. The death-tragedy of Chaim Weizmann the man, or what is left of him, has no bearing on the significance of his life. It would be just as superficial to point to his coffin and say: "Let envy look its fill." And his reluctance to go to his last long sleep was not, is not, a horror of death, a clinging to the flesh. Enormously as Weizmann enjoyed life, enormously as he suffered, his actions were not directed by his anticipated personal reactions. He rejoiced and suffered as the instrument of the Jewish people. What he could not bear, what he challenged as long as he could move his lips, was the annulment of his usefulness. As the end drew near, as the dismissal became more and more obviously irrevocable, the obsession grew on him: "I am being sent away when I am needed most."

He meant, of course: "It is just at this time of crisis in Israel that I should have been in my prime." But while a people can have many crises, a man can have only one prime, and we cannot doubt that the best of Weizmann's life—a long best, thank God—coincided with that long crisis of the first upbuilding for which it was predestined. Still, I believe with many others that if the Weizmann of twenty years ago had been with us today the crisis in Israel and world Jewry would be far less sharp, the prospects of recovery more immediate.

V

To a large extent this book is a justification of the preceding sentence. But it is not my purpose to lament the inevitable. Nor is my theme failure; it is rather the limitations and lessons of success. Moreover, I am concerned with the meaning of events, as well as with their substance. Contrasting the realities of the evening with the hopes and dreams of the morning, I shall also be stating a philosophy of Jewish life—my own, which was by no means identical with Weizmann's. But because he has been by far the greatest single influence in my own life, it is proper for me to begin, as I do, with a reference to the connection.

If I were to confine myself to the practical side of my dominant interest, I could say if I chose that I too have been a great success—in miniature. I attached myself forty years ago to a cause that was obscure, unintelligible, and despised. I have lived to see that which the intellectuals dismissed with contempt as "a historical absurdity" become a historical reality. I will not, of course, live long enough to hear them say: "How foolish we were"; but alas, it is simpler to win a battle than an argument. Still, I can report: "There is the Jewish State, member of the United Nations. It has fought its first war, and won it—against tremendous odds; it has absorbed nearly seven hundred thousand refugees; given reasonable help it will within a decade become a stable, self-supporting unit of civilization. My share in the building of the state has been a very small one, but it has been consistent, and it has formed part of my faith ever since I became a man. This I consider a successful life."

If I do not speak thus, it is because formal success is not enough. But what is enough? And what man has seen things work out the way he wanted them to? The very few—I am not among them—who can say with truth: "I did my best," are entitled to some satisfaction; but they are usually the last to enjoy it, for their nature is such that what matters to them is the result, not their merit. Weizman was certainly of those very few, and his dissatisfaction was as great as his achievement. This too will be explained in the following pages.

CHAPTER II

Refuge or Renaissance?

❀

I

WHEN war broke out between England and Germany in 1914—I was then nineteen—I saw no right and wrong in the struggle. I saw only economic forces at murderous play with deluded human masses. But to stay on in the England I loved and not enlist was only to make myself offensive to those I could not help, so I fled to America. When America joined in the war nearly three years later, I already saw considerable meaning in it. I therefore took out my first papers and was called up with the first draft. In three years a decisive change had taken place in my outlook.

I had ceased to believe that the spiritual motivation of man was fixed for him exclusively or even dominantly by the way he produced wealth. I had ceased to believe that all wars had to be interpreted exclusively as struggles for markets, or for sources of raw material, or for reserves of cheap labor. My steady absorption into Zionism and Jew-ishness had been accompanied by the increasing conviction that man was detaching himself from the animal or natural world, and that the process of detachment gave meaning to his existence.

I was also beginning to believe that in this vast process the most significant part had been played by the Jewish

Prophets; and to the extent that the Prophetic episode was incorporated in the Jewish people, or reinterpreted in Christianity, it was the dynamic element in Western civilization.

I saw the Western [1] world as the battleground of two concepts of ideal man: one of them Jewish, Prophetic, co-operative, Christlike, non-combative, non-competitive, and supremely hopeful; the other pagan, sportive, gallant, combative, honor-seeking, and supremely tragic.

These views I expressed crudely in *You Gentiles,* published in 1924, and more recently, with some improvement and additions, in *The Gentleman and the Jew,* published in 1950.

The hope of the world, it seemed to me in 1924—as it seems to me now—lies in the gradual recession of the pagan outlook and the gradual ascendancy of the Jewish and Christian outlook. I did not and do not believe that the Jews have a mission, in the sense that they were scattered throughout the world in order to teach or set an example. I did not believe that they were "better" than Christians. But I did believe that the non-pagan inspiration was better expressed in the body of Jewish doctrine and experience than in the doctrines and experiences of Christendom; I believed that the characteristic sin of the Jews was that of rebellion against the ideal, and the characteristic sin of the Christians that of misrepresentation of the ideal.

I believed further that, scattered as they are throughout the world, the Jews serve the good in so far as they exert themselves to incorporate the Jewish tradition in their way of life. Theoretically they can abandon this tradition to serve the good in other ways, but this very rarely happens. I also believed that the act of creating a Jewish home-

[1] Here Russia is included.

16

land, and the subsequent relations they would have with it, would help the Jews to hold on to the tradition.

I agreed wholeheartedly with the opinion of Lord Cecil, one of the founders of the League of Nations, that the two most important results of the First World War were the League of Nations and the projected Jewish homeland. These were to me expressions of aspiration toward a non-combative world, and instruments for its realization.

I believed that universal anti-Semitism, in its basic, folkloristic sense (as distinguished from local irritations) was the blind revolt of repressed paganism against the disciplines imposed in the name of Christ the Jew. I believed that anti-Semitism would last a long time, even after the establishment of a Jewish homeland, to disappear only when paganism ceased to masquerade as Christianity.

How much of the Zionist program did I hope to see completed within thirty-five or forty years? How much better did I expect the world to be at my life's end than at the beginning? To these naïve questions I can give only vague answers. I did not think I would live to see the proclamation of a Jewish State. Like most other Zionists —the great majority, I believe—I was not much concerned with the thought of a state as such until it became clear that the British Mandate over Palestine was being abused, and that without the freedom and instruments of statehood there was no possibility of continuing to build. What I expected of the Jewish homeland, what my hopes for it were, and what has actually come of it, will be set forth at length. As to the world at large, my illusions, disappointments, and continuing ideals were probably the same as those of millions of others who fought in the First World War and lived through the Second. But for me, and for many other Jews, there is a special meaning in the interplay between the world scene and the Jewish sector.

The grand central theme of human history is today interwoven with three fateful questions: Will our civilization continue to evolve toward higher forms? Will it be stamped out by totalitarianism of the left or right? Will it dissolve into chaos? To the extent that I did not understand the centricity of this all-human theme fifteen and twenty years ago, I did not know what faced the Jewish people everywhere, or the Jewish homeland in the making. As it happens, the problems of world Jewry and of Israel today are unintelligible except in connection with this theme. An entirely new set of co-ordinates must be applied —the co-ordinates of humanity's last choice.

II

Persecution has been called the motive power of Zionism, just as it has been held responsible for the survival of the Jewish people. My objection to this view is the same as my objection to the mechanistic concept of evolution. "This or that species *had* to develop such and such organs, otherwise it would not have survived," I was told. But no one told me why the species had to survive. And if persecution is enough to explain the survival of the Jewish people, there are other peoples of ancient days who should still be alive, and are not.

A challenge successfully met does not tell us where a people got the strength to meet it; and we shall not learn much by arguing whether the Jewish people would long ago have disappeared if it had not been persecuted. It is, however, instructive to observe that the Zionist movement was born in a period of comparative freedom from persecution (comparative by standards of long Jewish experience)—that is, around the middle of the nineteenth century. It was also a period of liberal illusions, even in

in addition to everything else, a political and moral setback for Palestine and the Jewish people, a *chillul ha-
Shem,* a desecration. Character alone had sustained the
Jewish people, character alone would build the Jewish
homeland properly. And while everyone would have agreed
with this statement, no one saw as profoundly as he (and
the Brandeisists hardly at all) that the Jewish homeland
would have no character, either in the moral or the de-
scriptive sense, would not even stand up in the physical
sense, if there were not brought into play, in the building
of it, the element of magic memory and of world meaning
then so much more alive in the Judaism of Pinsk than in
the Judaism of Washington; alive, but paralyzed by the
habits of the exile, and waiting to be stirred into action
by the Zionist appeal.

Character, quality, seriousness, reliability, craftsmanship
—these were obsessions with Weizmann, and he was forever straining to infect others with them. He knew only
too well the deficiencies of Jewish life; he knew also that
the will to overcome them had to be awakened by a renewed appeal to ancient and universal Jewish inspiration.
"Knew" is not an adequate description: he was himself the
perfect exemplification of what he wanted.

IV

Brandeis I had met as fleetingly as Weizmann, some
time before my enlistment. He had risen to sudden prominence in the Zionist world, a convert in his late fifties, and
he was later accused—in my opinion quite falsely—of having taken up Zionism in order to have a Jewish constitu-
ency, as it were, on being appointed by Wilson to the
Supreme Court. Brandeis was profoundly sincere in his
Zionist attachment, as the years were to prove. I saw him,
after my return to America, at two or three small, closed

meetings, and was struck by his single-mindedness: also by his complete inability to understand what the split in the Zionist movement was really about.

Nor was it something that the keenest intelligence, as such, could grasp; it was not a juristic or dialectical problem, it was not to be thrashed out in head-on debate. Expounding it to the reader, I must refer continuously to Zionist history, and to Weizmann's unique place in it.

There were three men whom Weizmann opposed throughout the years in Zionist leadership with all the weight of his personality and convictions. The first was Theodore Herzl, usually called the founder (I believe I am more correct in calling him the crystallizer) of political Zionism; the second was Louis D. Brandeis, by far the most distinguished American Jew to play a role in the movement; the third was Vladimir Jabotinsky, the brilliant Russian Jew who founded the Revisionist or ultra-nationalist wing of Zionism.

Herzl, who died in 1904 at the age of forty-four, was a gifted Viennese journalist who had grown up in casual contact with Judaism, and had had occasional and evanescent "ideas" about the Jewish problem. Witnessing at close range, as the representative of the *Wiener Neue Freie Presse,* the unrolling of the Dreyfus affair in Paris, he was seized suddenly with a vision, and went through a true "Saul-on-the-road-to-Damascus" experience. It came to him with the force—though not in the form—of a divine revelation that the solution of the Jewish problem lay in the creation of the Jewish State. His knowledge of Judaism, of Jewish history, of Messianic Jewish hopes, of the vast reservoirs of contemporary Jewish life in Russia, was fragmentary; he had not the remotest idea that there was already in existence a strong Zionist movement (not yet known by that name) and a Zionist literature. But the fury of the vision, and the dazzling appeal of his personality, placed him overnight at the head of the movement as he reorganized it through the first Zionist Congress, in 1897. So remote was Herzl from Jewish tradition that during the early phase of the "revelation" Palestine simply did not occur to him as the inevitable locale of the Jewish State to be. As far as he was concerned, it might as well be Timbuctoo. Even when he learned that these beggars were choosers, and nothing but Palestine would do for them, he had his own reservations, and by various phrases and proposals kept betraying his lack of rapport with the innermost forces of Judaism.

Thus, he looked to the *Judennot,* the misery of the Jews, to provide the great creative thrust. And just as it was the Dreyfus trial, and the anti-Semitic frenzy accompanying it, that set his Zionism in motion, so it was the Russian pogroms of 1903 that forced him, in a panic of need, to propose as the Zionist objective another territory than Palestine. Not Timbuctoo, to be sure, but another area in Northern Africa, namely, Uganda.

I was nine years old when Theodore Herzl died, in the midst of his struggle with the Zionists who threw back the Uganda offer that he had obtained from Joseph Chamberlain, the British Colonial Secretary. Weizmann, then thirty years old, was one of the leaders of that opposition and repudiation—the founder, too, of the Zionist Democratic Party, which later became practically synonymous with the Zionist Organization. I remember the black-bordered columns in the London Yiddish newspaper that my father took in, and the leonine Assyrian head of the dead leader. I remember, too, the pall of sadness, mingled with fright and incredulity, that descended on the household, and on our relatives. "Todor Herzl is dead!" In the seven or eight years of his Zionist career, years of mad labor and maddening frustration, Herzl had risen to the zenith of the Jewish firmament, a portent and a mystery. The masses worshipped him while he lived, deified him in his death, and did not understand him or respond to him. The Zionists too worshipped him—but they rejected his proposal to substitute Uganda for Palestine, even as a temporary measure in a time of great trouble.

Foremost among the opponents of the Uganda proposal were the pogromized Russian Jews; foremost among its protagonists were the Western Jews. Paradoxically enough, Herzl, in the safety of the West, suffered more profoundly from the pogroms than the Jews of Russia. *They* did not fly into a panic. Uganda *might* be more practicable than Palestine; England's was certainly a better government to deal with than the unfathomably corrupt Turk's; lives might indeed be saved by accepting Chamberlain's offer instead of continuing the endless, labyrinthine negotiations with the Sultan and his venal ministers. But, fantastic as it may sound, that was not the point. It was not need that drove the Jews toward Palestine. It might drive them somewhere else, but not toward Palestine, derelict, diseased, and despoiled. Need and panic were not creative forces. The admission of these motifs into Zionism meant a dilution of the ideal without which no Jewish homeland could be built anywhere; and the ideal, all-embracing as Jewish motif, meant the tradition, and therefore Palestine.

When Brandeis became a convert to Zionism the Uganda issue was of course dead; but not the spirit that had created it. For Brandeisism was Ugandism applied to Palestine. Brandeis was as sincere as Herzl; he was also as untuned to Jewish tradition. He showed it in his utilitarian view that Palestine could be built as a "practical proposition." It could not, of course. To envisage it merely as a practical proposition was to denaturize it. It could be built, it was built, only as an impractical proposition, by a people that had been impractical enough to go on existing for centuries when every consideration of practicality pro-

I am not averse to physical work, and I am not afraid of the simple life; but whatever interferes with a solid schedule of reading and writing becomes in a short time intolerable to me. I am not a bookworm; I have traveled a great deal, observed a great deal, mingled with people, enjoyed the world. But if I were prevented from breaking off any activity at will in order to pursue a line of study that suddenly appealed to me, or in order to work out, paragraph by paragraph, page by page, the presentation of a thesis, I would, I believe, fall sick. It has been so with me since I left school, and so it is now.

I have been drawn to, I have experimented with, other forms and materials; but my dominant interest for thirty years has been the essay on a Jewish subject, this book being typical. I have found moral satisfaction in spreading information on Jewish history, Jewish literature, Jewish folkways and ways of thought; in presenting as attractively and readably as I could the elements of Jewish problems; in pondering the nature of the relationship between the Jewish and the non-Jewish worlds. And since everybody is ready to psychoanalyze everybody else at the drop of a hat, I shall be told that my concern with the preservation of Judaism in the Diaspora was an identification of indulgence with duty: I rationalized my fear of the rigors of the Palestinian life and my hankering for the dollars and distinctions of a literary career. However that may be, I have always looked upon the building of the Jewish homeland as an enterprise to serve Jews who remained outside of it not less than those who went into it and became part of it. I have always felt that there would be needed channels of communication between the completed Jewish homeland and the Jewries scattered through the world. That the homeland in the making needed such intermediaries was obvious enough. That the need would continue when the task was completed—and it is not yet com-

pleted—occurred to few. Indeed, little attention was paid
to the ultimate implications of Zionism; or rather, no one
paused to consider Zionism in the total setting of Jewish
history and the Jewish future, to analyze it as a dynamic
process within which the creation of the Jewish homeland
was only a phase.

IV

There is on the surface a contradiction between what I
have written here on the Chalutzim and on Weizmann. Of
them I say: "I regarded theirs as the continuity of the essential Jewish morality," and of him: "Had he died before
his time I would have remembered him as the personifica-
tion of what I held to be the essential nature of Zionism."
Yet Weizmann was not a Chalutz; he was not even a
socialist. Until past the age of sixty he did not settle in
Palestine, though he paid frequent and extended visits.
Like myself, but in an infinitely larger measure, he had
creative needs that a life entirely rooted in Palestine would
have frustrated. It is perhaps proper to say that his greatest
creative need was to become the leader of world Jewry;
and this he could never have satisfied without spending
most of his time in the West, which harbored the effective
Jewish majority. Moreover he was by nature even more
incapable than I of the disciplines and abnegations which
the Chalutzim took upon themselves, the chief of these
being the submergence of the self, the surrender of privacy,
the complete renunciation of the graces and warmths of the
best kind of middle-class life.

In this last respect I was nearer to the Chalutzim than
he. I have always had a contempt for what is called
"gracious living." But whereas I once thought that my
contempt was purely moral in origin, I have since con-

cluded that some of it was rooted in æsthetic deficiency; I was lacking in plastic appreciation. It is still true that costly home surroundings repel me, even when they are in good taste. But at least I understand now that there is something more in them than ostentation or affectation. Weizmann, the man of form, was never guilty of my one-sidedness. He regarded as a grave fault the general indifference of the east European Jew to the discipline of form, whether it was due to ancient prohibitions or to recent privations in the history of the Jewish people, or to a mixture of the two. Moreover, he extended the idea of form beyond the plastic to the ceremonial. He was attentive to the choreography of courtesy, and to the tone of human contacts.

All the more meaningful, therefore, was his understanding for the Chalutzim of the collectivist movement, among whom my attitude toward "gracious living" dominated. Their rejection was not simply adaptation, the reflex of primitive conditions in which the simplest luxury was unthinkable, let alone "graciousness." They had rejected it on principle, as "bourgeois." And even simple luxury was suspect. But Weizmann was not alone in his understanding and sympathy. It was characteristic of the classic period of Zionism, the period of Weizmann's leadership, that the Chalutzim of the collectives were regarded by the majority of Zionists, of practically all shades, as the supreme manifestation of the Zionist will. The Chalutzim were a minority, a small minority, but they were in a congenial environment, both within the new Palestine and within the Zionist movement as a whole. In all this, however, Weizmann's role was more than representative. He was in part responsible for the protective atmosphere thrown about the kibbutzim, the moshavim, and labor generally.

The outspoken enemies of the kibbutzim came from various strata. There was an "old" Jewish Palestine side by side with the "new" Palestine. As late as the time of my first visit, in 1924, the pre-Zionist Jewish population in Palestine was still in the majority, largely untouched by the activating influences of Zionism. The religious groups that had come out in the early nineteenth century, which may be called proto-Zionist, had not produced any change in the lethargic ways of the earlier population. Settling in Hebron, Jerusalem, Safad, and Tiberias, the purely religious "Zionists" had themselves drifted into the Sargasso Sea of the old Jewish life. Among all of these, and particularly among those who lived on alms sent from Europe, the hostility to Zionism, and to the Chalutzim in particular, was implacable. The "irreligiousness" of the newcomers was more than an offense to the natives. It was an interference with their Messianic strategy. To begin with, the new type of work for Palestine might divert to secular and therefore worthless enterprises the money which had hitherto been devoted to the support of the pious; worse than that, however, the Messiah whom the old-timers had planned to attract with piety and prayer would assuredly be frightened off by the spades and shovels of the Godless.

All Zionists were anathema to the medieval and semi-medieval Jews of Palestine; the Chalutzim were however the chief targets of their resentment. But among the modern Zionists too the Chalutzim had their opponents. In 1925 Polish anti-Semitic legislation sent toward Palestine tens of thousands of Jews of the lower middle class, people unfit for pioneering in any sense, many of them quite indifferent to the social ideals of Zionism. Weizmann warned the movement against the importation of the Nalevkis (Warsaw's inner ghetto) into the new Palestine. He was denounced for leftist un-Jewishness. But he spoke for the majority feeling in the movement; and he was pursuing, with farsighted consistency, the policy of selection and education which he opposed to the indiscriminate stampede tendencies in the movement.

Again, opponents of the Chalutzim were to be found among the individualist settlers who had come to Palestine in the early days of modern Zionism, in the eighteen eighties and nineties, and had prospered in a modest way, helped by Baron Edmond de Rothschild and cheap Arab labor. And there had crept into the Zionist movement, even as far back as the eighties, a touch of panic, a view of Zionism as refugeeism, as a plan for taking care of the persecuted and the helpless. Increasing anti-Jewishness in eastern Europe was strengthening a Zionism that had nothing to do with renaissance, and was simply a natural scramble for survival, a tragic competition among unfortunates. It was the kind of Zionism which Weizmann had fought in the Uganda proposal. It was in its way the Zionism of Brandeisism and Revisionism. For though Brandeis and Jabotinsky wanted a self-supporting Jewish homeland or state (Jabotinsky thought only in terms of state), they did not think of Zionism as world-wide Jewish renaissance and Jewish homeland in organic oneness. So, for the Brandeisists the kibbutzim were unbusinesslike, hence a bad example to the Zionist movement, and a discouragement to the investment of private capital. The Revisionists regarded the kibbutzim as a mixture of childishness and dangerous Marxist anti-Jewishness. What they found hardest to bear was the contempt of the Chalutzim for the half-sinister, half-comical jingoism that the Revisionists developed in the Zionist movement.

Brandeisism was a passing phase, and Revisionism never attracted more than a minority. The Zionist movement as a whole was proud of the Chalutzim and the collectives. Even religious Jews, who were shocked by the ritualistic shortcomings of the Chalutzim, respected their idealism.

Well-to-do Jews of Europe and America and the few—the very few—wealthy ones who contributed to the Zionist funds, knew that a large proportion of the modest budget was allocated by the Zionist Congresses to the collectives and co-operatives. Most of the donors were content that it should be so. Those that were not submitted to the moral authority of the Zionist Congresses. A thoroughgoing reactionary like Baron Edmond de Rothschild (the late Republican Felix Warburg, also a contributor to the funds, was pinkish by comparison) was quite alert to what was going on; but like many others he contrived not to let his rightist hand know what his leftist hand was doing. He had helped create the individualist farmer type that opposed the Chalutzim; he now helped to establish the Chalutzim.

If we take the Zionist movement as a whole, with all its negative elements, its nationalist extremists, its anti-social adventurers, and its refugee misfits, it stands up as a remarkably affirmative phenomenon. And the rule may be laid down that its moral content, or charge, may be gauged by its attitude toward the kibbutzim and labor generally. It is proper to judge a city or community by the character of the elite which it respects without emulating it; in the same way it is also proper to judge a city or country by the amount of criminality which it tolerates, even if the great majority of citizens are perfectly honest. The kibbutzim are the barometer of Zionist morale, and the changes in their position will enable us to understand what has happened to the movement as a whole.

V

I am continuously aware of the danger of idealizing the past and so distorting the history of our development.

Therefore I do my best to call up an objective picture of the conditions from which we started out. But among these conditions not the least important was our state of mind. Concerning this, I draw upon personal memories and records.

We Zionists believed in those days that we really had a new form of life to give to the world; not the less new because ancient forces went into its making. Perhaps all the newer, in fact, because it was a unique blend of powerful tradition and modern techniques. Palestine was to be a Jewish contribution in the multiple and complicated development of civilization. It gripped us powerfully, this faith in the continued creative potency of the Jewish heritage; and we felt it was an extraordinary privilege to be associated with it.

True, Zionism was a minority movement among the Jewish people; but we were convinced that it represented the latent will of the majority. There were other minority movements in Jewish life, some genuine, having a goal and inspiring effort, others spurious, being only drift disguised as purpose. A genuine movement was the revolutionary leftist opposition to Zionism; a spurious movement was bourgeois assimilation. But on the whole the obstacle to active Zionism was inertia rather than hostility. My boyhood environment in Manchester was typical. My parents and relatives thought the Zionists wonderful people, but the enterprise was too awesome for simple folk. That Jews should return to their own land, and rebuild it; that Jews should actually become farmers—it was all too extraordinary. They were held fast in the paralysis of centuries. They waited for the Messiah. Even if not literally so, even if they were not complete pietists, they unconsciously waited for something cataclysmic to start off, to signalize, so tremendous a revolution in status and habit. "A great thing, a great thing," they said, somewhat dazed. They gave

49

their blessing, and the few pennies they could spare. But joining a movement was not for them. Jews did not belong to movements. Jews had protectors. The rich and powerful intervened for them, and God decided the issue. As for actually going to Palestine—that was for saints. Of settling on the land, though admittedly Jews should be farmers, they would not even speak. What? Isaac the shoemaker, and Berel the tailor, and Moishe the shopkeeper following the plow, like peasants? Yes, it was as alluring as the End of Days itself but it was also incredible—and slightly comical.

And so they approved, they admired, they wondered; they helped a little, and they watched. And from year to year the phenomenon became more familiar, from year to year their confidence in themselves, their people, and their future grew stronger. They saw evidence, in this effort, of the renewability of Jewish life; and they became increasingly a part of what they saw. *"Am Yisroel chai,"* they said. "The Jewish people lives."

And it was an altogether remarkable thing that this ancient organism called the Jewish people should have been able, at this juncture, to put forth the necessary effort for its own remaking; to produce a pioneering class as it were to order; and on the very brink of its dissolution in the oceans of modern life, to pull itself together, and reassert itself.

We were immensely optimistic; we refused to believe that such visions and emotions could be inspired by a fata morgana; we were confident that there was strength enough in the Zionist upsurge to overcome all the difficulties on our path. And we allowed for quite a number of them. Unfortunately—or was it fortunately?—we did not foresee the most important ones.

CHAPTER IV

We Didn't Plan It This Way

❀

I

I WOULD like to scotch once and for all the lie that is growing up in the Jewish world and elsewhere: that the pioneers of the kibbutzim and their supporters were slightly insane idealists who stumbled into achievement by a mixture of obstinacy and accident. The lie sometimes has a larger spread: the entire Zionist movement is sometimes looked on as a freak episode which sensible people don't have to account for. The corrective to the lie is of course a knowledge of the facts.

There was a good deal of conscious as well as instinctive shrewdness in the planning of the Zionist program. Mistakes were made, but they were such mistakes as practical people make. On the whole we were astoundingly successful colonizers and statebuilders, as the issue shows. The difficulties that today beset the Jewish State are not primarily the result of basic errors in the time of building. On the contrary, they are largely—not wholly—due to more or less compulsory deviations from the original principles of action, the result of unforeseeable events. The fact is that if the foundations had not been so well laid, these deviations would have ruined all the work of the past.

The collectivist-idealistic cast of the Chalutz mind was

itself a high practicality. No other form of life could have coped with the cruel condition of the early pioneering times. Call this, if you like, instinctive shrewdness. On the other hand, it was conscious shrewdness and farsighted calculation which directed the Zionist policy of land purchases. The areas were so chosen and spaced that they took an enclosing grip on the country, from Galilee down into the Valley of Jezreel, then round the Carmel and down the coastal Sharon Plain to southern Judea. If the buying was done irregularly, that was due to lack of funds, not of foresight.

It is not easy to classify the "strategic" meaning of the Jewish National Fund. This instrument of national policy was created by one of the early Zionist Congresses, in 1901. But its character was already outlined by the pre-Zionist or proto-Zionist Conference of Kattowicz in 1884. It called for public purchase of land as the inalienable property of the Jewish people—land to be leased to settlers, never sold, never thrown on the market. In short, nationalization by purchase. It was a genuinely idealistic measure, and it was inspired far more by the ancient Jewish relationship to the meaning of land than by modern single-tax or socialist theories. It took the Jewish National Fund a long time to get under way, and it did not acquire its first million dollars until after the First World War. But if there had not been this fund at the disposal of the movement, the strategic purchases could not have been made. Individual settlers or development companies would have bought land at random, according to individual calculation and competitive interest. Group settlements on strategically purchased areas would have been unknown; group action would have been stifled at its birth.

Was this accident, instinctive shrewdness, conscious shrewdness, the adaptation of a vigorous organism to its surroundings? It was a mixture of all four. Certainly it was down-to-earth practicality that impelled the idealistic, pacifist-minded Chalutzim to set up their own military self-defense. The Israeli army of today is the continuation of the Jewish self-defense of yesterday; the Jewish self-defense evolved out of the Shomer or Guard movement of the earliest labor settlements.

II

The idealism of the Zionist movement was not born of ignorance of the facts of life; and if certain events were not foreseen by the Zionist leaders, they were not foreseen, either, by practical men of affairs inside and outside of Jewish life.

We were always anxious to negotiate with the Arab world; and at one time we had grounds for believing that a mutually beneficial arrangement could be reached. That was in the days immediately following the First World War, when Feisal, the then undisputed leader of the Arab world, saw the advantage of a Jewish-Arab alliance, and offered to enter into one. Later he backed down. We believed in such an alliance, we saw it as part of our historic function. But we did not rely blindly on this possibility. We were aware that peoples do not always act on an intelligent perception of their own interests. And so we were prepared to fight. Of special significance is the fact that the idealistic kibbutzim were the reservoirs of our best fighting material. This was not an accident.

What we did not foresee was that, achieving the Jewish State, we would have to fight off seven Arab nations, outnumbering us in the proportion of thirty to one. Our army had been created more or less furtively, our equipment was makeshift, and even our last minute preparations were crippled by British interference. We also did not foresee what would be the political consequences of such an attack, and the internal psychological consequences of victory.

III

We were never so naïve as to think that the Jewish homeland would emerge smoothly, and of itself, from the joint efforts of the Mandatory Power and the Jews. Very soon after England was given the Mandate over Palestine, on the basis of her own Balfour Declaration, which called for the establishment of the Jewish homeland, we realized that there would be a lot of pushing and tugging and maneuvering between the occupying government and the Jews. Most of us believed in England's basic good will; that is, in the preponderantly favorable attitude of British public opinion. We knew however that there were conflicting opinions in England about the value of a Jewish homeland in the scheme of imperial interests. We knew that high British officials "on the spot," that is, in Palestine, could undo, if they were so inclined, much of the good intended by authorities at home. We knew that there would have to be "incidents"; perhaps there would be riots against British obstructionism. But it was not in our calculations that England would one day flatly repudiate the obligations she had assumed under the Balfour Declaration and the Mandate. We did not believe that a Tory government would do it; and quite inconceivable was the actuality: our having to fight for our lives against a British *Labour* government. For if the old British ruling class was deeply tinged with pro-Zionism of a semi-religious variety, the Labour Party had been with us—and furiously critical of Tory vacillation and repudiation—because of the social meaning of our work. And it was the Labour Party that, without the excuse of a Nazi threat hanging over England, continued, after the victory, the Near Eastern anti-Zionist policy of its Cairo experts, and condemned the Jewish homeland to destruction.

I am not putting it too strongly. We had reached a point at which anything less than the independence that we claimed, and which had been promised us—anything less than independence and the chance to organize our own defense—meant massacre by the Arabs.

This betrayal, coming upon us as it did after the horrors of Hitlerism, had a profoundly depressive effect on Zionist morality. It had not been in our plans, so to speak, to have an anti-British terrorist movement in Palestine. But it almost looked as if the British Labourites insisted on our having one. Their policy was apparently to drive us mad. It was as if they were saying: "Under no circumstances will we let you build your homeland in a decent spirit. You must prove first that you are good killers. That you are social idealists of our stripe is more or less irrelevant."

The wonder of it is that the terror, with its glorification of the killer, did not become a national movement among the Jews; and that it did not is testimony to the toughness of the Zionist ideal. The overwhelming majority of the Jews of Israel put their faith in the responsible people's resistance. But it is not to be denied that the cynicism of Ernest Bevin's anti-Israel policy had a deleterious effect on the moral standards of the Zionist movement.

The mere fact that social idealists like the British Labourites could play the low game of international intrigue without seeming to be conscious of turpitude was bad enough. It undermined the moral self-confidence of Zionist liberals—as of liberal opinion in all peoples—and it refreshed the cynicism of Zionist reactionaries. But the maneuver was directed against ideological "comrades-in-arms," against the forward-looking Jewish homeland whose praises the British Labourites had been singing for a generation. Therein lay the special sting. The results within the Zionist movement were not all immediately visible, nor can they always be traced back to their source. But among the disillusionments against which we must struggle today, amidst the damage we must repair, the effects of the British Labour default are not the least.

It cannot be doubted that part of the deterioration in the standards of the kibbutzim and of the labor institutions in Israel are the direct but concealed consequence of the betrayal by British labor. Perhaps the stupidity and futility of the betrayal should be mentioned, too; for the welching Labourites had not even the virtue of shrewdness. They tried to be Machiavellian villains and turned out to be shlimihls; whence it was made to appear in retrospect that even their earlier good intentions had been the product of incompetence rather than character.

In the general moral letdown that followed the Second World War, this particular incident occupies a place of its own. It did England no good, it did the world no good. For the Jews it was particularly harmful, most of all in the moral field. Here was another of the contingencies we had not reckoned with.

IV

Although we denied that Jewish persecution was the mainspring of the rebuilding of Palestine, we did not deny it a certain limited role. We feared the Jewish self-pity that lowered the moral standard of Zionism; we fought against the kind of Jewish "pride" which is a cover to self-hatred; but we knew that anti-Semitism had its part in activating Jews, and we tried to sublimate the reaction, to convert it from resentment and rancor, mixed with mendicancy, into an ideal worth following for its own sake.

That was a long struggle within the movement; and it will be seen, when I come to describe it at greater length, that we were not always successful. In fact, we were not always faithful to our principles, and often yielded to the lower motivation when we need not and should not have done so.

We were at all times prepared for sporadic resurgences of anti-Semitism; and we were at all times afraid of their moral effects on Zionism. I have cited instances of Weizmann's resistance to the panic councils that were inspired by desperation or impatience. But we were not prepared for, we did not reckon with, the mounting horror of the Nazi blood-madness, and the aftermath of frenzy in the masses of the Jews.

At first we did not recognize the Hitler threat as something new of its kind. We looked upon it as an extreme case of an all-too-familiar evil. Even so, the unexpectedness and the programmatic fury of the attack astounded us. This was not the random, epidemic malice of the Czarist regimes; it was not, either, the sporadic rage, part superstition, part greed, part animalism, of the medieval mobs. It had a consistency that made us tremble. Whether it was ready for this role or not, Palestine became the most important center of refugee relief. By 1934 and 1935 it was receiving a volume of immigration which threatened the structural stability of the homeland in the making. More disturbing was the threat to its spiritual stability, its morale, its power to continue evolving creatively and healthily. We were frightened by an influx of Jews who had previously abandoned their ties with their people in a systematic attempt to pass as non-Jews. They were a minority among the German Jewish and other Jews—but their numbers ran into thousands. The Jewish ideals to which they owed their physical rescue were repugnant to them. We were afraid that in a time of danger to the homeland they would side with our enemies. But there was no question of refusing asylum to any Jew who applied for it. We only hoped that, given the time, we would be able to absorb them spiritually as well as economically. This is in fact what came to pass. But we must bear in mind that in 1935 we admitted not more than some sixty-five thousand Jews—a fifth of the Jewish populational base. For the years 1934-5-6 the total proportion was about a third. But between 1948 and 1951, inclusive, we *doubled* the population of the Jewish State. Moreover, if among the newcomers in that earlier, smaller flood many were indifferent or hostile to our ideals and purposes, the general standards of education and intellectual adaptability were high. And as it happened, we were given a whole decade in which to assimilate this material. It occurred to none of us that this was only the beginning of the Hitler assault on the Jewish people and the Jewish homeland.

V

Ought we to include, among the developments we could not foresee or provide against, the East-West division of the world and its effects on Israel? At first it would seem that this is not one of the peculiarities of the Jewish situation. Nevertheless we have been affected in peculiar ways by the common totalitarian threat to civilization.

We suffered the first of a frightful series of calamities when the Communists cut off from world Jewry that section of it which was richest in Jewish tradition and most advanced in Zionist understanding and practice. Russian Jewry had given us Chaim Weizmann, Achad Ha-Am, Chaim Nachman Bialik, Shmarya Levin, and a host of others; later it had sent forth the younger generation of Chalutzim which today constitutes the leadership of Israel; it unquestionably had a third generation in hand for us, but this has been withheld by interdiction.

One of the reasons that kept the Chalutzim pro-Russian for a long time was their belief that the intolerance of communism was a passing phase; the dictatorship would relax, Zionism would be legalized in Russia, the vast reservoirs of Russian Jewry would be opened up for Palestine. It was hoped that the Jewish traitors of the Yevsektzia— the Russian Jewish Communist Party, more bitterly anti-Zionist than the general Communist Party—would relent. It was hoped, also, that Russia would see the injustice of making Palestine, Jewish Palestine, the innocent victim of her quarrel with England. In those days we were in fact neutral. If we were anti-Communist, we also had our quarrel with the British Empire. Only after a couple of decades did we finally understand—I exclude myself, as never having succumbed to any illusions—that the totalitarianism of Russia could not tolerate a movement like Zionism whatever the external political constellation, and that Russian Jewry had been doomed from the beginning to forcible assimilation.

Thus the first blow came from the totalitarian left; the second and third came from the totalitarian right. It would be truer to say that there were five or six blows. Rightist totalitarianism began by plundering and expelling German Jewry and placing a heavy burden on Palestine and the Zionist movement. It compelled Zionists to lower their sights, to think as philanthropists instead of as statebuilders and carriers of a renaissance. It gave a powerful impetus to world anti-Semitism, and weakened Jewish morale generally. It gave the upper hand to those British elements that were opposed to the fulfillment of the promise made in the Balfour Declaration. All this before the actual outbreak of the Second World War.

Then, with horrible acceleration, things happened that twisted us more and more from our original purpose. Maddening stories of Jewish mass annihilations in Nazi-held

Europe came through to us. Ships with illegal cargoes of escaping Jews wandered about the world, unable to make port because no port was open to them. The British navy hunted them down in the Mediterranean, and if one of them beached on the Palestinian shore the passengers were arrested and deported. The democratic nations, themselves imperiled, bade us wait until the successful close of the war.

The Zionist movement suffered further dilution and adulteration. Masses of Jews who had never given a thought—or a penny—to the Jewish homeland, suddenly declared themselves Zionists, or pro-Zionists. They brought into the movement, together with their donations, their indignation, and their pity for refugees, a wild mob spirit, and a complete ignorance of the great aims of Zionism. *We* had wanted the co-operation of the Jewish masses on another level.

This situation, too, we had not foreseen, this "success." Moreover, among veterans, informed and trained Zionists, the new spirit had its own destructive effects. Some were genuinely carried away by it. Others found a new road to popularity.

VI

What happened after the Jewish Declaration of Independence and the victory over the Arab nations climaxed the process of deviation from basic Zionist purpose and method. For we won freedom, we won the war, and we lost our heads.

Many rivers of emotion came together in the torrent that carried us away in the time of our triumph. There was the sheer marvel of the Jewish State itself. We ransacked the Bible for miracle literature to express our wonder—and our incredulity. We enjoyed the bewildered applause of the world, and we went about in a daze, repeating: "Look —we did it!" And there was the sheer reaction from the uncertainty of the preceding years: it had looked for a time as though the whole dream of a Jewish homeland was about to be extinguished in—supreme irony!—the victory of the democracies over Hitlerism. But wilder still was the reaction from the indescribable horror of the Hitler episode. We had survived: battered, crippled, reduced by a third of our numbers but still—ourselves. We had survived, and like a sign from above, like a word of consolation and approval, there came—the Jewish State.

In the delirium of those hours, in the almost megalomaniac seizure, we felt that we could do anything, overcome any obstacles, undertake any enterprise. And it was in this mood that we launched the operation known as *Kibbutz Galuyot,* the Ingathering of the Exiles, the bringing into the Jewish State of the scattered Jewish people.

And now we must be very careful to distinguish between what may be called the legitimate and sensible and honorable exploitation of the new situation, and the abuse of it. Without this we shall not understand to what extent we were the victims of circumstance, and to what extent ourselves responsible for a costly error. And it need hardly be added that in the present discussions on the problems of Israel, of Zionism, of world Jewry, some of us want to create a large, all-embracing confusion, and to make everything appear the consequence of *force majeure.*

When, with brilliant courage, the Jews of Israel declared their independence, they threw open the gates of their country to all world Jewry. Henceforth, as long as there was a Jewish State, any Jew, anywhere in the world, had the right to enter it and to become a citizen. This was a magnificent gesture, corresponding to the sublimity of the occasion. There went into it, besides the appropriate exaltation, a kind of revengeful joy. We felt a furious desire to indulge the appetite that England had so long and so obstinately starved: the appetite for Jews, the appetite for the central privilege that had so long been withheld from us—that of the control of our immigration. There was also in it a somewhat infantile flourish of suddenly acquired authority. "There is no one to stop us now!"

There were more intimate, more personal forces at work. Tens of thousands of Israeli Jews—as they now called themselves—yearned for their relatives in Europe, the survivors of the Great Pogrom. Anyone who has seen a boatload of postwar Jewish refugees approaching the harbor of Haifa, and has stood amid the feverish crowds on the docks awaiting the approach of the loved ones whom they had once thought lost, will know what this *force majeure* meant. Here the phrase is certainly used with full justification. And it was used with equal justification for those Jews who were brought to Israel from certain areas without the intervention of anxious brothers, sisters, sons, daughters. There were some countries that threatened the extermination of their Jewries. On others the Iron Curtain might descend any day, adding their numbers to the lost millions of Russian Jewry. There were also hundreds of thousands of survivors of the Hitler years for whom the soil of Europe was impregnated with poisonous memories, and for whom restoration to sanity and usefulness could be accomplished only in Israel. In all of these instances we can say that if Israel had to be flooded beyond its structural capacity, the issue was out of our control.

I do not mean this in the technical literal sense. There was nothing to prevent the Israelis from saying: "We declare in principle that any Jew, anywhere, has the right to enter this country and to become a citizen. But we are compelled for safety's sake to space out the privilege, being able at the present time to absorb no more than a hundred thousand immigrants a year. By this prudent measure we shall, incidentally, ensure a fuller immigration in ten or fifteen years than if no control is exercised at the beginning." There was nothing to prevent the Israelis from saying this—nothing except the irresistible pressure of emotion. Practical considerations, too, urged the Israelis to stretch to the utmost the absorptive capacity of the country —a hundred thousand immigrants a year, a hundred and twenty-five thousand, even a hundred and fifty thousand— as long as the pulls and pressures were genuine; that is, as long as Israeli Jews clamored for their surviving European relatives, as long as certain Jewries were threatened with extreme oppression, or were in danger of being lost to us forever by imprisonment. All this would have come under the heading of the unforeseeable developments to which we had to adapt ourselves as best we could.

But the operation called *Kibbutz Galuyot* went beyond the genuine pulls and pressures. There was an indiscriminate piling in of immigrants which was neither Zionism nor rescue. An artificial stampede was imposed on top of the natural one, and swept along tens of thousands of Jews who did not have to come to Israel at this time, and without excessive provocation and cajolery would not have come. *Kibbutz Galuyot* proclaimed, moreover, that Jews ought not to want to live anywhere but in the Jewish State, and Jews who did not pull up stakes, wherever they were, and head for Israel, were letting their people down.

The overwhelming majority of the newcomers lacked both the indoctrination of the earlier Zionist settlers, with their strong core of Chalutzim, and the technical, educational advantages which, among some of the later, non-Zionist settlers, were a partial offset to the absence of Zionist sentiment. The majority of the post-statehood immigrants consisted, it is true, of those whom Israel had to take anyway with the least possible delay; but a bulky minority, perhaps one quarter of the total, could have been deferred for a number of years without dishonor. Whether urgent or not in that sense, the newcomers were heavily loaded with problem types: the men and women and children who had survived under the abnormal and deforming conditions of Hitler's Europe and the D.P. camps; the aged and useless, for whom comfortable provision might, in many cases, have been made elsewhere than in Israel; the untrained of the West and East; and, especially from the East, those masses that issued from a medieval world and needed long preparation for the new environment.

It is not enough to say that large numbers of the immigrants had no feeling whatsoever for the Jewish State, and knew nothing of the spirit that had built the country for them. Many had, understandably enough, acquired the deep-seated conviction that government, any government, was something sinister, something to be circumvented. For them a state was an evil thing, plotting evil against the individual. Or else, if they came from the East, they could not conceive the existence of government officials who were not licenced thieves, though of course a Jewish state and Jewish officials were preferable to non-Jewish. Over and above all this, there were also criminal elements looking for new fields of operation.

The ecstasy of the Israelis left no room for foresight. If half a million Jews would have applied in the first year, room would somehow have been found for them. The Israelis read their own high mood into the intentions of the newcomers. That so many of them would turn out to be ungrateful, intractable, suspicious, demanding, was not part of the calculation. The worst that the refugees had to endure in the improvised reception camps and transitional shanty towns compared favorably with what the Chalutzim had put up with joyously in their day. But the protests of the newcomers rang through the Jewish world. The difference in character, conditions, health, and preparation was, indeed, anticipated theoretically; its acceptance in practice was another matter. And now, to that which the years had done of their own accord to the original builders of Israel—the natural wearing down of their enthusiasm and endurance—were added the undermining effects of this crushing burden. The heroic intentions of the old-timers could not stand up to such an undertaking. There was needed a patience which they could not summon, and had no right to expect of themselves. There were needed financial means beyond anything supplied by world Jewry. But even infinite patience coupled with infinite skill and unlimited means would not have performed the miracle they expected. There are human processes in which time is an essential ingredient. Where this ingredient is ignored evils may be created which, later, time itself will not cure. But as it happens, besides lacking infinite patience, skill, and means, the Israelis already had difficult spiritual problems of their own before the enormous upheaval of the new mass immigration.

Before the assault on the framework of the country and its institutions, before the frenzied adaptation of the economy to the flood tide, there were already serious challenges to the old standards—to all the principles of the classic time which Weizmann had represented. These standards, we must remember, had not been abstractly moralistic, ivory-tower luxuries and monastic salvations of the individual soul. They had been the *practical* foundations of the country. They were standards that had stood firm against formless mass and number, against haste, pretence, façade, all the shoddiness of quick results on insecure foundations. Difficult to maintain under favorable circumstances, these standards were now subjected to mob assault under the most unfavorable circumstances conceivable.

65

There is probably no parallel for it in the experience of any other country: the doubling of the population, *and with specifically unsuitable material,* within a period of three years. The deviation with a touch of panic now became the norm in a frenzy of panic. Whatever Weizmann had fought in Ugandism, Brandeisism, and Revisionism was now come upon Israel magnified ten- and twentyfold. It was the original danger, the inherent threat of self-defeat, risen against us with apparently overwhelming force in the hour of our triumph.

VII

An error of judgment that cannot be reversed must be accepted; its effects must be faced and remedied. But it must be acknowledged first. It is necessary therefore to deal with the principal arguments in total defense of the operation *Kibbutz Galuyot.*

There is first of all a high scorn for a policy of selective immigration. If it is a basic principle of the Jewish State that every Jew has the right to enter it as a resident, at any time, then there can be no picking and choosing, there can be no discriminating on the basis of fitness or desirability. But whatever the principle, reality asserts itself. Israel simply could not go on taking these numbers, and these problem types, in such volume. The time was bound to come— it is here now—when we *would* pick and choose, simply because the absorptive apparatus and the finances were breaking down. But it really was not a question of selecting from among spontaneous applicants. We went out of our way to stimulate and overstimulate immigration. We paid for the transportation. If one hundred and fifty to two hundred thousand immigrants, from various areas that need not be specified, had been left where they were, much of the financial stringency of Israel could have been avoided—and the immigrants could have waited with no harm to them. We shall, however, see that the financial problem is far less important than the spiritual.

We are told, also, that mingled with the great exaltation which made possible—and imperative—*Kibbutz Galuyot,* there were shrewd considerations, at least in the minds of the leaders. For instance, if Israel was to exploit to the full the tide of American enthusiasm, it had to set an example of uncalculating generosity. Unlimited immigration into Israel, unlimited aid from American Jewry; the Israeli sacrifice of comfort and ease to be matched by American Jewry's financial sacrifice.

This is the most specious of the self-deceptions. The mood of admiration and pride which came over American Jewry in those days would have yielded the same financial results for any reasonably generous policy of immigration. A slogan of "One Hundred Thousand a Year"—it was the number that President Truman had suggested as a one-time and final concession by England in the pre-Independence nightmare of negotiations—would have given the same maximum results.

More serious seems to be the argument from security. We needed the maximum number of additional Jews in the minimum amount of time in order to discourage the Arabs from attempting a second round. But doubling our numbers from 700,000 to 1,400,000 in three years without regard to the quality of the new human material, or the effects on the economic and productive structure of the country—not to mention its morale—was not a guarantee of optimum increase in strength. It is true that it was touch and go during the Israeli-Arab war, and that five thousand more men in the field on their side, one or two thousand fewer on ours, might easily have turned the scale. But the lesson taught in that ferocious little war, as clearly as in any other that has ever disgraced the human species, was the incomparable value of morale. It applied to the civilian not less than to the military area. In the midst of the operation *Kibbutz Galuyot* Prime Minister ben Gurion cried out that the country was in danger of Levantinization because the flood of primitive, panicky Oriental Jews was not matched by a comparable flow of volunteer Jews from the trained West. But the Arabs were beaten precisely because they are Levantinized; and if there was no prospect of a compensating contribution from the West, the tide of Eastern immigration into Israel should have been controlled as far as it could be, and not whipped up artificially. We are weaker, not stronger, because of that unnecessary addition to the natural and inevitable influx.

There is, finally, an argument that is usually brought up —for no reason that I can see—in a discreet undertone. We had to get in the maximum number of Jews, helter-skelter, from everywhere and anywhere, fit and unfit, endangered and not endangered, convinced or merely cajoled, because it was necessary to fill up without delay the areas vacated by the hundreds of thousands of Arabs who had fled from their homes. If those towns and villages and fields had been left vacant there would have been no resisting the argument for the return of the Arab refugees; and to have permitted their return would have been to commit national suicide.

Now precisely because the last statement above is overwhelmingly true there is no need to speak furtively of our refusal to readmit the bulk of the Arabs. The circumstances under which they fled would have made their return a successful military maneuver on the part of the Arab States. It was, indeed, proper and practical for us to occupy the places they had abandoned. But, first, the filling up of the populational vacuum did *not* call for a policy of stampede immigration. There were tens of thousands of Jewish immigrants without decent quarters—in tents and shanty towns—over and above those quartered in Arab areas. And second, if it was a matter of life and death for us that the Arabs should not be readmitted, we had only to say so, and stand firm. The U.N., which had lacked the power to protect us from invasion by the Arab nations, lacked the power to force the Arab refugees upon us. The Arabs who were responsible for the Arab refugee problem—their creation of it had been part of their military strategy—had gambled with the lives of three quarters of a million Palestinian kinsmen, and had lost. It was proposed, then, that we pay voluntarily the fatal price that they had not been able to exact by force of arms. Miserable as the situation was, leaving us, God knows, no room for moral satisfaction, we did not have to be evasive and devious about it. We *could* not readmit the Arabs; we would have to fight the war all over again to prevent it. This was the naked truth, which needed no adornment. To be Machiavellian when there is no need for it, to create secondary and afterthought excuses when the true and primary reason is sufficient, indicates inner confusion. The confusion here had to do not with the Arab problem, and our justification before the world; it was part of the effort to give an appearance of necessity and inevitability to the policy of all-out *Kibbutz Galuyot*.

For what dominated the minds of those in control was not, at this moment, the affirmative Zionist ideal, but a sudden, wild belief in their ability to rush Providence off its feet, or (again) to force the hand of the Messiah, to crown the miracle of independence with the miracle of overnight completion of the task.

There were men in the Israeli government who understood the dangers of this course. They protested privately to the man in control—to Prime Minister ben Gurion. But Prime Minister ben Gurion was the acknowledged artificer of independence and victory. In the fateful days of decision he had been—no one will be found to challenge this even now—the God-sent inspiration. Among those who today protested against the policy of unlimited, over-stimulated immigration, were men who yesterday had feared to issue the Declaration of Independence, had hesitated to flout America's advice, or to risk war with the Arabs. Ben Gurion had carried them along—to triumph. Discredited on one cardinal issue, they could not, without an interval for recovery, pronounce firmly on another. But besides this natural timidity, there were motives not so easily forgivable.

VIII

The one man who could have put a brake on the stampede was Weizmann—if he had been twenty years younger. He was seventy-four when in 1948 Israel declared its independence, and at the moment he was not on the spot but in America, negotiating with the government and the U.N. He was nearer seventy-five when he was inducted as the first President of Israel. This is not a very advanced age. His friend and contemporary, Winston Churchill, was later to fight his way back to the premiership of England. But Weizmann had almost used himself up. During the summer months of 1947, when I worked with him in Rehovot, Palestine—he was dictating the second half of his autobiography—I saw with what an effort he concentrated. Half blind with cataracts on both eyes, he drove himself far beyond the safety point.

The autobiography was a side activity. He was the director of our strategy vis-à-vis the UNSCOP, the United Nations Special Commission on Palestine, which was then in the country. He was also absorbed in the creation of

the Weizmann Institute of Science. He was still the most
fascinating and persuasive personality in the Jewish world.
Those who saw him testifying at the Jerusalem sessions of
the UNSCOP that summer carried away an unforgettable
impression of spiritual and personal prestige. Unquestionably his mere reputation had something to do with it; but
that accounted for only part of the respect, or rather awe,
which he visibly inspired. I remembered, as I watched
him, an incident out of his prime. It had been proposed
to an opponent of the Zionist movement that he pay a
visit to Weizmann. The man refused, declaring that he
dared not venture within the ambit of Weizmann's powers
of fascination. Arthur James Balfour, Weizmann's greatest
support in England, heard the story, and denounced the
man for cowardice. During the UNSCOP sessions I remembered the man, whoever he was, and sympathized
with him. It was particularly curious to see the Indian
member of the UNSCOP, white-haired, short-tempered,
hostile, who had badgered every other witness quite above
the call of duty, sit almost open-mouthed during Weizmann's testimony, venturing an occasional question with
timid courtesy.

Weizmann was sick during those days. He had prepared
a statement to read out, and it had been printed for him
in letters half an inch high. When he had been helped to
the platform he put the statement aside and improvised
in his old manner. We who sat in the auditorium, and
could barely hear him, were miserably uneasy. But within
a few moments his ascendancy was established. We had the
feeling that if he had been introduced to the Committee as
one Mr. Cohen, he would have produced the same effect.

Weizmann's sickness was not only of the body. His spirit
was being tried almost beyond endurance. It was the time
of the anti-British terror in Palestine. Thousands of young
Jews had become fiercely convinced that only by con-

tinuous assassinations of British officials and soldiers could the gates be forced open for Jewish immigration. For some of the terrorists killing had become a sacred duty, a high fulfillment in itself, a redemption of the Jewish people, which through them was declaring to the world that it had overcome ancient taboo and paralysis. To kill was a demonstration of independence, a repudiation of passivity, an advertisement of Jewish normalcy. A mad literature of killer-glorification already existed. The majority of the terrorists, consciously, half-consciously, and explicitly, had motives of other kinds. They were largely members of the old reactionary movement, Revisionism. They had internal political purposes; it was important that *they* should seem to be the real liberators of Palestine, so that when the hour struck the people would turn to them for a government, and not to the leadership of labor. And so their propaganda of violence was even more insidious in its effects than the violence itself.

The real and effective resistance, the people's resistance of the Haganah and the older leaders, disciplined and calculated, was derided as footling cowardice, or denounced as collaborationism. The walls were daubed with slogans: "Down with Petain-Weizmann." And: "This Is the Only Way," side by side with a stenciled design of an arm brandishing a gun.

It is necessary to dwell on that episode in the making of the Jewish State, because it illumines the spiritual problem of the movement. The mass of the population in Palestine, for all its desperation, was anti-terrorist, on both tactical and moral grounds. But it would not turn stool pigeon for the British, and it refused to help in the hunting down of the terrorists. Despite itself, however, it permitted a haunting doubt to eat at its moral and political convictions. Suppose the terrorists were right? Suppose freedom could be won, and hundreds of thousands of Jews saved, only by relentless assassinations? Suppose the world was so bad, or had become so bad recently, that nothing impressed it more than the ability and willingness to kill—indiscriminately, contemptuously.

In America the Zionist leadership played a double game to the new, enormous, and uninstructed membership of the organization. It rebuked the terrorists in formal resolutions, but it managed to convey to the masses a sympathetic attitude toward terrorism. Once again there appeared prominently, in the Zionist enterprise, Jews who had made their reputations outside the Jewish field, and who, having suddenly found their Jewishness, were not content to learn first, but brought in their own solutions to the Jewish problem. The most active of these converts made common cause with the terrorists, and worked openly—or rather, in a blaze of publicity—with their representatives in America. To these converts Zionism as a great movement meant nothing at all. They wanted revenge on the enemies of the Jews and they wanted to save Jewish lives. It is hard to tell which motive came first. Whichever it was, they helped to create an atmosphere of respectability around the terrorist movement; and it was in the pattern of the type that as soon as Israeli independence had been achieved, they should lose interest in the problems of the Jewish people; and if they expressed any further opinions, these were to the effect that with the existence of a Jewish State in Palestine, Jews outside of it had no reason for remaining Jewish.

Weizmann's hatred of the terror was of a piece with his lifelong interpretation of Zionism. His resolute and unequivocal statements helped keep down the dangerous influence that the terror had unloosed, and I feel strongly that but for him the inroads into the character of the Jewish homeland and the Jewish people would have been considerably deeper than they were.

He was not, during that period, the president of the World Zionist Organization. He had been voted out of office at the last World Zionist Congress of 1946. The avowed purpose of the British Labour government (elected in 1945) was to continue the White Paper of the Conservatives and crush the idea of an independent Jewish State. Weizmann had for more than a generation represented Jewish trust in the ultimate good will of England; and his dismissal therefore signallized the collapse of that trust. It was a sound and necessary move, even though personal ambitions and rancors played, as they always do, their own complicated role among the representative figures. Weizmann let these ambitions and rancors affect him unduly, and he took his demission badly. He felt—wrongly, I think—that his removal from office diminished his usefulness; also that his leadership was being challenged in an over-all sense. That he misjudged the meaning of the defeat was made manifest when the Jewish State was declared, and the Presidency was offered him, or rather conferred upon him, automatically, no other candidate being remotely conceivable. And since his real leadership did not depend on his official position, he was as effective outside of office as within it. Nevertheless, the rankling in his heart between 1946 and 1948 helped drain his energies. His labors for the movement did not relax; they only took more out of him.

The last time I saw Weizmann more or less in command of his old self was in America, at the time of the Israeli Declaration of Independence. When we met a year later in Rehovot there had been a startling change. The President of the State of Israel was a sick old man, and when I bent over his chair to embrace him I had to hold back my tears. From now on he had to husband his declining powers with as much skill as he had once shown in deploying them on a dozen fronts simultaneously. His mind was still sharp,

74

his vision clear. He simply had not the physical strength to give the vision utterance in the old way. Gone, too, was the magnetism that had once streamed from him, and which had prepared his listeners for conviction before they had heard him speak.

In 1948, writing the last chapter of his autobiography, he had expressed the hope that the Presidency of the State of Israel would be conceived on the American model, and not on the French or Swiss. His hope was not realized; and even if it had been, he could not have put the Presidency to effective use. He was past that. He had attained the summit of formal power and prestige: all that this eminence enabled him to do was to take in as no one else did the full extent of the errors being committed by lesser men. Henceforth his contribution to Israel and world Jewry would have to flow from his record and his tradition.

His last years were heavily overclouded by physical and spiritual suffering. What he had feared all his life was coming to pass—a stampede immigration, and on an unimaginable scale. The *Judennot* had taken charge of the Zionist movement! Affliction, not inspiration, was the counselor, Messianism was eclipsed by mendicancy.

Only for an instant was there a heavenly touch of the early vision. There was a sudden opening up of historic vistas, a pealing of memorable prophetic words across the ages, a fusion of identity between the self and everlasting travail of Judaism. There seemed to be no sufficient reason why we little people should find ourselves associated with so prodigious a phenomenon. Nothing can take away from us the recollection of that instant; and I still think that the experience will be vindicated. But what followed immediately was, in its extreme form, an unnecessary, an unavoidable descent.

I repeat that an ingathering of the exiles, in a volume and of a kind hurtful to the new state was morally and physically unavoidable. Only a Moses leading his six hundred thousand refugees out of Egypt could tell them that they were unfit for liberty, unfit to lay the foundations of a Jewish State, and that they would have to perish in the wilderness so that their children might have time to be trained for the enormous responsibility. And who knows whether the account we have received is a literal one? What, in our case, was improper, unneeded, uncalled for, was our surrender to the negative feature of the situation, the failure to warn, to prepare for a stand. If at least the leaders had proclaimed: "We cannot discourage a single Jew from coming here, let alone refuse him admission if he applies. There is danger in what is happening, and we must do the best we can." But no! They went out of their way to increase the danger, and not least by representing a perilous necessity as a providential fulfillment. There were far-reaching consequences to this misrepresentation; the ultimate purpose of the Jewish State, its uniqueness as a state, its role in Jewish history and for world Jewry—all this was thrust still further away from the center; the Zionist movement throughout the world, swamped by spiritual refugees as Israel was being swamped by physical refugees, lost more and more of its regenerative function. The work must be begun again.

I believe that Chaim Weizmann would have agreed with most of what I have written here. He would have put it more pointedly, less diffusely, certainly more convincingly. But with him it was never a question of merely stating a view; he was never the kind of teacher who could issue directives from a retreat. He had always to go out among men, to persuade in person, to charm, to infect with insight; and, above all, to set an example in a specific practical way. For it was characteristic of him that in addition to his over-all leadership of the movement, he always had some special enterprise, a "project," which was a lesson as well as a substantial contribution. Into such projects he would pour his entire philosophy; and even when he was burdened with all the responsibilities of office he had time for such additional illustrative activities. Toward the end he suffered because he could not be effective in the only way he understood. Even if he had had the strength for a sustained statement, a sort of last testament, he could not have contented himself with it. It was not in his style to issue pronunciamentos. His autobiography comes nearest to being a spiritual testament; but he dictated it while busy implementing it in action. Debarred from action, he lost the inclination to speech; this explains the silence of the last two years.

CHAPTER V

Winds of Change

❀

I

WHAT I have written so far may read to some like an alibi: "We haven't done better because we didn't get the breaks. Or, rather, luck was overwhelmingly against us." But it is not my intention to enter a defense. The achievement does not need it. I would like, instead, to show where we could have done better than we did. Also, believing that we are about to enter the second phase of the Jewish renaissance, I want to examine our shortcomings and determine what was due to circumstance, what to error.

To do this I must turn once more to the history of practical Zionist achievement, and restate under a fresh aspect the case of the Chalutzim. I am concerned to show here that the burst of moral inspiration which accompanied the going up of the Chalutzim onto the soil of Palestine, and sustained them for decades of creation, was essential to the accomplishment of the task assigned to them, as it were, by Jewish history. I speak here not of the organizational forms they used, themselves uniquely adapted to the task, but of the preconditioning spiritual enthusiasm.

Overwhelmingly urban by direct and indirect compulsion, the Jews in the Exile lived for centuries an agricultural shadow-life in their religious ritual and culture. They celebrated regularly imaginary harvests; the more learned studied the Talmudic minutiæ of ancient Palestinian rural law, usage, and economy—in the ghettoes of European cities; they were forbidden to plant certain seeds side by side on soil they did not possess, and to graft upon each other trees that they could not have identified. The Jewish people as a whole, homeless as a people even though individuals and communities found temporary homes, thought of a life on the land as the ideal contrast to its millennial vagabondage. It was something unreal, Messianic, unattainable in ordinary circumstances. The Biblical verses that all knew spoke of every man under his own vine and his own fig tree, with none to make him afraid; but this was the millennial vision. Even rural Jews were not of the soil. I have often dwelt on the curious fact that my parents lived for many years in a Rumanian village among Rumanian peasants; and in fact we even had a climbing vine in our own back yard and often sat under it! But we remained quite unrural in habits and knowledge. My parents could not have told an oak from a pine tree, or a field of wheat from a field of barley. The reason for this split between longing and reality, between the land-hankering and the unexploited land contact, lies partly in the second half of the prophetic verse: "And there shall be none to make him afraid." We could sit under our vine—but we were not free from fear.

There are on record many instances of Jewish effort to build an agricultural life in the Diaspora. We know that the famous medieval scholar Rashi was a cultivator of the vine; we know that Russian Jews of the nineteenth century founded little colonies; and Baron de Hirsch launched a great scheme, more than half a century ago, to transplant Jews from Europe to the Americas, from the cities to the soil. In the transplanting of Jews to America history displaced Baron de Hirsch on an enormous scale; and his plans for the agriculturalizing of tens of thousands of Jews failed after a brief initial success, even as the less ambitious, more scattered efforts of individual Jews had failed before. A permanent and significant Jewish life on the soil could not be created without a total-revolutionary concept and a total-revolutionary mood to blow up, as with dynamite, the psychological blocks of the centuries.

To carry through, Jews had to think of the transformation Messianically—and Messianically meant also in terms of moral redemption. In short, there could never have been a successful move on to the soil of Palestine without the conviction of a unique moral purpose. Unweighted by this conviction, the effort would have petered out even in Palestine as it had petered out elsewhere.

Even in Palestine it had hard going. The colonies of the oldest Zionists, those founded largely with the help of Baron Rothschild, could not hold on to the younger generation; and at one time it looked as though the attempt would wind up, as it had done elsewhere, with a scattering of farms and hamlets manned largely by older people. It was the collectivist Chalutzim who set up an agricultural life that spanned the generations, inspiring others to the same achievement; and the Chalutzim were the elite of the movement as a whole.

"Messianically" had, in this connection, curious overtones of meaning. Remembering the attitude of my parents and relatives toward the subjects "Exile," "Diaspora," "homelessness," remembering the poignancy of their lamentations on the day of the Black Fast, which commemorates the Destruction, I am struck by something transpersonal which was not evident to me in earlier years. It was not always the homelessness of persons that they lamented, and not the vagabondage of the flesh. When they turned their eyes to God and asked: *"Ven vet der golus nemmen a sof?*—When will this exile of ours end?"* they were not necessarily referring to their own lot. What weighed on

80

them was the sense of the Jewish national unrootedness. It was Judaism that was homeless, more than Jews; it was the humiliation and frustration of their people's identity that hurt, not less than the persecutions and expulsions. The Return was a great restitution on a historic and cosmic scale. This was their belief, and if the Chalutzim, the core of the builders of Palestine, represented the Jewish people in this mood, they also represented the core of its belief. With regard to themselves, the Chalutzim felt they were dedicated to the special or central expression of the redemption; it did not mean that the Jewish people would, of its own free will, and in its entirety, withdraw from every part of the world, to reconcentrate in Palestine.

The moral drive of the Chalutzim came, as we have seen, from their Jewish side; their Marxism was part rationalization, part technical theory. The technical theory—and particularly the theory of surplus value—played, and continues to play, a great part in the thinking and planning of the kibbutzim. But Marxism was hostile to their Jewishness. The Zionist movement, on the other hand, was friendly to their social idealism. It furnished them the means. Without the Jewish National Fund, without other financial assistance, the Chalutzim could not have taken the first steps toward the realization of their plans.

It would be easy to put a cynical interpretation on this historic episode, and some have done it. They have pictured the Baron Rothschilds and Felix Warburgs and Chaim Weizmanns and the rest of the bourgeois Zionists as watching and encouraging the socialistic Chalutzim with a sly smile, thinking: "Let them go ahead, since they are first-class human material and are determined to sacrifice themselves. Let them fight the deserts and the swamps. Their collectivism will fail—the land will remain Jewish." The interpretation is as shallow as it is melodramatic. The sympathy of bourgeois Zionism with the Chalutzim was

81

genuine, and was of high moral worth. The deterioration of the kibbutzim, the decline of their moral *élan,* and the confusion that has fallen on them, do not represent a triumph for bourgeois Zionism, nor, except among those Zionists who have never understood the purpose of Zionism, is it felt to be one. Further, I believe that the force of the Chalutzic inspiration is far from spent. We are at the trough of the wave in Zionism and its mission. I shall not evade any of the implications of this fact. But neither will I yield to the temptation—all the more attractive because it is clothed in exhibitionistic intellectual honesty —to declare that the kibbutz movement is bankrupt.

II

"Let judgment run down as waters, and righteousness as a mighty stream," cried the Prophet Amos. In this spirit the Chalutzim conceived the character of the renewed Jewish homeland. But how could there be either judgment or righteousness as long as there existed the accursed thing called "surplus value," the gap between the value of what the worker creates by his labor, and the pay he receives? This is the Ahriman of society, the basic evil, the irremediable affliction—irremediable, that is, without the total and revolutionary remaking of society. It was Karl Marx who identified and nailed down the abomination. He cut through all the theorizings of earlier economists on the subject of profit, and where they had given it various names he bluntly called it theft. Profit is what the employer holds back, with the protection of the law, from the value created by the worker. With the tools owned by the employer, the employee, the worker, produces wealth. He gets only a part of that. The remainder is retained as tribute by the employer. And every effort to clothe this enforced tribute with respectability, every search for justification, is in the Marxian view evasion and chicanery.

And so they took an oath, these Chalutzim, that the Jewish civilization they were rebuilding would be free from the father of all evils, from surplus value. Or at least in their associations—the kibbutzim on the land, the cooperatives in the cities—no man would be an employer or an employee. All, jointly, and in equality, would be the owners of the instruments of production; the full value of their labor would return to them as their earnings.

The father of evil being thus eliminated, his capitalistic offspring would vanish too. A numerous and varied offspring it was: oppression, domination, snobbery of possession, envy, enslavement of woman, poverty for the many, insolent luxury for the few, enmity of the classes, enmity between the nations, war, cycles of want, the periodic crises of the capitalistic world—these are some of them. But of course the worst of them was the corruption of man himself, the encouragement of his baser impulses. And so, in setting up the working models of the perfect society, the Chalutzim engaged themselves not only to exclude this *primum mobile* of evil, but to demonstrate in their own lives that with its exclusion human relations blossomed naturally into goodness.

One of the crucial points on which they differed from orthodox Marxists was that of compulsion, or dictatorship. They did not aspire to seize power through a government; they would not impose their system on reluctant masses. In their view laws had a limited potency, and without continuous inspiration from another source, man could not rise above the level of legality. They therefore relied on voluntary association. It was their intention to set an irresistible example of moral purity and economic effectiveness. This was the double meaning of the kibbutz.

Every intense human activity develops ornamental flourishes that are both symbolism and self-propaganda.

Often it is hard to tell in detail what is "unnecessary flourish" and what essential motion. It is also hard to determine at what point the flourishes lose whatever usefulness they may have had, and become harmful. It was, for instance, something like a virtue among the early collectivist Chalutzim to suffer privations for the sake of the cause. They felt called upon to repudiate demonstratively the amenities that they associated with the corruptions of bourgeois life. Such was their hatred of the acquisitive instinct that they literally would not call their shirts their own. All articles of clothing were in a common store; shirts, dresses, trousers, socks, were distributed according to approximate sizes, were returned to the laundry, and redistributed; and it was with something like moral satisfaction that they ran a hundred yards through mud or dust to the primitive outhouse.

Now it is quite certain that the first outhouses had to be primitive, and sometimes badly located; also it was cheaper to do the communal laundry unsorted. Therefore it was perhaps "necessary" to be convinced that such privations were goods in themselves, the permanent asceticisms of the right life. But at a certain point these practices became too costly in human wear and tear; and their abandonment was a matter of common sense. Unfortunately revolutionaries have their own conservatism. A history of the kibbutzim can be written around the struggles that accompanied the retreat from outlived asceticisms.

One is afraid to take the first step backward; for there will be a second and a third—and where will it end? Will not a private shirt and a private pair of trousers, and—even more—a private blouse, reawaken the immemorial evil of conspicuous consumption? Will not a private room and a private shower lead back naturally to the old, hateful bourgeois love of luxury, with its debilitating moral effects? Will not the privilege of having one's meal occasionally in one's own separate room, added to the other concessions, re-create the separatisms and egotistical individualisms of the capitalistic world? Lead, in short, to "gracious living"? Give way on these points, and there will follow competition for possessions, the enslavement of woman in the home and—the return of surplus value, that is, of exploitation.

Now what has actually happened seems to justify the forebodings of the revolutionary conservatives. Nearly all the collectives—and all the older and more affluent ones —have private rooms even for the unmarried, and private shirts, trousers, and blouses for everyone. The outhouses still leave something to be desired, but private showers are common. The debate *has*, in fact, moved into the crucial area of surplus value; and the exploitative principle—to use their terminology—has been adopted in practice by most of the kibbutzim. This phenomenon, and its meaning for the kibbutzim and Israel, will be treated at some length in a later chapter.

III

Here I shall deal with the first planned and principled modification of the collectivist movement—something very different from the unplanned modifications that came about with the years.

The kibbutzim demanded an immediate total transformation in the lifeways of its members. It was assumed that as soon as a society was created free from the profit motif, the psychological and moral effects would at once become operative. Or, if not, the members of the society would, on plan, behave as if the effects had become operative. Now, in trying to anticipate these effects, the Chalutzim had to rely on moral intuition—and guesswork;

and if they guessed wrong they would be doing the opposite of what they wanted: they would be imposing on the revolution those patterns and dreams which were born in the bad old world. For we must remember that what the oppressed worker dreams of in the capitalist world is itself a capitalist product; and in truth it is impossible for him to guess what he will feel like in a communist world. The family may serve as an instance.

As Marxists the Chalutzim saw in the old family life many evils implanted in it by the capitalistic and pre-capitalistic history of man: the degradation and enslavement of the wife and mother; the tyranny of the father, himself a slave in the outer world when he was not a slave-driver; the egotistical separateness of this little primitive, biological unit in the larger social setting; the debasement of sexual ideals in the struggle for possession and prestige—and others. A socialist life meant the end of these evils. Family life—for that would still exist—would have new forms within which the old evils simply would not arise. The mother would no longer be enslaved, for the burden of the home would be lifted off her shoulders and she would be the equal of her husband in the work of the kibbutz; the father would not be a tyrant, for to begin with he would not need to take out on his family the humiliations he suffered as a wage-slave; the family would not develop egotisms and gangster separatisms, for it would be integrated with the social unit—the children would all live together in the kindergartens or dormitories, there would be no social distinctions, no graduated standards of living, no displays of possession; sexual life would be pure because marriages would be ruled by love and not by economic and social ambitions and repressions. And it must be stressed again that these effects were expected to manifest themselves with the very founding of the kibbutz. No conditioning for generations was called for. By an effort of vision and will the Chalutzim would conjure up the psychological and moral results of socialism in advance of the economic conditions that were supposed to produce them.

And as with the family, so with the community of property, with equality of reward for labor, with the absence of the acquisitive impulses.

In this process two questions arose tacitly to which the answers had to be guesses. How much good was being thrown out with the bad? And how much of the bad could human beings get suddenly and permanently out of their systems? Even the formulation of these two questions assumed a general agreement on what was good and what was bad.

It was however universally agreed that it was bad for one man to hire another and make a profit on his labor; so bad, in fact, as to be inadmissible, however strong the temptation. This was—surplus value. Perhaps it was also bad that a man should want his own piece of land to work, rather than agree to move around from plot to plot, from task to task, according to the resolutions passed in the meetings of the kibbutz. It was a sad thing, but somehow (said the dissidents) a man worked with more *cheshek*, more will, and energy, and understanding, on a piece of land that was his, that he became familiar with, attached to. It was bad, perhaps, to be the victim of such possessive fixations—but there you were. A man hankered for self-identification with a particular stretch of soil. He also hankered for a retreat for himself, his woman, and his offspring. Perhaps that was bad, too. But oddly enough, though it all meant a return to the old enslavement to kitchen and children, many of the women, too, hankered for it.

The dissidents from the kibbutz movement were not, as might have been expected, newcomers. The founders of Nahalal, the first and most famous moshav ovdim (co-operative settlement, as distinguished from the kibbutz, the collectivist settlement) had in fact been the founders of Daganiah, the first and most famous kibbutz. The movement toward the moshav ovdim was fed from the membership of the kibbutz. Today the two forms flourish side by side.

The co-operationists (as I shall call them) differed from the collectivists not in the ultimate socialist ideal, but in their conception of the possible at a given stage in social development. They laid down for the moshav these four principles:

(1) Individual small holdings, which every man (with his family) worked for himself, being forbidden to hire wage labor.

(2) National, inalienable land; that is, land owned by the Jewish National Fund, and leased in perpetuity to the member of the moshav.

(3) Mutual help.

(4) Co-operative buying and selling.

The moshav, then, is also conceived on a high moral level; but it does not pretend to the perfectionism of the kibbutz. It rejects the collectivist techniques that reach into certain privacies. These may be legitimate, or they may be anti-social, but they are privacies that, say the co-operationists, human beings simply cannot surrender on demand. Thus the moshav recognizes and accepts differences of reward for labor; and in the moshav system the more diligent and intelligent a farmer and his family, the more they will earn. However, a limit is placed on earning capacity, and a distinction established between permissible and impermissible use of skill and shrewdness. The farmer may see a way of earning more by hiring a laborer and making a profit on him. But as a member of the moshav he agrees not to do so. He also agrees not to play the market for himself, but to buy and sell together with his

88

neighbors. The differences in earning capacity, and therefore in standards of living, limited by these regulations, are also mitigated by the principle of mutual help.

The moshavniks, like the kibbutzniks, found their ethical inspiration in the Biblical literature. But it must be admitted that on the whole the kibbutzim had the greatest appeal, and commanded the deepest respect, among the Zionists, even when it was felt that in the long run they would have to retreat from their extremist ideals. There was about the kibbutzim a moral consistency, an absoluteness of self-surrender, which was genuinely awesome. Moreover, the fact that most of the converts to the cooperatives had received their training in the collectives, proved that the collectives were fulfilling a special function. They were converting city dwellers into land workers. They were the necessary trial by fire for most pioneers, and only the elite remained in them. If they were wrong, they were wrong in the right direction.

Nor was it the moshavim alone that received many of their recruits from the kibbutzim. Thousands of workers passed through the kibbutzim and moshavim to the moshavot, the individualist settlements. It must be kept in mind that the simple, primal pioneering urge of earthy peoples was unknown to Zionism. The Chalutzim had to be drawn by an idea and an ideal before they could feel the actual attraction of the soil. Even those that went direct into the moshavah, accepting the individualist struggle, were actuated by something more than a crude instinct of self-preservation. All three types of pioneers suffered hunger, loneliness, and violent if temporary maladjustment; the kibbutzniks and moshavniks for Jewish social and national ideals, and individualist farmers for an ideal of personal and national dignity. The diversity of ideals did not obscure the unifying Jewishness common to all of them.

IV

Weizmann did not share my partisan attitude toward the collectives. His partiality was for the co-operative moshavim, and his favorites were, I think, the men of Nahalal. But his all-embracing love of creative elements in Jewish and Palestinian life eclipsed his preferences for particular forms.

During the struggle with the Brandeis group in America, when the cry was for the application of "business principles" in the building of Palestine, and when British administrators worried about the leftism of the kibbutzim, Weizmann stood firmly with the left. But he justified it by something more than a leftist outlook. Of that period he writes in his autobiography:

> British officials and Zionist visitors to Palestine returned to advise us to put an end to "all these fancy experiments" in agriculture, and concentrate on building up industry and trade—in other words, take the line of least resistance and relapse into the old diaspora habit of creating towns to receive an urbanized population. . . . I resisted all this advice strenuously, and sometimes in my eagerness to defend my point of view I may have been less than just to the lower middle class people who came to settle in Jerusalem, Tel Aviv and Haifa, since they too were pioneers, in their fashion. They built up hundreds of small industries, investing their small life-time savings, brought with difficulty out of Poland or the Ukraine; and they too were building up the National Home of their people. Even so, I believe that the backbone of our work is and must always be agricultural colonization. It is in the village that the real soul of a people—its language, its poetry, its literature, its tra-

ditions—springs up from the intimate contact between
men and soil. The towns do no more than "process"
the fruits of the village. So, for more than a quarter of
a century now, it has been given to me to watch, with
a deep and growing exultation, the steady development of our village life in Palestine. I have watched
the Emek's marshes drying out, and gradually growing
firm enough to support more and more clusters of red-
roofed cottages, whose lights sparkle in the falling
dusk like so many beacons on our long road home.
The thought of those spreading clusters of lights has
been my reward for many weary months of travel and
disappointment in the world outside.

Here we see clearly the motivation of his support for
the "fancy experiments." They were creative—and that
was what mattered. Weizmann's upbringing and general
orientation were not leftist; and he certainly did not agree
with the kibbutz interpretation of family life. Readers of
his autobiography will remember that he retained to the
end a deep affection for his childhood home setting, and
for his parents, his brothers, and sisters. Nor had he ever
passed through a phase of rebellion and hostility. His had
been an orthodox middle-class Jewish home in the finest
classic tradition. His father, the village timber merchant
of Motol, near Pinsk, barely made a decent living for his
family, which grew through the years to tribal proportions.
But in the face of many worldly handicaps there was maintained in the Weizmann house an attractive blend of reasonable ritual observance and high intellectuality. The
father's favorite reading was *The Guide for the Perplexed*,
by Maimonides, and the *Code* of Caro. Weizmann loved
to talk of Motol, of the synagogue, of the festivals; and he
had a thousand little stories to tell, a thousand sayings to
repeat, of his parents and grandparents, his uncles and

aunts. He was a "family man" through and through, but without any of the churchwarden self-righteousness we associate with that phrase. I suppose he would have been content to see Jewish Palestine filled with homes like his father's, with couples as lovable and high-minded as his parents, even if not quite as pious and prolific. (Weizmann's mother bore seventeen children, of whom twelve grew to useful manhood and womanhood; and she lived happily into the middle eighties.) He therefore had a profound affection for those bourgeois, individualist settlers on the land who clung to the ethical and intellectual tradition of Judaism. And there were such. But there were many who departed from the spirit of the tradition while keeping the form; they had neither the love of learning nor the love of fellowman, neither respect for the spirit nor kinship with the workingman. But form was for Weizmann, the great lover of form, the inescapable utterance of the content. The form of a bourgeois home simply did not exist for him apart from the best in bourgeois ideals. The talk at table, the intellectual level of the home, the web of emotional relationships—these were aspects of form. Thus Weizmann had a scarcely concealed contempt for pietistic gesticulation as such. He despised the parade of religious conviction, and since religious political parties must make a vote-catching device of their superior piety, he despised them, too. His interpretation of religion gave a higher place to the Chalutzim who called themselves agnostics than to the clerical politicians who wore their phylacteries on the hustings. But he did make a distinction between the collectives and the co-operatives. His attitude toward the former was one of consistent admiration; but in his view the moshav came, at the time, nearer to the right combination of the possible and the desirable in the new colonization of Palestine.

The passage I have quoted from the autobiography is

dated 1947. I believe that if Weizmann were writing today about the colonies he would refer to the gap between his hopes and their fulfillment. The hundreds of kibbutzim and moshavim which dot Israel are indeed marvelous demonstrations of the creative will; the traveler through the Emek and Galilee and the Sharon—and now latterly the Negev, too—feels about him the thrust of energies that bespeak a healthy people wrestling with brutal natural handicaps. He too, if he is at all sensitive to human values, is aware of a kind of exultation as evening falls, and the clusters of lights to the right and left of the road, on height and in valley, sweep past him. But if he is more than a visitor, if he has been here many times, and has watched the development of the country, he is aware that the high place which the collectives and the co-operatives held in the regard of the people has been forfeited. The first inspiration of Chalutzism is no longer there, and we shall have to look into the reasons for this failure.

CHAPTER VI

In Process of Time

I

THE problems of the kibbutz fall, as we have seen, into two groups: those inherent in the nature of the institution, and those that were created by unexpected and cataclysmic changes in external circumstances, and by resulting pressures on Jewry, Palestine, and the kibbutzim. The division, made for purpose of study, is in some ways artificial, for there was a constant crossing of effects, and in life itself the picture was never so clear as I shall try to make it.

The inherent problems emerged in the process of time. As the kibbutzim, with the help of general Zionist funds, struggled out of their first poverty, their demonstrative asceticism, asceticism as anti-bourgeois strategy, as ideal, faded. The kibbutzniks were better off, they were also older and more efficient. There was a change in tone and outlook, which was not the less significant because it could not always be defined. There was, heaven knows, debate enough —passionate, even acrimonious—over every modification, which was usually accepted over the dwindling protest of a large and outraged minority. But somehow in the end there was no consciousness of important cumulative concession. As each modification settled into habit it fitted itself by degrees into a revised concept of the total original ideal.

Sometimes the problem would crystallize around an

apparent triviality. For many years a custom called the *kumsitz* was debated with immense earnestness. This portmanteau word (from the Yiddish for "come sit") appeared in the early days. Between hours of labor a group of men and women would hold an impromptu little social, which consisted of very light refreshments and very much talk: assuredly a harmless indulgence. But since the social could not be attended by all the members of the kibbutz, even if it was a small one, the *kumsitz* had about it a touch of extracurricular luxury. It might also carry, ever so faintly, a suggestion of separatism, of something put over, of a tiny festivity sneaked in by a group, not shared with all the members. As the kibbutz grew in numbers, and as accommodations and amenities improved, these objectionable features became more marked. With a hundred families or more in the kibbutz, with *nudniks* (bores) identified and catalogued, with friendships localized, one already had lists, so to speak. Who was to be invited to the cup of tea, which this time was served in the private room of the host, and prepared on the electric kettle? Also, instead of gathering in the dining-hall to listen to the communal radio, the group of "insiders" could resort to someone's room to listen to a *private* radio. When "distinguished visitors" came to deliver a lecture at the kibbutz, they would find a hierarchy. Actually, it is impossible for a visitor to place himself, for two or three evenings in succession, at the communal disposition of an entire village. He will pass much of his time in the rooms of two or three "important" kibbutz members, and the privilege of meeting him will be restricted to the V.I.P.'s. Presumably anyone can drop in. But out of the *kumsitz,* or partly by its means, has developed the group, the clique—intellectual-social barriers against the free flow of all-round comradeship. It was one more move away from the original ideal of the kibbutz as a single, undifferentiated family.

Much more obviously dangerous was the tendency to revert to the bourgeois family unit, another crystallized resistance to the perfect intermingling of group interests and affections. It turned out that parents wanted to have more of their children than kibbutz life allowed them. The scheduled visits to the nursery and kindergarten, the fixed evening hour on the green, other occasional contacts, were not enough, especially for the mothers. Emotions refused to be rationed. Then began a movement for withdrawal of the children from the communal accommodations sacred to the ideology and traditions and technique of the kibbutz, the reconstitution of something more like the old-fashioned home. It was not a concerted movement; there was no systematic revision of principles—only a divergence of practice. In one of the oldest kibbutzim the children are taken into the expanded quarters of the parents from the kindergarten; in a new kibbutz the private quarters include from the outset a second room for infants taken from the nursery. These scattered developments have wide bearings. The mother is now partially restricted in choice of occupation. What becomes of her complete equality with her husband? The child leans more on the family. What will happen to its total social integration? Will not ancient complexes reappear, matrices of egotisms, rivalries, ambitions?

There are learned and earnest discussions on these subjects, statistics are cited, laws of infant psychology invoked. It is argued by some that the kibbutz child develops slowly out of infantilism because it is too much in the company of children, not enough in a natural environment of grownups. Young mothers report that they feel better, work better, if they are permitted to handle their babies more frequently, to bathe and fondle them as well as breast-feed them.

In each separate kibbutz such changes are introduced

only after long discussion and by a majority vote binding on the minority. Once the decision is made there is not much room for individual variation of temperament.

The tradition and ideology of the communal dining-room have also been affected by the years. When ten or fifteen or even twenty young people sat together at a table —friends and intimates with common views, and years of common experience—the hastiest meal was something of a festive occasion. But when a hundred, two hundred, three hundred are served simultaneously in a huge Howard-Johnson hall we have only technological efficiency of feeding—if that. Although poverty made communal meals inevitable in the beginning, it was not intended that they should be merely public conveniences, assembly lines of consumption. The partaking of food in common is universally associated with some higher purpose. There is an ancient Jewish saying that if as few as three eat at one table and do not discuss things of the spirit they might as well be idol-worshippers. The uproar and confusion of the big communal meals of the kibbutzim deprive them of all social value. Time and again I have seen members carry home a plate of food—this could only take place in the evening—to consume it privately. Sometimes the wife or husband was not feeling well; but just as often it was out of weariness with the hullabaloo of the dining-room. Here and there an effort is made to mitigate the effect of numbers by dividing the dining-room into semi-alcoves—but this exactly was what the kibbutz never intended: the cliques begin to appear.

Common to the alcove, the *kumsitz*—itself a kind of protest against the dining-room—the little *private* libraries, the private radios, the family urge, is something very deep—the flight from the pressure on the personality. All village life, whatever its form, exercises a tyranny; the kibbutz village is especially liable to this evil because it wields such power over its inhabitants. This close living together, this living on top of each other, this compulsory, indiscriminate comradeliness, is beyond the nervous adaptability of most people. Tolerance on the surface may conceal repressions; or it may go deep and create an unhealthy insensibility.

II

The noblest over-all feature of the kibbutz idea is its voluntarism. It is also its most important strategically; for the kibbutz cannot serve as example if it lapses into compulsion; neither will it obtain the maximum effort from its members. Moreover, a kibbutz is a state in miniature, and the ideal state is one in which compulsion has withered away; all is understanding and good will.

Such is the theory; such presumably is the practice. For if a man does not like kibbutz life, he is free to leave it, to join a moshav or go back into the capitalist world. And as long as kibbutzim and their members are young, theory and practice coincide. But suppose a man has put ten, fifteen, twenty years into the development of a kibbutz, has invested his youth in the creation of this rich life-form in a place that was desert, and in the end finds the life no longer bearable. Where is he to go, depleted of his strength? How is he to start again? Is he not a prisoner of the "state"?

The reasons that make him want to leave are irrelevant. He may have discovered that he no longer has the nervous strength to live this intermingled life; the implacable intimacies, the unprocurability of solitude, may be too much for him. Perhaps it is rural life as such that has become unbearable in a powerful awakening of urban nostalgia. But let us consider positive, not negative reasons. At thirty, or thirty-five, a man may be seized with an irresistible impulse to write, study, paint, compose. I do not speak of recognizable talents that can get a hearing, but of the right that any man has to gather up his belongings and reinvest them in the desperate gamble of a "call."

But what belongings has such a man? None at all. He must go out of the kibbutz as naked as he came in—and the ten or fifteen most vigorous years of his life expended.

The kibbutz can say to him: "You joined us freely, knowing what it was all about." But no man knows at twenty what it is all going to be about at thirty-five or forty. He has changed. For that matter, the kibbutz too has changed. A man may even reach the conclusion that the moral standards of the kibbutz are now below those of the city. Perhaps the spectacle of kibbutzim now expelling members on purely ideological grounds not connected with kibbutz life itself is too much for him. He would rather face the frank competitive system than what seems to him to be the hypocrisies of the kibbutz.

It is in fact being suggested in some kibbutzim that a fund be set apart in which members share according to the years of their service; so that a man, or a couple, will not have to go out empty-handed, leaving to others the fruits of ten or fifteen years of labor. On the other hand, the kibbutz cannot be turned into a savings institution, an invitation to smart young men and women who want to earn while they learn.

The problem may be unanswerable, but its existence cannot be ignored. It is impossible to say how many kibbutzniks would move into moshavim, or try their luck in the cities, if they could start out with a reasonable part of the surplus wealth they have created. The number is certainly not negligible, though we can only guess vaguely at the effect on the vitality of the kibbutz.

More revealing than any other single development in kibbutz life is the movement to draw up a "bill of rights" for the individual, protection from the tyranny of majorities. We have come far from the implicit trust of the early days. Thirty years ago, when the question of a formal intramural "constitution" was raised, the implicit insult was resented, the suggestion rejected out of hand. What had comrades of the spirit to do with juridical guarantees against each other? Was it not of the essence of the collective that mutual affection and a common purpose should make formal regulation—state compulsion—an anachronism? But the years have shown that if without continuous inspiration from another source man cannot rise above the level of legality, neither can he rely on continuity of inspiration.

There are many kibbutzim that will deny the importance, even the existence, in their midst, of some or all of the foregoing problems. And kibbutzim do in fact vary, in age, history, composition, and tone. But not to that extent. There are undoubtedly many kibbutzim where these problems are not discussed—but that is another matter, to be dealt with separately. However, problems go on existing even when their existence is not acknowledged, and that may constitute the most important problem of all.

III

If we add up all the foregoing changes in the form and spirit of kibbutz life, or rather life on well-established kibbutzim, we still do not have a fundamental criticism. The Chalutzim believed they could create a social system that would bring into automatic harmony the needs of the individual and the needs of the group. They did not succeed in this project. What of it? It is an impossible Messianic ideal. It is perhaps not a desirable ideal, for a man without moral and social problems is not a man; and perhaps the essence of morality is continuous struggle and search. There are of course doctrinaires who tell us that the kibbutzim were bound to fail, imbedded as they were in a capitalistic environment. The whole country, they say, perhaps the whole world, has to be reorganized in order that such a social organism shall succeed and endure locally. On these grounds they condemn the Chalutzim for even making the attempt—amateurish, unpolitical, utopian, un-Marxian, counter-revolutionary—when they should have devoted their energies to transforming the national and world organisms as wholes—and that not by stages but by sudden violence. At the other extreme are those who condemn the Chalutzim for trying to do that which is impossible on any scale, by any method, and in any setting, local, national, or world-wide. The ideal, they say, may have been a noble one; the attempt was foolish; it showed ignorance of human limitations.

Here I am interested in the second view, because it is prevalent today in the Jewish and Zionist world. It is, I think, a narrow and harmful view. Certainly we ought to take account of our limitations, psychological, social, and habitual; but it is also a good thing, a necessary thing, to probe them; not abstractly, in discussion, but by social experiments conducted in the right spirit—a spirit born of the moral impulse, and not of the will to dominate. Such experiments always do something to change our limitations, diminish their circumference, expose *their* limitations. And this should be borne in mind regarding the kibbutzim quite apart from their practical historical deposits—the villages, farms, and factories which would never have been created without them, the tens of thousands of workers who would never have been trained; quite apart, also, from the high mood of inspiration which the Chalutzim, as its extreme expression, helped to maintain in the classic days of Zionism.

But it is an error and an injustice to confine our appreciation to the past. If we speak of the kibbutz as a form of life, an addition to the experience and to the moral instrumentalities of the Jewish State, we may say that too much was attempted, but much was done. We may add that too much had to be attempted in order that much might be done. For what remains after the many retreats from the first stand is considerable and irreplaceable.

I have described so far only the most important of the retreats, and only such as I consider inevitable and organic, belonging to the nature of the experiment. These are the retreats on which a great part of current hostility to the kibbutzim is concentrated in argument. But it is a hostility that in reality has nothing to do with the failure of the ideal. The success of the ideal would not have been acclaimed, either, in the present Zionist mood. There is a general letdown in morale throughout the world, and the Jewish people is not exempt from it. Neither is the Zionist movement. In this letdown people find satisfaction in showing where an ideal has failed, and in exaggerating the failure. We are reminded on every side that the kibbutzim attract very few members nowadays. This is true, and is part of the crisis of the kibbutz movement. But if the kibbutzim were today what they were twenty years ago they would attract even fewer members. Newcomers to Israel shy away from the kibbutzim not because of the ideals which have been dropped, but because of those which have been retained.

On one point there is no disagreement among observers, Israelis and visitors alike. The kibbutzim have brought forth and nurtured a generation of youngsters who are a delight to the eye and the spirit. They are sturdy, industrious, friendly, conscious of their social duties, and free from the complexes of city life. They have of course their own complexes, the consequences of a narrow intellectual environment. Also, they share the common Israeli alienation from the sense of a world Jewish people. But they are inspiring human material. Their biggest defect is—their fewness. The kibbutzim have not, so far, shown themselves capable of expanding by natural increase. We rarely find families of three and four. The number of children needed, according to vital statisticians, to maintain a population is 2.8. This average is not reached in the kibbutzim. It strikes one as extraordinary that in such surroundings, where children are wanted, and where parents do not have to worry about "another mouth to feed," the birth rate should not be higher. However, a kibbutz experience of twenty or twenty-five years—very few of the kibbutzim go back further than thirty years—is perhaps not enough for definite conclusions on this point.

But if the youth of the kibbutzim fall short in number, they show one crucial advantage over the youth of all other forms of agricultural colonization; they show the fewest defections from the soil. In this respect one part of the dream of the Chalutzim, the creation of a rooted landworking class, has become a triumphant reality. The lure of the city has no meaning for the youngsters of the kibbutz. I make the surmise—it is nothing more—that one reason for this tremendous success is the devotion showered upon the children of the kibbutzim. Childhood life there has always been happy; and attachment is strongest where memories are happiest.

I cannot help making a digression—if it is one—on the subject of the "imported" youth of the kibbutzim, the children brought in by the Youth Aliyah movement, the remnants of the last generation saved from Hitler Europe. Here is one of the most moving achievements in creative rehabilitation to be found anywhere in the annals of social service. The enterprise was begun under the leadership of the great Henrietta Szold, and has been sponsored by

Hadassah, the Women's Zionist Organization of America, and the Women's International Zionist Organization (WIZO). The spiritual recuperative capacities of the young, their responsiveness to affectionate, patient treatment, have never been so brilliantly demonstrated, as in the thousands of Youth Aliyah members of the collectives. One would say that a world had conspired to turn a generation of Jewish children into monsters, and that the Youth Aliyah movement was the successful counter-conspiracy. If an international congress of inspired social workers had sat long and earnestly on the problems of these children when they were rescued from ruined Europe, they could not have devised an instrument of mass therapy anywhere near as effective as the kibbutzim have been.

IV

What has happened to the kibbutzim cannot be described simply; the forces that have played upon and within them are too many and too interlocked. The enumeration and description here given must be reshuffled by the reader so that all the factors appear simultaneously before his mind's eye.

This much is certain: fifteen and twenty years ago a kibbutznik appearing in the city on a visit was looked on with respect, even with a little awe. He was a man apart, playing a special and exalted role. Today the kibbutznik attracts no particular attention; his role in the national life no longer has a high significance for the large majority. If he comes from one of the new kibbutzim, on the northern frontier, or in the desert Negev, he is respected as a pioneer —but that has nothing to do with kibbutz life as such.

The public attitude is unjust; it is touched with

Schadenfreude, an angry satisfaction that conceals a half-forgotten resentment with laborites in England, with British socialists who betrayed their Zionist-socialist comrades in Palestine. "Socialists are all right until they get the power. . . ." The kibbutzniks, on the defensive, are themselves depressed by the recollection of what the British Labour government tried to do to Israel. Their external status shaken, they are insecure within. And so they are excessively concerned with defending a reputation and demonstrating their consistency.

But the kibbutzniks also suffer from an old tendency to over-defend themselves. They were never able to accept with good grace those inevitable modifications of kibbutz life, those proper, natural, human modifications which we have just considered. They fought over them humorlessly; in the debates harsh words were used like "betrayal," "corruption." When the modifications were finally accepted, when the changes were digested, and became a "normal" part of kibbutz life, the debates were forgotten. Even the dissenting minority fitted itself into the new dispensation, and in time was ready to assert that nothing of importance had happened; the "kibbutz" was still the "kibbutz." Well, it was, and it was not. The changes were and were not important. They were important because they were sensible adjustments to psychological inevitabilities; they were unimportant because they left intact the major principles of economic equality within the kibbutz. But though the debates were forgotten, their effects lingered somewhere in the mind, and nourished an obscure feeling of guilt, retreat, and defection.

This intellectual and moral confusion constitutes one difficulty in respect of the internal modifications of kibbutz life. When it came to other and more significant modifications the kibbutzniks were unable to face the new issues squarely, sensibly, with complete honesty.

The result, from this and other causes, has been the loss of that moral leadership in Zionism which the kibbutzim once exercised. Weizmann wrote, as we remember: "It is in the village that the real soul of a people—its language, its poetry, its literature, its traditions—springs up from intimate contact with the soil." This function of Israel's rural life may belong to the far-off future. It has been in quite another sense that the villages of Palestine have hitherto been the soul of the people. The kibbutzim reversed the immemorial political relationship between town and country; the kibbutzim and their offspring, the moshavim, representing more than half of the rural population, were the liberal socialist core of Jewish Palestine. If Weizmann's vision of Israel's village life will ever clothe itself in reality, it will be by other processes than those of past history. For the kibbutzim and moshavim did not intend to create a classic peasantry; and they have not done so. Let this too be written down to their everlasting credit. It is quite possible that in the modern mechanized world, with its improving communications, its press, radio, and television, the classic peasantry is on the way out in every country. The Zionist pioneers were determined that in their new land there should never exist the kind of peasantry that, whatever its folkloristic virtues, has to be lifted by the cities out of its political and economic bondage. On the contrary, it would be the new land life which would set the liberating pace for the cities. "The towns do no more than 'process' the fruits of the village," wrote Weizmann. It could be said that this was already happening in Jewish Palestine, not yet as Weizmann meant it, but in an equally important sense. Now it is no longer happening, and part of the cause is in the confused thinking of the kibbutzim, in a failure of nerve and of intellectual courage.

Behind the cyclic letdown of mood in kibbutz and city alike, in Israel as a whole, there is another great factor that receives little attention in public discussion. As subject matter it does not belong to this chapter, but it must be mentioned here. For many reasons the awareness of Israeli Jews that they are the expression of the aspirations of world Jewry has been receding into forgetfulness. The pioneers and other emigrants of the early Zionist days felt themselves carried by a tidal wave moving through Jewish history and through world Jewry, even when world Jewry was not explicitly conscious of it. They were Jewry adapting itself to the modern world, finding a new technique of survival. It was a common article of Zionist faith that a Jewish homeland would confer new meaning on Jewish life everywhere, and would reinterpret in modern terms —like a living *midrash*—the permanent values of Judaism. The actions of the Zionists therefore had a majestic significance, ranging through time and space, embracing the universal Jewish phenomenon. This significance has now been lost, and its restoration is the business of the second renaissance.

CHAPTER VII

After the Stampede

❀

I

THEY are still remarkable places, these kibbutzim, the old ones and the new ones, each in its own way. Even to a detached observer, for whom Biblical prophecy and Jewish dreams of a thousand years are only literary expressions, not personal experience, they are remarkable. Especialy is it so if he has made his visits at long intervals, and has clocked the older kibbutzim twenty or twenty-five years apart. This is not merely conquest of desert and swamp and man-made infertility of the earth; it is likewise the conquest of human helplessness, the undoing of physical-psychological handicaps. In terms of the earth's panorama, it is also the advance of high civilization into derelict areas. Let such an observer remember the desolation he once saw in the Huleh Valley and the Valley of Jezreel, in the Galilean hills and the Plain of Sharon; and let him now climb the same hills, descend into the same valleys, and linger amid the fields and orchards and homes of the older settlements. In a world as threatened as ours is by destructive skills, it warms the heart and steadies the outlook to stand in the midst of the purely creative tradition of Genesis.

In the respect just spoken of the kibbutzim are not more remarkable than other achievements on the land, moshavim, or moshavot, modified socialistic or purely individualistic settlements. But rightly or wrongly I consider the kibbutzim to be the chief original driving force in Israel; moreover, their reinfusion of fertility into neglected earth and frustrated men was accompanied by a special vision and plan, the fate of which is now under scrutiny.

A well-established kibbutz is a complex and fascinating organism. As the visitor is conducted through it, through the grainfields and orchards and vegetable gardens, the workshops, the factory (clothespins, or plywood, or furniture, or packing-boxes, or preserves, or electrical appliances), past the artificial fishponds (a number of kibbutzim have these), the machine shop, the barns, the stables, the chicken houses, the dairy, the laundry, the tailoring-shop, the shoe-making shop, the storage bins, then into the great dining-room, the nursery buildings, the meeting-hall, the children's dormitories, the cultural institutions, the memorial for the fallen in the War of Independence, the flowerbeds, the playgrounds, the little forest, the green common, the homes (graduated from the early shacks, which are being replaced steadily, to the comfortable little apartments of the veterans), the public showers, the school, the secretariat, it becomes clear to him that this is no amateur enterprise. Much ability, management, calculation, a great deal of trial and error, went into the creation of this unit of life. It is big business now. The unit has an annual turnover of hundreds of thousands of dollars a year. It is linked with hundreds of similar units throughout the country, acting together with them, for the purchase of supplies, for the sale of produce, through co-operatives owned in common. Or, more exactly, owned by the over-all labor organization of the country, operating in the cities as well as on the land.

Very definitely the kibbutz could not have been created without the help of the general Zionist funds. But all the financial help in the world would have been useless if the kibbutzniks had not been such an extraordinary amalgam of vision, practicality, and endurance. Everywhere the early years were brutally difficult; the funds were never more than a trickle; there was hunger, loneliness, inexperience; but there was the Jewish and the socialist vision. And it was only by common effort, common suffering, common planning, and a hope in common, that the enterprise could be established. No success was ever more richly merited.

And in spite of the changes and falling away I have described, the simplicity of life in the kibbutz is a refreshing and impressive thing. There is no sign of that kind of demonstrative luxury from which the Chalutzim fled; food, clothing, accommodation are the same everywhere, except in so far as the veterans are given the first use of new and improved apartments; possessions are the same, reward for labor, skilled and unskilled, is the same; there is no competition of consumption; there are no temptations to wasteful consumption.

What the visitor begins to wonder about, after he has digested the first heartening impression, is whether this simple and austere life, this equality in physical frugality, still maintains the original standards of economic effectiveness in other respects. The kibbutzniks do not eat better than the city workers; do not dress better—if as well; have no extravagances. Their accommodations are not superior —that is, not until one begins to analyze. Where the children have not been brought home (and that is still in the large majority of kibbutzim) the parents have a room to themselves, and the children are taken care of in the nursery, kindergarten, or dormitory. Since there is no cooking done privately a kitchen is not needed. We may say, then, that the smallest kibbutz family enjoys the equivalent of two rooms and a kitchen. The city working-family seldom gets more. As against this, the woman in the kibbutz puts in a full day's work, like a man, and presumably this is more than an offset to the cost of boarding and caring for the children from the cradle to the age of eighteen.

But is it? The whole question of kibbutz costs is a dark and complicated one. I for one cannot form an opinion. But I must point out that in the kibbutzim the service staff is enormous: there is the nursery with its trained attendants, and the kindergarten teachers for the next stage. There is the care of the dormitories. There is the communal kitchen and the communal laundry. There is the administration. And the calculation of comparative consumption as between the kibbutz member and the city worker is so difficult in the separate details that the over-all comparison will probably be debated forever. And of course the figures will vary from kibbutz to kibbutz.

Even a simple business like communal kitchen defies real analysis. I received four estimates on kitchen service costs. From the average—to which all estimates approximated—it appears that one person working eight hours a day can serve three meals for eighteen persons, cook, wash up, and clean the place. The preparation of fifty-four meals in separate homes would take—here the estimates varied widely, but certainly it could not be done with less than twenty working hours. From the point of view of cost, then, the communal kitchen is a great advantage. But one never knows what to make of these figures. Morning and noon meals in the working-class family entail little real effort; often they fit at practically no labor cost into the interstices of the routine. The important evening meal is something else; but in the working-class family the children help. On the other hand, there is the buying of supplies, in these days of austerity and standing in line an exhausting and ennervating task, of which the kibbutz relieves the woman. We may perhaps grant that as an isolated item the communal kitchen is an economy. But if we add up the communal kitchen and the nursery and the kindergarten and the dormitory, we do not know what the over-all result is in terms of comparative costs. (I omit here the ideological side.)

But the kibbutz, with all the simplicity of its life, has its own "extravagances." Its cultural demands are higher than the city's. It spends more on its institutions than city workers do. Its schools cost more; its little museum, fine and useful as it is, represents a far higher proportion of the kibbutz income than cities spend on similar public services. This is all to the credit of the kibbutz. But we are led back to a fundamental question:

Among the justifications of the collective experiment in the national purpose was its economic effectiveness. It cost less to integrate an immigrant into a kibbutz than into any other type of settlement. But suppose the kibbutz has now canceled this advantage in the high standard of service enjoyed by its members?

It is widely held, in circles not unfriendly to kibbutz ideology, that the kibbutzim have a higher standard of living than their production justifies, and it is only thanks to an exceptionally favorable market that they have so far maintained this standard and have nevertheless been able to put part of their income into the expansion of their units.

This complaint accounts for a good part of the public decline of the collectives.

II

The kibbutzniks will not admit that they spend too much on themselves. They point to their expanded productivity. Nevertheless they are troubled by the accusation. Coming on top of the internal changes I have described, it adds to their inner uneasiness; it strikes at their faith in the continuing historic validity of the kibbutz;

above all, it deprives them of the courage to face the crucial problem of the present phase in the development of Israel—the problem of the stampede immigration and its effects on the collectivist sector.

Whatever may be said about the kibbutzim, no one can accuse them of not having tried hard to hold on to their basic principle—the total rejection of *Mehrwert,* surplus value, profit on hired labor. Now it is true that even before the emergence of the Jewish State, and the present crisis, before the frantic need to find employment for hundreds of thousands of newcomers, some kibbutzim had—like the socialist co-operatives in the city—deviated now and again from the basic principle; had hired outside workers at a wage; had "taken advantage" of the proletariat, which has nothing to live on but its labor—and made a profit on it. When the kibbutz decided to add industry to agriculture it created for itself an inescapable alternative between occasional deviation and the risk of costly failure. It might need a good cook for its little health resort (which served the general public), or an expert for its canning factory or its machine shop, and was unable either to find one among its members or to persuade an outsider with the right qualifications to join the kibbutz as a member. Sickness might suddenly interfere with production. A rush job courageously contracted for could not be completed without temporary hired assistance. The issue was met rather furtively; the transgression was slurred over. There was no thought of abandoning the principle; it was only a question of adjustment pending the development by the kibbutz of the necessary skills and facilities. And indeed, the adjustment was made as soon as possible. The kibbutzim never liked to have hired workers in their midst.

Today, however, there are thousands of hired workers in the kibbutzim. There is nothing furtive about their presence. They are a distinct and important feature of the kibbutz economy. And a serious quarrel has developed between the kibbutzim and the public. The kibbutzim are protesting: "We don't want hired laborers in our midst. It is against our faith and traditional practice. We are going to get rid of them as soon as possible." The public replies angrily: "These are not the old times. You'll have to get off your ideological high horse, and give up the pretense of socialism. We're in a national crisis. You're going to keep these workers, and take more."

III

All previous modifications in the kibbutz form of life were more or less voluntary. They were the result of inner experience and of calculated adaptations to changes in external circumstance. It was an evolutionary process. One could not speak of an assault by the outside world.

But now vast masses of immigrants have appeared in the country, at the invitation, or rather earnest solicitation, of every segment of the old population, including the kibbutzim. Most of the newcomers are entirely without means, without skills, and without tools. The country as a whole lacks tools, instruments of production, as well as training personnel. But the kibbutzim *are* and *have* instruments of production; and they are as interested as anyone else in putting the newcomers to work. What can they do about it?

The first, most obvious suggestion is: draw the newcomers, or a certain proportion of them, into the kibbutzim as members. The answer is: the newcomers won't come into the kibbutzim as members. Those from the Oriental countries have brought with them a patriarchal family outlook to which the kibbutz form of life is incomprehensible; those from behind the Iron Curtain countries

114

have had experiences with compulsory collectivism which
make them start with traumatic dread from voluntary collectivism. Such newcomers as are ready to work—some are
not—can often be persuaded to go on the land. But they
will not hear of the kibbutz. They can be persuaded to settle on their own pieces of land, in moshavim (but it remains to be seen whether these settlements have a future);
and they are willing to hire themselves out as laborers. But
they want to be paid in money, and allowed to spend or
save their earnings as they see fit. They will live in the
maabarot (transit camps), near the employing kibbutz, or
in new villages, or in the city, *and they will live in their
own way*.

In many cases the attitude of the newcomers is not even
an implied criticism of the kibbutz way of life, an ideological rejection, even in simple terms. It is a primitive or
primal demand to have as little as possible to do with social
obligations and involvements. Were the kibbutzim everything they have ever dreamed of being, this attitude would
be unaffected.

But the kibbutzim are short of members, both relatively
and absolutely. Relatively because they are getting very
few of the newcomers, and so they are becoming a smaller
and smaller proportion of the population; absolutely, because they are not getting enough members from the old
population to maintain their programs of development.
The kibbutzim are not, have never been, mere showplaces,
monastic retreats of the right life. They have always looked
upon themselves as a dynamic element in the country.
They have reached out into new forms of production, they
have increased their unit memberships far beyond the
early concepts, precisely because they placed equal emphasis on the two slogans: *to build*, and *to build right*. But on
the one hand, they will not be building if they do not go
on expanding; and on the other hand they will not be

building right if they expand by abandoning wholesale and programmatically the principle of "no exploitation, no profit on other people's labor."

The kibbutzim feel as deeply as anyone else about the newcomers. The productivization of these hundreds of thousands is a life-and-death problem for the state, and the kibbutzim want to have their part in solving the problem. In so far as it is a question of land work, they are prepared to supply training cadres for new kibbutzim; they supply instructors—thereby depleting themselves of manpower— even when it is not a question of creating new kibbutzim. But they cannot bring themselves to throw open the established kibbutzim to the unlimited employment of the newcomers.

The second obvious suggestion is: "Employ as many newcomers as you can, but do not make a profit on them. Retain no surplus value. Pay them for their work, not at the market rate, or the rate fixed by the Histadrut (the Labor Federation), but according to the full value of their labor, keeping nothing back for the kibbutz."

Again the obvious happens to be the impossible.

A kibbutz that turns itself into a systematic employer of hired labor on a large scale and makes nothing on the transaction condemns itself to a static condition. It cannot expand because the hired workers, drawing out every piastre's worth of value created, leave nothing behind for expansion. The kibbutz is thus placed at a fatal disadvantage vis-à-vis the competition of private enterprise on the land. The kibbutz becomes in fact a combination socialist and private enterprise retaining the most disadvantageous features of both. (In a discussion of these alternatives a kibbutznik reminded me of Zangwill's definition of a Jewish pessimist—one who, faced with a choice of two evils, takes both.)

There are objections of wider scope to this second suggestion that the kibbutzim save their socialist principles by giving their hired workers the full value of their labor. Instead of spreading the socialist gospel, the kibbutzim will be confirming their employees in the capitalist outlook. The word will go round: "The best employers are the kibbutzim. . . ." Who will want to join a kibbutz if he can be the unexploited employee of the kibbutz, enjoy all of its economic advantages, suffer none of its self-imposed disciplines? The workers will in this case become the exploiters of the idealism of the kibbutzniks, whom in the end they will come to regard, with a mixture of incomprehension and pity, as plain suckers. Unless, indeed, they suspect that it is all a racket.

Actually the foregoing proposal is a trifle silly, and I mention it only because it has been put forward with some earnestness. It ignores the effect on the general labor market and the wage scales fixed by the Histadrut—of which the kibbutzim are a part! In a couple of kibbutzim the following practice has been suggested. Hired workers, in field or factory, will be paid at the government fixed or market rate; but the kibbutz will turn over the surplus value to some labor institution, or to some fund devoted to the settlement of the newcomers. This does, indeed, clear the individual kibbutz from the charge of capitalist exploitation. But what happens to the problem of expansion? It might be argued, of course, that the kibbutz should be satisfied to expand only in so far as its own members do not consume all the wealth *their* labor creates. But surplus value, retained and unspent, is the very foundation of economic progress. And it is a constant discouragement to the kibbutz to see a considerable part—perhaps the major part —of its reinvestable production disappearing regularly. For it must be remembered that the greater number of kibbutz workers are employed in the services, and are not direct creators of reinvestable wealth. The newcomers might easily outnumber those kibbutz members from whose work something is left for expansion.

We are reaching what I believe to be the heart of the problem—the psychological element. The bulk of the resistance which I found in the kibbutzim to the mass employment of outsiders, the transformation of the kibbutz into an absorber of labor, arose from fear. "We do not want," they protested, "to become systematic users of hired labor. We have sometimes used hired labor in the past under pressure. We never liked it. We are using hired labor now, partly because we are critically short of hands, partly because we have been maneuvered into it. But our ideal, our very *raison d'être,* demands that we reverse this trend. Instead, we are being asked to encourage it, turn it into a system. We are being asked to make a principle of what has always been a compromise, to pledge ourselves to permanent and increasing use of something that strikes at the root of kibbutz ideology and practice. We are told that we must learn to think in a new way of our production problem, and of our national function, our role in the development of the country. Instead of pacing the growth of an agricultural class, as we once did, we are now blocking it— they tell us—by doctrinaire rigidity. We must therefore change fundamentally: we—the kibbutzniks—must become something we have always thought of with horror: an employing class. We must develop an employer-employee psychology."

I asked: "Isn't it a question of degree? Also of a passing phase? You admit you've had to use hired labor in the past; you're using it now. Well, you are being asked to use more of it, for a longer time."

They said: "What we are really being asked to do is set up a system that would kill the prospects for a renaissance of the kibbutz movement. The camps of the transients which are planted close to the kibbutzim will transform themselves into permanent workers' villages integrated with the kibbutzim. The system will take root, become ineradicable. And we, the kibbutzim, will become closed corporations. We will have equality of ownership among ourselves; but we shall all be employers of outside labor from the attached villages. We are, in short, being asked to liquidate the whole kibbutz system."

After many talks with old and new acquaintances in the kibbutzim I began to feel that a basic difficulty was the loss of moral self-confidence. The kibbutzniks do not trust themselves to withstand the psychological effects of prolonged employer-employee relations. Here and there I have heard quiet confessions: "When you have a body of strangers in your midst, hired workers who don't understand the kibbutz, have no interest in its welfare, you look down on them. Also, you tend to give them the unpleasant and monotonous work. You know they'll leave you the moment they can get a better job elsewhere. And there's something else: it's very easy to get into the habit of including surplus values in your calculations. Say we've used five thousand hired working days during the year; in the factory, or at harvest time. We've paid out an average of two and a half pounds a day—we know that the work was worth at least three and a half. We're five thousand pounds to the good. It's much too pleasant a feeling to encourage."

But the corruption will not be confined to adults. The effect on the youth of the kibbutzim might well be even more disastrous. Grownups can perhaps handle a compromise by holding on to a perspective. Young people receive a permanent bent from a passing phase. Thus, if objective conditions a few years hence should favor a renaissance of kibbutz activity, the morale of the kibbutzim might by then be ruined.

And so they continue to wrestle with the problem. So far the only practical solution is really an evasion. There has been set up a special organ to take over the handling of hired labor in the kibbutzim. This organ will be the intermediary contractor, and the kibbutzim will not figure in the role of employers. No doubt a certain amount of unpleasantness can thus be avoided; but the problem is still there. And it cannot be solved by organizational devices.

IV

The problem of hired labor in the kibbutzim was not created by the stampede immigration; but the stampede immigration (and all the more that part of it which was artificially stimulated) has deprived the kibbutzim of the hope of finding an evolutionary solution. One can hardly speak now of a voluntary adaptation. The kibbutzim are compelled to give as it were at pistol-point immediate answers to question that go to the heart of their social philosophy.

And the challenge came at a time of internal moral crisis. The kibbutzniks cling to their social philosophy, but they are not the self-assured idealists of twenty years ago. They are, moreover, aware that the moral climate within the Zionist movement is no longer favorable to their original dreams. That has changed together with the moral climate of the world at large. And again I must make advance mention of the great over-all factor to be described in a later chapter: the recession of the feeling that once inspired the vast majority of Palestinian immigrants, that they were carried by the tidal wave moving through Jewish history and through world Jewry.

CHAPTER VIII

The World Division

❀

I

THE severest blow to the inner morale and the public standing of the kibbutz form of life is the breakup of a number of kibbutzim on the East-West issue. Here we have a mixture of inherent, organic development—the inevitability of character—and external, world-wide forces. I shall speak of the breakups that came *before* the Prague trial and the Case of the Poisoning Doctors. The additional splits which followed that bungled anti-Semitic maneuver are only special illustrations of the older process described here, and they have nothing additional to tell us with respect to the adverse effect on the kibbutz ideal.

There are three principle federations of kibbutzim. One is Kibbutz Artzi of the Hashomer Hatzair (the Young Guard). The members of its constituent kibbutzim are pro-Communist leftists. A second is Ichud Ha-Kibbutzim (Union of Kibbutzim); the constituent members of its kibbutzim are anti-Communist leftists. The third, Kibbutz Ha-Meuchad (the United Kibbutz) did not, until recently, recognize any such classification among the members of its constituent kibbutzim. (I shall refer to the federations as Hashomer, Ichud, and Ha-Meuchad, for the sake of brevity. The names have no intrinsic significance.) Hashomer belongs to the pro-Communist Mapam political party of

Israel, forming its left wing. Ichud (like the moshavim) belongs to the anti-Communist Mapai, which was until recently the government-controlling party and is now the major partner in the labor-centrist coalition. Ha-Meuchad was technically neutral.

It was natural that men and women of similar social and political philosophies should form the groups of comrades which became the kibbutzim; it was natural, therefore, that kibbutzim should fall into groups of right and left. It was, however, not quite so natural that the kibbutzim of the moderate left and those of the extreme left should form themselves into separate federations. But they did. And it was partly in protest against this error that a third federation came into existence, which declared that the Palestinian kibbutz as such, whatever the individual political coloration of its members was—I emphasize, *in its quality as kibbutz*—a Jewish Palestinian life-form, an instrument of moral-social regeneration in Palestine, or Israel. It should be observed that other factors entered into the formation of the federations, but they need not and should not have coincided with the political division.

The fact is that the conduct and purpose of the kibbutz have nothing to do with this political division. One seeks in vain a Marxist explanation, or that contrast of economic interest which makes a Hashomer kibbutz pro-Communist, an Ichud kibbutz anti-Communist. The structure, the organization, the schedules, the internal problems are the same in both. In both, as they grow older, there is the retreat from the early asceticism. If there are differences of practice as between kibbutz and kibbutz, these are not classifiable by federation. There are Hashomer kibbutzim that use hired labor; there are kibbutzim of the Ichud and Ha-Meuchad which do not. If, in the total, the Hashomer kibbutzim do use less hired labor than Ichud kibbutzim (which seems to be the case), the difference is not of real significance.

Of real significance is the fact that Hashomer members do not admit to using hired labor, and make a great to-do about the Marxian purity of their kibbutzim. Actually they show some skill in disguising the practice, as the following instance will show. A kibbutz of Hashomer enters into partnership with a neighboring Arab village to work a hundred dunams (twenty five acres) of tobacco land. The kibbutz supplies the tractors and drivers, the Arabs do the more tedious work, part of it unskilled, part of it skilled. All workers, Jewish and Arab, are paid alike, the profits are divided equally. But in this partnership there is nothing to prevent the Arabs from using hired hands and even child labor. The profits accruing to the kibbutz are as surely tainted with surplus value as if it had hired the Arab laborers direct.

Hashomer members have told me over and over again—with a unanimity that I found disturbing and suspicious—that there is also a great difference between their kibbutzim and those of the Ichud in something even more important than techniques—namely, the spirit. Oddly enough, this is true, but not at all as they meant it. Like all Communists and near-Communists the Hashomer kibbutzniks pretend to have no basic ideological perplexities. They have only "practical problems." But I have already observed in this connection that perplexities which are repressed do not cease thereby to exist. They only become more complicated and dangerous within the setting of a new over-all perplexity. On the surface the Hashomer kibbutzim show more unanimity of outlook than kibbutzim of the Ichud. This gives them a slight edge in competing for the few newcomers available for kibbutz life. The authority of leadership (strange phenomenon in a kibbutz) is stronger in Hashomer than elsewhere, and explanations from above take the place of agreement from below.

We also have here, in miniature, the device of a strong "foreign policy" to offset or cover up the difficulties of domestic changes. The political battle with the government of Israel, the continuous playing up of pro-Russian sentiment, absorb intellectual energies that might otherwise be directed inwards. It is this difference, so precious to Hashomer, so obstructive in solving kibbutz problems, which is perhaps central. The fact remains that Hashomer kibbutzim are not on the whole more efficient, more productive, more self-sacrificing (except of their intellectual faculties) than the kibbutzim of Ichud.

II

Standardization of ideology and daily opinions in the Hashomer kibbutzim has always been more rigid than in any other section of Russian-orientated Mapam, which has always had its moderate wing. Now that Hashomer and Mapam have been shaken to their foundations by the bewildering Russian strategy of the winter of 1952–3, new patterns and alignments are forming. What we have here is, in a loose way, an abbreviated and truncated repetition of the confusion produced by the strategy of 1939–41. Russia proclaims an open alliance with anti-Semitism, avoiding only the name. Communists and pro-Communists are taken unawares. Some rebel from the move (as did the large majority of Mapam and Hashomer). Some (the majority of non-Jewish Communists throughout the world) endorse it. Russia then makes a partial retraction; she clears the doctors, and leaves Prague untouched. That is enough for the faithful, and for many of the dissidents. There is immense rejoicing, which reminds one of the pauper, the rabbi, and the goat.[1] In the hullabaloo two things are forgotten: first that the retraction is partial; second (far more important) the astounding fact that the alliance could have been made at all. However, I am concerned here not with the intrinsic case, but with the intrusion into the kibbutzim of violent group divisions irrelevant to kibbutz management and life; and we shall best understand the nature of the damage done to the kibbutz movement by considering the story of the mixed or "neutral" units of Ha-Meuchad.

Standardization of views is not a Communist or pro-Communist monopoly. Few people are independent thinkers. We generally drift into our opinions under group pressures of various kinds, and political discussions are nearly always a collection of dreary "releases." The majority of rebels, too, only take a popular opinion and stand it on its head; which gives them the impression that they have thought the matter through. The pro-Communist standardization has, however, certain peculiarities. It is, to begin with, more complete. It is interpenetrated, also, with a certain rancorous self-righteousness from which there is no appeal, and which equates dissent with viciousness of purpose and character. It is an opiate—more correctly a hashish—for masses in search of that kind of self-assurance which no human being is entitled to. It is especially attractive to those hyperthyroid types for whom an insensitive and monomaniac activism is a necessity. The objective of discussion and action is not, for these, a reasonable improvement, but total victory *for its own sake.*

[1] A Yiddish folk-tale. A pauper came weeping to a rabbi: "Help me! My life is unbearable. I live with my wife and seven children in a one-room hut. We are dying of suffocation." The Rabbi: "Take in a goat." The bewildered pauper obeys, and returns a week later half dead. He manages to wheeze: "Rabbi! That finishes us." The Rabbi: "Take out the goat." The pauper obeys and returns a few days later beaming: "Rabbi! You're wonderful! You've simply saved our lives."

Kibbutz people, who must work and live together, who must consult continuously on assignments of work, on offices, public policies, sales and purchases, cultural programs and institutional plans, people who run across each other in the field, the factory, the dining-room, the assembly hall, a dozen times daily—people thus intertangled with each other week in week out, year in year out, must not be subjected to the strain of a Communist-anti-Communist atmosphere. Unfortunately, Communists and pro-Communists pride themselves on their party devotion or devotion to the line, their vigilance, their never-relaxing activity. If it was a question of choosing a delegate to an inter-kibbutz conference, appointing a secretary, inducting a teacher, electing a chairman, arranging a celebration, inviting a speaker or an artist—*they* were always on the job, in their own, special way. One had to watch them like a hawk. The chairmanship or secretaryship would be without political significance; so would the choice of speaker or artist. But of significance was the appointment of the Mapam-orientated, or at least the Mapam-proposed member of the kibbutz. Significant was the mere fact that the Mapam group had had its way, and thus asserted its ascendancy.

It is surely not necessary by now to multiply the instances of Communist-front practice; anyone with a touch of political sophistication is familiar with them and their meaning. So there emerged in the "neutral" kibbutzim of Ha-Meuchad the familiar odious pattern that is the degradation of political life in every part of the world: the merits of a problem or proposition are overridden by the political exploitation of it. The guilt or innocence of Scottsboro boys, of an Alger Hiss, ceases to be the real purpose of investigation; and the conclusion of the bystander is discredited in advance by the sickening unanimity of the Communists. When one considers them wrong on the particular point, one is buried under their abuse; when one considers them right one is infected by their endorsement. At the other end of the scale Nazis and Fascists, the mirror-twins of the Communists, create the same dilemma. Except for the absence of Nazis and Fascists in the kibbutzim here being described, these miniature worlds became replicas of the world at large in the struggle to retain intellectual objectivity.

For everywhere in the world the savage contempt of Communists and near-Communists for leftist liberals is part of the accepted revolutionary technique: and with reason. As power-seekers the Communists have far more to fear from sincere reformism than from outright, thickwitted, brittle, suicidal reaction. What a nightmare to the extremist are the Mirabeaus and Kerenskys, and what a sigh of relief bursts from him when these fall. And what a nightmare to the Communists and near-Communists of Israel are the reformist efforts of the admittedly far from perfect Mapai and the Mapai kibbutzim.

III

Interwoven with the general skirmishing in the mixed kibbutzim was the continuous battle for the control of the schools. It is questionable whether, even without the crucial problem of the young, the near-Communists of the Mapam and the anti-Communists of the Mapai could have gone on living together in the neutral kibbutzim. Fifteen and twenty years ago there was already strain enough, and incidents took place which foretold the present crisis. Since the Second World War, with the polarization of the world struggle, the aggression of the near-Communists had become an intolerable nervous imposition even apart from the sensitive school question.

The Jewish youth of Palestine has always been subjected

prematurely to ideological pressures. From the beginning, religious groups founded their separate schools with a separate curriculum and separate prayer-schedules; schools of the half-secularized middle class modeled themselves on the secular traditions of the Western world, with a natural emphasis, however, on Hebrew literature, which cannot quite be regarded as secular; schools of the left were founded by the kibbutzim and of the labor movement generally. The British Mandatory Power, doing little in the way of education either for the Jews or the Arabs, had no control over the schools.

All this was bad enough. In a land with settled traditions, experimental and parochial schools are, in my opinion, an excellent thing, a safeguard against standardization. In a land in the making such variations are dangerous. It is hard to determine whether the early Palestinian Jewish groups can be blamed for the misfortune of the divided school system; there is a complicated and confusing history behind it. Whatever the blame for these beginnings, and wherever it falls, this much is certain: the continuation of the division, in full force, into the opening period of statehood, is a calamity.

But as if the existing divisions were not enough, there crept into the kibbutzim a new one—the division between extreme left and moderate left; and the world situation being what it is, this meant pro-Communism and anti-Communism. I will not go into a detailed account of developments; I will only state my opinion that in the new fission, the one which occurred within the educational system of the kibbutzim, I cannot find extenuating circumstances, as I do in the old divisions throughout the Jewish community. In the kibbutzim the intrusion of the fractionating force was conscious, deliberate, programmatic, and reckless of consequences. It came from the extreme left.

In kibbutzim entirely Mapai or Mapam the problem did not reveal itself; in each case the unanimity on the spot concealed it. In the "neutral" kibbutzim, in Ha-Meuchad, that federation which was to correct the error of left and right kibbutzim, the problem exploded before the eyes of the whole country.

In few societies has the upbringing of children been so programmatic and passionate a concern as in the kibbutz; their physical and moral welfare was the first charge on the attention and resources of the parents; and from the beginning the kibbutzniks knew that if the youth did not grow up to follow gladly in their footsteps, their dream was a hollow one, their life of sacrifice a vanity.

In the kindergarten political philosophies do not play an obvious role; but in the first elementary classes there are already possibilities for the fanatical teacher. The curriculum itself will not give us a full picture of the division, which will only be suggested by certain differences in reading-material, by emphases on certain subjects. It is the tone, and the extracurricular activities, which will reveal the full extent of the intrusion. It is the expression on the teacher's face when certain personalities are mentioned; it is the preparation for festivals and celebrations; it is the sharpening of controversial issues that the children hear discussed by their parents. Is the picture of Lenin or Stalin to hang side by side with that of Herzl and Weizmann in the assembly room? Is the Red Flag to fly over the kibbutz side by side with the Israeli flag on Independence Day? The teacher's attitude on these questions would be known or inferred. If he did not state openly in class that the Mapai leaders, who make up most of the present government and have been the core of Israel's builders, are reactionaries, warmongers, American imperialists, betrayers of the working class, aggressors in Korea, condoners of bacteriological warfare—if he did not state this in class, his enthusiasm for certain extracurricular activities, the relative allotments of time given to May Day celebrations and Independence Day celebrations, were indications enough. The Mapam leadership—and the leadership preceding it before Mapam was formed—saw to it that they should be.

IV

Finally the tensions in the mixed kibbutzim of Ha-Meuchad reached the snapping-point; and then the country was treated to the astounding spectacle of an internal transfer of populations. Hundreds of Mapam sympathizers withdrew from kibbutzim with Mapai majorities, hundreds of Mapai sympathizers from kibbutzim with Mapai majorities. Men and women who had worked side by side for a score of years, transforming the wilderness into a garden, picked up their few personal belongings, and fled like refugees from impossible surroundings. Families were broken up, children turned against parents, old friendships went up in flames. Two or three large kibbutzim with evenly balanced Mapai and Mapam members proposed physical fission, and to one of these I went, dejectedly, to try and grasp what was happening.

It was a kibbutz illustrious in the annals of Zionism. I had seen it first nearly thirty years ago, a heroic little brotherhood in the desolation which was then the Valley of Jezreel. It had grown steadily for three decades, conquering one problem after another, passing through all the now familiar phases, from the floundering and hungry beginnings of unskilled pioneers to the efficiency and self-assurance of veteran builders. They had worked together under the British administration, they had resisted together its latter-day usurpations; they had fought off the attacks of Arabs in the rebellions of 1936–9, they had—together with their grown-up sons and daughters—defended themselves against the attack of the Arab nation in 1948 and 1949. And now I saw something that satire itself could not have invented: the common dining-room, that obstinately sustained symbol and instrument of brotherhood, had divided off into two parts, with three long rows of tables in each. On one side of "the Thirty-Eighth Parallel" ate the members of the Mapam, on the other the members of the Mapai. In the kitchen two groups of workers with two sets of dishes cooked for them—one for each political party.

The school had been divided, and there were two sets of classes, Mapai and Mapam; there were two dining-rooms for the children; and some married sons and daughters who disagreed with their parents—as perhaps with brothers and sisters—also took their children with them to their respective halves of the colonies; and the grandparents had to watch the grandchildren, the little cousins, being mobilized into hostile camps.

I left the kibbutz like one stunned. I had known all about it before; I had heard and read about the quarrels, the insults, the fist fights; but seeing it it was something else. And it was something else to hear a grizzled father tell me: "Oh, yes, the children visit us from time to time, but we have to be very careful not to mention or hint at certain subjects."

V

Some kibbutzniks are foolishly trying to minimize the tragedy of the breakup by pointing to figures. "After all, it affects only one federation, Ha-Meuchad, and even here the kibbutzim were so preponderantly Mapai or Mapam that the transfers were mostly insignificant. Once the transfers and splits are affected, normal kibbutz life will be resumed, the scandal will be forgotten, everything will be as before."

Nothing will be as before. The old unanimity in the various Mapai and Mapam kibbutzim was at least presumed to be natural; an accident, not a law. Henceforth it is known to be a fiat. Particularly shattering is the effect in the Hashomer kibbutzim from which minorities were *expelled* for refusing to join by vote in condemning the anti-Semitic implications of the Prague and doctors' trials. A shocking bankruptcy has been exposed. The kibbutz form of life is now known to be incapable, in its present form, or under present conditions, of uniting men and women in an overriding common task, which as it happens, is in no way affected in practice by the philosophies which divide them. This is what hurts: the knowledge that there is no *practical* difference involved. What we have here is a tyranny of ideas, a discipline of utterance, which foreshadows the true totalitarian state. When one remembers what the pioneers started out to build in the way of ideal social organisms, when one looks at this development, one finds no consolation in statistics.

Some consolation may be found in the fact that we have to do here with one of those world forces which we could not take into account at the beginning. The cold war has reproduced itself in the kibbutzim (which, I insist again and again, have no economic divisions and competitive rivalries to explain the split) by a kind of electrical induction. The subsidence of the cold war in the world macrocosm will also mean its subsidence in the kibbutz microcosm.

CHAPTER IX

The Future of the Kibbutz

❀

I

THESE, then, are the principal negations that have appeared in kibbutz life. There have been other fallings away from the kibbutz standard which are part of the general decline, but are not in themselves organic; their intrinsic importance has in my opinion been exaggerated. Kibbutzim have been caught trafficking in the black market, buying and selling outside of their own co-operatives and in defiance of the law. But the severity of the crisis sometimes made this practically unavoidable. Let us suppose that a consignment of cattle is expected in a kibbutz; the material for the stall has not been delivered on time; the contractor cannot deliver it, or pretends he cannot, without an "under the counter" payment. The kibbutz is faced with the alternative of breaking the law or losing its new livestock by exposure. I do not suppose that all the black market cases of kibbutzim could be classified thus; but the pressure has often been unbearable; and I have not heard it suggested anywhere, even among the harshest critics of the kibbutzim, that these have become infected with the black market spirit, that they are black marketeers. One would have liked to think of all the kibbutzim as capable of facing any discomfort, any loss of their property, in their incorruptible fidelity to the law. But it is too easy to make a principle of other people's exemplary conduct. And kibbutz property is public property, too. For my own part, I was less disturbed by these reports after frequent visits to kibbutzim. Among these, as among some businessmen, I have had glimpses into circumstances that are not only difficult, but are sometimes rendered intolerably infuriating by administrative tangles and delays.

The kibbutzim are widely accused of occupying a special position in regard to the system of taxation. The same complaint is leveled at the co-operatives of the Histadrut. It is very difficult to form an opinion on such subjects; and I hope that what I have written so far about the kibbutzim will be accepted as proof that I am not evading the problems of the black market and of taxation out of bias. I feel genuinely that the black market is not a disease of the kibbutzim; and that even if they have a favored position in the tax system it is at worst an administrative inequity rather than a moral lapse.

These misdemeanors or aberrations are often brought up excitedly in discussion on the kibbutzim, but even as arguments they are supplementary, not primary. A far larger role in public thinking is played by the fundamental drift I have described. The cry of the critics is: "The kibbutzim aren't what they used to be." Neither are the critics, of course, though they are apt to forget it. There is not, in the Jewish, the Zionist, the Israeli public, that general mood which could produce as its focus the Chalutzic phenomenon. But the secondary and primary arguments are buttressed by an objective fact: the kibbutz is not playing an important role in resolving the current crisis of the stampede immigration. The kibbutz is not part of the dynamic of Israel.

I have been given various estimates of the optimum proportion of land workers to urban workers in Israel. I accept a compromise figure of twenty per cent. The present ratio is about thirteen per cent. The shortage, in a population of about a million and a half, is over a hundred thousand. The kibbutzniks are as genuinely concerned as other Israelis with the maintenance of this balance. The question is: can they do anything about it?

We have seen their reluctance to turn themselves into systematic large-scale employers of hired agricultural labor; and I have referred to the refusal of the newcomers to become members of kibbutzim. A leader of the moshav land-settlement movement in Israel informed me that forty thousand postwar immigrants are in moshavim. He admits that only ten per cent of them can be regarded as genuine moshavniks—people who understand and accept the high principles of co-operative land settlement as practiced and preached by the moshavim. Another well-informed agricultural leader, a director of land settlement, with whom I have frequently traveled throughout Israel, visiting widely scattered points (as I used to travel, in the far-off past, with the great colonizer, Arthur Rupin) also accepts this estimate. The latter speaks of thousands of new immigrants in the *maabarot* (transition camps) who will neither go on the land nor develop into urban workers. Hundreds of them who were cajoled or bullied into trying agricultural work fled back to their tent-and-shanty towns (sometimes paying key-money to be readmitted!), and they show no inclination toward labor or craftsmanship of any kind. Hundreds more have never been tempted to leave the *maabarot*. Thousands have gone into the cities, to live halfway between work and mendicancy—if not worse—and constitute a new *Lumpenproletariat* of the most dangerous kind; this to say nothing of the large admixture of outright criminals. The estimates of the almost irreclaimable element now (autumn 1952) in the country vary between one and two hundred thousand—that is, between seven and a half and fifteen per cent of the population. I say *almost* irreclaimable because no doubt with vast means and personnel, which there is no prospect of obtaining, most of them could be made useful, productive members of society. And unfortunately we must add to their number a proportion of those now settled as moshavniks. Of these some will remain co-operative settlers, some will develop useful individualist villages, and some will drift into shiftlessness when they have used up the credits and other forms of help extended to them by the colonizing agency.

Of those newcomers who have been willing to go on the land, more than half are being trained in the moshav system; the remainder are scattered chiefly in individualist settlements; a few are clustered round the kibbutzim as hired labor. The kibbutzim play the smallest role in absorbing the new immigration agriculturally.

The cry has therefore gone up that the kibbutz is an anachronism. It has no role to play in the future of Israel. Its virtues were those of a given period, a given set of circumstances, and a given generation; all three are gone. The time has come for the liquidation of this form of Israeli life.

II

Sometimes this talk is insincere. I am amused to hear it on the lips of those who have always opposed the kibbutz, but who every year have regretfully withdrawn from it the support that they did not give it the year before. Nevertheless the feeling is widespread among those who have been friends and admirers of the kibbutz way of life, even if unwilling to share it.

We have noted earlier fluctuations in the standing of the collectivist Chalutzim. They would always move into the background whenever there seemed to be prospects that large private investments were about ready to enter Palestine and were only waiting for a decline of socialist influence in the country and movement. They would move back into the foreground when, in a critical moment of Palestinian life, their unique dynamic role was again made manifest.

Thus, in the Arab riots of 1929, and again in the uprisings of 1936-7-8, the courage and daring of the collective and co-operative settlements sent a thrill of pride through the Jewish world; and it was noted with deep satisfaction that the Chalutzic colonies had taken up strategic positions that until then had escaped the attention of the public. The part they played in the post-Independence Arab invasion is a chapter in itself. But more significant than the military role of the Chalutzim was the adaptability of their form of colonization to unforeseen situations.

The Arab uprising of the spring of 1936 fitted into the grand pattern of the Nazi-Fascist assault on the democracies. The Mufti of Jerusalem, who later became an open partisan and coadjutor of Hitler, led the uprising. Its purpose was twofold: first, to arrest Jewish expansion and colonization. Second, to make England's position in Palestine untenable: that is—do what the Jews later did in 1945-8. Had the Jews of Palestine merely remained on the defensive from 1936 on, waiting for the storm to blow over, the first half of the Mufti's purpose would have been fulfilled at once.

Militarily the Jews did remain on the defensive; they saw the trap that the Mufti laid for them—progressive civil war, abandonment of colonization—and avoided it. Despite the long, maddening provocations, the ambushes, night attacks, roadside assassinations, uprooting of orchards, and despite the efforts of Jewish extremists, forerunners of the anti-British terrorists of 1945-8, the Jews refused to be lured into reprisals that would have set the whole country aflame. They kept before them the defeat of the Mufti's first objective, and realized that on the colonization front they dared not take up a defensive position. There they had to advance; they had to increase the number of settlements whatever the dangers, however insecure communication was, however precarious the position of each new point.

It was then that the kibbutz developed the *chomah u-migdal* (wall-and-tower) method of occupation—a lightning technique that was the answer to the Arab terror. In a para-military operation a group of Chalutzim would advance in the night on a piece of land owned by the Jewish National Fund; they would bring with them, ready for assembly, enclosing walls, watch-tower, and the most necessary buildings; from before dawn until the afternoon they would work, under their own fire cover, at the fencing off of the field and the erecting of the buildings; before nightfall they would be in entrenched possession, ready to work the land—and to fight off invaders. Thus, while Arab bands roamed the country, and descended from the hills, in a concerted effort to terrorize the Jews into immobility, the Chalutzim would break out in a dozen new places, to the bewilderment of the Arab strategists. And no form other than the kibbutz could have answered simultaneously both of the two equally necessary purposes of occupation *and* colonization. The first could be achieved by a military group, the second by farmers. The two together called for a combination of qualities found only in the kibbutz.

Actually this peculiar and as it were providential value of the kibbutz had been demonstrated before—as in the occupation of a northern point, Tel Chai, and a point, Bet Alpha, commanding the entrance to the Valley of Jezreel, soon after the First World War. There was, however, this crucial difference: what had been occasional now became systematic; what had been unnoticed was now recognized and applauded. Nor had Tel Chai and Bet Alpha been occupied with the same dramatic and technological swiftness, or under such dramatic circumstances. Nevertheless the principle was the same.

Another instance of adaptability peculiar to the kibbutz form is more recent; is, in fact, still in the experimental stage. Again it is—or may be—the answer to the combination problem of security plus economic development. The industrial centers of Israel are as far away as possible from the land borders—which is not very far in that tiny country. The borders themselves must be lined by strong settlements. But strength means numbers, population. The little purely agricultural kvutzah of a generation ago is not the answer. The new kibbutz, combining industry with agriculture, could be. Individualist industries will not, probably should not, enter the risky border zones to provide a denser population. Kibbutz industries in the Chalutzic spirit, communal, not guided by the profit motive, would seem to be meant for just such a situation.

It is not as simple as all that, of course. City industry does not like the competition of kibbutz industries, and it is hard to reconcile the two. The latter has a public claim and an economic advantage over the former; but the former has a public claim of another kind: it will, after all, be the principle provider of jobs in the country. Far more baffling is the paradoxical position of the kibbutzim. They cannot run fair-sized industries without hired labor; and the larger the proportion of hired labor, the weaker the kibbutz spirit.

III

No one has yet explained clearly what is meant by "liquidating" the kibbutzim. Shall a law be passed compelling them to adopt new constitutions? Shall the existing kibbutzim be left alone, and no assistance given to new ones? The first suggestion is really meaningless; the second is unwise. Not only because the kibbutzim may still harbor great possibilities, but because they are still doing excellent work, even if not on the scale they once dreamed of. In any case, one simply does not liquidate in a hurry a life-form with so recent a history of leadership. It would be a good thing if this loose talk came to an end, both in Israel and in America; and particularly in America, where it is fed by a reactionary mood having little to do with the moral success or failure of the kibbutzim.

Though the kibbutzim are losing ground they are still a pioneering factor. They are not, and in the nature of things cannot be, the unique phenomenon that their forerunners were. It is not the same adventure any more; and we must not reproach them, as they spring up on the borders, and in the Negev, for not producing among us the effect that their forerunners did twenty and thirty years ago. To the extent that there is blame, it falls more on us, the spectators, than on them.

In the new kibbutzim you will find:

(a) Children of the old kibbutzim;

(b) Children of the Palestinian cities, recruited by the youth movements;

(c) The youth from abroad.

(a) The children of the old kibbutzim have always known a life on the land, and a life free from exile pressures. They do not have to remake themselves while they remake the country; they do not have to learn Hebrew while they learn farming, adapt themselves to an unfamiliar clime, invent a social form, and live themselves into it. They take upon themselves a harder life; but it is a matter of degree, not of kind.

140

(b) Part of this applies to the children of the Israeli cities; but they must be more consciously and willfully idealistic than the children of the kibbutzim.

(c) The youth from abroad came either as refugee children, or as idealists from lands of freedom. It is the latter who come nearest to the spirit of the earlier Chalutzim.

But even the young idealists from lands of freedom, who threw up security, comfort, and career (they are mostly of the middle class), and struggled out of their urban and climatic patterns, cannot repeat the miracle of the past. The adventure is less absolute. To begin with, it has been shown beyond a doubt *that the thing can be done.* And then, there is a body of experience, there is a machinery. There is wider approval. Latterly there has been the authority and encouragement of the state. Also, the young Chalutzim of today are circumscribed in their dreams by the vision of themselves twenty years from now, as presented by the older kibbutzim.

Except for the youth from lands of freedom, the young kibbutzniks are not aware of themselves as part of world Jewry, as having a meaning for world Judaism. They do not care for world Judaism; they are puzzled and irritated by talk of it. As far as they can see the ten million Jews of the outside world are either unfortunates who cannot get to Israel, or renegades who do not want to; and the renegades are by far the larger group. World Jewry is ceasing to exist for the young people of Israel.

It is impossible, I think, to overestimate the discouraging effect of such an outlook. It makes the achievement of the new kibbutzim all the more remarkable. But the limitations on their vision will gradually sap their vitality; and with less vitality, with less of a feeling of significance in their work, they will not work out new forms. In respect of this development we have no right to talk of organic necessity or of world forces beyond our control. It fell

within the controllable area of Zionism; and if the best of
the Israeli youth is for the time being alienated from
world Jewry, and from historic Judaism, we must acknowledge an error in the Zionist movement, and consider how it
shall be rectified.

IV

It is useless to try to forecast the future of the kibbutz;
and this in part because it depends, like every other form of
Israeli life, on the future of the relationship between
Israeli and Diaspora Jewries, on the fate of Jewish world
unity. For the time being, the collectivist movement is still
carried by the inspiration of the past. The kibbutzim and
the moshavim, their offspring, gave Jewish Palestine its
forward moral thrust. However welcome the individualist
settlements are, it cannot be claimed that they represented
a source of national inspiration. *They* expressed only the
Jewish longing to be normal; but had they pre-empted the
Jewish scene Zionism would have lost its energizing principle twenty or thirty years ago. The Jews did not want a
peasantry in their homeland; they wanted something
hitherto unknown: a rural-life setting the pace for urban
life. And that was created by the kibbutzim and moshavim.

With all the negative features that I have described, I
would still say that in the kibbutzim the sense of social
service and of national responsibility is higher than in the
general population. Many individuals with high ideals are
to be found in Israel; nowhere are they collected in such
groups. The readiness of the kibbutzim and the moshavim
to contribute manpower to the task of integrating newcomers with the land is a remarkable, and in some ways a
paradoxical phenomenon. While they were harassed by
shortages of manpower, and were being pressed to take on

hired labor, they placed themselves at a disadvantage by sending out members to train the immigrants. If they hoped in this way to win over considerable numbers of converts they soon discovered their mistake. But the supplying of *madrichim,* or guides, still continues.

When the enormous task of opening up the Negev confronted the State of Israel, and relatively vast areas had to be taken over swiftly, the kibbutzim further depleted their manpower. Teams went down from Judea and Galilee to plow and sow a half million dunams of land; and rotating shifts harvested over a hundred thousand tons of grain. Certainly it paid the kibbutzim to do this; but it was not the profit that attracted them. They were excited by the prospect of bringing so much more of the derelict southern semi-desert under the plow.

Like patriotism, public spirit and the sense of civic responsibility are not enough. There is needed also an inspiration; and this inspiration does not flow, either, from mere physical achievement. The propaganda of the State of Israel properly makes a big play round the redemption of the soil and the rehabilitation of human beings. It is a solid satisfaction to linger in kibbutzim, whatever their political coloration, and to listen to technical discussions; on return per man-hour of labor, on yield per dunam, on cash crops versus food crops, on orchard versus grain, on artificial fishpond versus canning factory, on protein and carbohydrate content, on managerial costs and hired labor, on buying and marketing, on soil chemistry, rainfall, cubic meters of irrigation water, intensive and extensive cultivation, rotation, seasonal demands, fluctuating demands, banking rates, taxes, regional co-operative units. This is good, solid, normal. But once it is established, what is it all for? The extension of it provides some employment for the spirit, but the question persists. We cure people to enable them to create; the cure is only a preliminary. Public spirit and civic responsibility are channels, not goals. They are goals only while they are being constructed. The drive that led to their construction, and which will provide them with purpose, is something else.

We cannot, either, look to organizational adjustments as a source of renewal of the spirit. There has been in existence for some years a new form of kibbutz, the partnership kibbutz, which is being preached as "the answer." It is a halfway house between the kibbutz and the moshav. The land is not parceled out, but owned and worked in common, as in the kibbutz; so is the industrial enterprise. As in the kibbutz every member gets the same pay, whatever his skill; but it is made in cash. He is free to spend his earnings as he likes. To each house, which everyone builds for himself according to his taste and means, is attached half an acre of land. The wife does not join in the common work. She attends to the house and, with the help of the husband, earns extra money on the half acre— vegetables, chickens, corn, etc. In this combination form we have the kibbutz advantage of communal ownership as basis, and community of the larger interest. It seeks to avoid the divergences of economic status which have already appeared in many of the moshavim. It is free from some of the pressures of the kibbutz, such as the communal dining-room and the rationed family life. Here, as in kibbutz and moshav, hired labor is of course forbidden.

It is certainly a useful and promising variant in the co-operative rural life of Israel, and though it has not yet caught on, it may have a future. But this, too, is not the heart of the question, which is the restoration to the idealistic land settlements of a sense of purpose transcending the local scene and the temporal struggle. When the answer comes, it will have to show the three co-ordinates of Israel, world Jewry, and the total meaning of Judaism in world history.

V

In my wanderings among younger kibbutzim I would encounter flashbacks to the old spirit, but only in such as had a heavy admixture of newcomers from lands of freedom, and were not of the Shomer type. For in these latter an experience such as I am about to describe is impossible; the problems raised, and the spirit in which they were raised, are alien to a pro-Communist philosophy, which regards them as unreal, in the same way as Christian Scientists regard sickness as unreal.

There stands out in my memory one night in western Galilee. I had been asked to lecture on a literary subject, but I begged off, being anxious to gather information. I therefore gave a summary of my views on certain practical matters, hired labor, the new organization for the outside management of hired labor on the kibbutzim, the competition between city and kibbutz industries, and the like. For a time the discussion after the lecture stayed put; then it broke off suddenly, and before we knew it we were questioning each other on first and last things: the meaning of the good life, the good Jewish life, the life aptest to bring out in us the highest possibilities in social relations, individual being, and the awareness of purpose.

These young people were deeply troubled by the inadequacy of their efforts, which they were inclined to blame on inadequacy of insight. It seemed to them that if they had done all they could, they would be at peace with themselves; and since they were not at peace with themselves it proved that they had fallen short of their best. They spoke of *Ish* and *Makom,* of man and God; and of the old riddle whether man's relationship to man could of itself fulfill all of man's relationship to God. It might be that they had erred in taking just that view, inhibiting thereby a flow of insight from the ultimate source.

Let me make it clear that these were not sentimental boys and girls mooning soulfully in the twilight. They were hard and able workers; they had committed themselves to creating a settlement in a waste place, and their willing hands matched their practical minds. But the "what for" had not been pushed aside by the "how." It concerned them that the manner of their life should have meaning and congruence for the world-wide House of Israel, not less than that the planting of their trees should give them the maximum return per dunam. They had come from American cities strung across the continent from the Pacific to the Atlantic; and they were here, in the land of their people's origin and destiny, not in separation from those who would not accompany them, but as their fulfillment. They were well aware that the fulfillment was concealed from the vast majority of American Jews; but inasmuch as this handful had been awakened to a new Jewish life in the midst of the American Jewish community, one was compelled to believe in the latent powers of that community. Moreover, the fulfillment would not mean the transference to Israel's soil of the majority of American Jews, but of as many of them as Israel and America would need for a permanent interpenetration of the reawakened Jewish spirit.

I stood before them, and they sat in a semicircle on the grass. Behind me was the Mediterranean, before me the hill country of western Galilee, with the lights of townlets and settlements scattered through the night. Safed and Nazareth and Tiberias and Gilead were nearby, beyond the slopes. Even within this little section of Israel an everlasting search had been conducted for the way of life and the purpose of Israel's people. Hereabouts Elijah had been born, here Jesus and His disciples had been active, the Tannaitic teachers had taught after the destruction. Here Jewish mystics of the Middle Ages, drawn back from the

146

exile, had settled. And now these young people were here, one with the Prophets and the Tannaim and the mystics, and one also with the intervening ages and with the community beyond two oceans.

And it was as if I were rehearsing, in my own life, this concentration of the life of a whole people, because suddenly I was thirty years younger, and the Chalutzim who surrounded me were those I had strolled with on the banks of the Vistula, or through the streets of Lodz, and had met again a little while later in Ain Charod and K'far Gileadi and Bet Alpha. This alone apparently was real, since it alone persisted, while the accidents that we miscall history fell away and the purpose that they had obscured again became visible.

CHAPTER X

Multitude

❀

I

From Chaim Nachman Bialik I received the following interpretation, his own or traditional, of the Book of Jonah: it is primarily a protest against the indiscriminate asceticisms of the Prophets, many of whom, born in the desert and bred to its brutalities, despised the amenities of city life as evils in themselves. It is a protest against the rancorous and grudging philosophy that a diet of locusts and a covering of animal skins are the necessary conditions of the virtuous life. It is also a double-edged satire on the professional pride of the Prophets and their hypocrisy.

God sent Jonah to announce the doom of the Ninevites: "Arise, go to Nineveh, that great city, and cry against it; for their wickedness is come up before me." But Jonah had some knowledge of God, and anticipated an act of underhanded benevolence. So he fled from before God, and took ship, and was swallowed by a great fish. (That picturesque bit of embroidery has had the unfortunate effect of diverting the world's attention from a profound parable into the silliest conceivable controversies.) Delivered from this unusual durance, Jonah received the message a second time, and went to Ninevah and cried against it: "Yet forty days and Nineveh shall be overthrown."

Thereupon the Ninevites repented, and God saw that they had turned from their evil way, and he too repented of the evil that he had intended. But it displeased Jonah exceedingly, and he was very angry, and he remembered his suspicions. "I told you so," he stormed. "Was not this my saying when I was yet in my country? Therefore I fled. For I knew that thou art a gracious God, and merciful, slow to anger, and of great kindness. Therefore now, O Lord, take I beseech thee, my life from me: for it is better for me to die than to live."

Better, thought Jonah, that Nineveh should perish than that a Prophet of God should be made such a fool of.

Then God asked: "Doest thou well to be angry?"

Jonah did not answer. He only went out of the frustrating city and made himself a booth and sat in its shadow, "till he might see what had become of the city." For it appears that he was an obstinate man, and still hoped that his reputation might be re-established. And in the night God caused a gourd to grow up and clamber over the booth, to increase the shadow; and in the midst of his chagrin "Jonah was exceedingly glad of the gourd." But in the night that followed God prepared a worm, which ate at the gourd and caused it to wither as fast as it had grown. "And it came to pass, when the sun did arise, that God prepared a vehement east wind; and the sun beat upon the head of Jonah, that he fainted, and wished in himself to die, and said: It is better for me to die than to live. And God said to Jonah: Doest thou well to be angry for the gourd? And he said: I do well to be angry. Then said the Lord: Thou hast had pity on the gourd, for the which thou hast not laboured, neither madest it grow; which came up in a night, and perished in a night: and should I not spare Nineveh, that great city, wherein are more than sixscore thousand persons that cannot discern between their right hand and their left hand; and also much cattle?"

II

This lesson and reading had its *propos*. We were discussing the demonstrative asceticism of the early Chalutzim, and their flight from the cities; and Bialik surmised that this had something to do with the love of the Prophetic books which dominated the Chalutzic outlook. Now Bialik was an admirer of the Chalutzim, but he belonged to the cities; a great poet, and a very able businessman. He was a lover of books and libraries, and a printer-publisher by profession. He understood the zeal of the Chalutzim, without which they could not have carried out their mission. Nevertheless, he said, the city, with its comfortable houses, its shops and gardens and libraries and theaters, was as legitimate a way of life as that of the nomad and the farmer. "I am not apologizing for the cities when I say 'as legitimate,'" he explained. "I mean that they are as high an expression of man's divine possibilities. God is born in the desert, but he becomes civilized in the cities. Was he not prepared to spare even Sodom if there had been at least ten just men in it? But Jonah would have rained fire and brimstone on Nineveh even though the king and the people put on sackcloth and ashes, and cried mightily unto God. He was a *nit-farginner,* a grudging soul; it irked him to see people well-dressed, at ease, smiling, flirting. We are not told that he was a Wahabbi, a desert man, but that was his spirit."

"Isaiah the Prince certainly wasn't a desert man," I said, "but we have his chapter three."

I was referring to that celebrated attack, delivered in such murderous detail, on the elegances of the ladies of Jerusalem:

> Because the daughters of Zion are haughty, and
> walk with stretched forth necks and wanton eyes,

walking and mincing as they go, and making a tinkling with feet; therefore the Lord will smite with a scab the crown of the head of the daughters of Zion and the Lord will discover their secret parts. In that day the Lord will take away the bravery of the tinkling ornaments about their feet, and their cauls, and their round tires like the moon, and the chains and the bracelets, and the mufflers, the bonnets, and the ornaments of the legs, and the headbands, and the tablets, and the earrings, the rings, and nose-jewels, the changeable suits of apparel, and the mantles, and the wimples, and the crisping pins, the glasses, and the fine linen, and the hoods and the vails. And it shall come to pass that instead of sweet smell there shall be a stink.

"He wasn't a desert man," admitted Bialik. "But like the Chalutzim he was fed up with the cities. And notice how he throws everything together. Even a change of apparel is impermissible."

"He meant," I suggested, "that if they abused such things, they were not to have them at all."

"You don't mend too much with too little," he answered. "And you don't answer a problem by destroying its terms. The problem of mankind is that of living together in large numbers. The problem will recur again and again because certain high forms of human self-expression are possible only as the result of numbers. The Chalutzim are afraid of the problem of numbers; but some day they will have to face it. One of the greatest laws formulated by Moses—a much neglected one—is: 'Thou shalt not follow a multitude to wrong.' This means: thou shalt not be part of a mob. The mob! The dreadful thing that emerges in the twinkling of an eye from a crowd of human beings, to bind them together in order that it may separate them: to interpose itself between individual and individual, and also between individual and God. For in a crowd a man is not aware of his neighbor as a person. He is aware only of the big, anonymous intoxication. He doesn't think with his own brain, taste with his own tongue, listen with his own ears. Have you ever reflected how wise it was of God to make Moses, the creator of the Jewish people, a stammerer, while giving Aaron, the maker of the golden calf, the gift of the gab?"

He used the phrase, *"a geschliffen tzingel,"* because for conversation this supreme master of Hebrew was—like many distinguished protagonists of Hebrew in those days —more at home in Yiddish. Of Bialik it certainly could not be said that he had the gift of the gab, yet he was, in private and on the platform, one of the most fascinating talkers I have met. He spoke in a heavy staccato, throwing out phrases which exploded like grenades. He would summarize a world of circumstance and ideas in a sentence, and though he held an audience spellbound it was not by that oratorical charm which produces a mob, but by the individual engagement of each listener in the discipline and delight of his ideas. I once traveled with him to a number of American cities, addressing the same audiences, he speaking Yiddish, I English, and I have preserved notes of our conversations. I brought him a copy of a popular five-cent magazine which had more than two hundred pages of text and advertising. His observation was: "Here's the contrast between America and Palestine. In Palestine, when we publish a magazine we ask: 'How much dare we charge without losing our circulation?' Here they ask: 'How little dare we charge without losing our advertising value?'" He knew no English, and my talks, which always preceded his, would sound to him something like: "Mumble-jumble-grumble Chaim Nachman Bialik, tumble-rumble-bumble Bialik . . ." He said, after one of them: "I heard the footsteps of my friend Samuel conducting me through lightless corridors."

This gift of crystallization he employed in its happiest form at the *Oneg Shabbat*—the Joy of the Sabbath—the Saturday afternoon assemblies in Tel Aviv at which he and Shmarya Levin and others would hold forth on literary and intellectual subjects. The *Oneg Shabbat* of Tel Aviv became a famous institution, and its merit was not only in its spiritual content. It was a high expression of Zionist purpose and fulfillment; it brought together bourgeois and worker, the well-off and the badly-off, in community of spirit, the difference between what they had forgotten in the similarity of what they were. And this community helped to diminish the difference—not too big to begin with—and increase the similarity. It was part of that moral climate that gave to "general Zionism"—politically speaking—its natural sympathy with labor Zionism.

It was also linked with a widespread awareness of the spiritual function that Palestinian Jewry had to fulfill in relation to world Jewry. The proportion of idealists in the middle class was high, even though Polish anti-Semitic legislation had brought into the country, after 1925, thousands of unindoctrinated refugees. We have seen how Weizmann confesses to having perhaps been unfair to the middle class. The honorific word "Chalutz" has been tacitly reserved for those who went on to the soil, and especially for the collectivists among them. But that part of the small bourgeoisie which migrated voluntarily to the primitive cities and villages of Palestine as artisans and professionals and even as shopkeepers, had not chosen the easiest path, either. For the patient and persistent it was still possible to get to America. It took longer, but the reward in worldly prospects was more than worth it. The majority of immigrants was still, in those days, motivated by a good deal more than the blind instinct of personal self-preservation.

It is only fair to make a distinction between those whose idealism was all-embracing, and entailed the special sacrificial efforts of the Chalutzim, and those whose vision was more limited, or whose will was weaker. But it was characteristic of the urban middle class as a whole that it was inclined to acknowledge the distinction, even when it disagreed with the theories of the collectives. The moral and intellectual tone of the new Palestinian cities was extraordinarily high. It corresponded, on its particular level, to the phenomenon of the Jewish renaissance.

III

It is not enough to say that the Jewish population of Palestine had, in those days, the lowest criminal record in the world. It must be added that we would have been completely baffled otherwise. We used to joke about it. There is a widely known story in Israel that once, some twenty years ago, when a Jewish burglar was caught—the first—Bialik recited the prayer appropriate to a rare privilege: "Blessed art Thou, O Lord, Who hast preserved us to this day," adding: "Thank God we are a normal people, and don't have to depend on others (*onkummen tzu andere*) for our supply of criminals." This joke of Bialik's is, unfortunately, being taken quite seriously today; and there are those who nod approvingly, and add: "Of course such a high standard of morality was abnormal." Which only serves to remind us of the Mishnah's warning: "Sages, be heedful of your words"; or perhaps of Thomas Arnold's admonition to the youngsters he was playing with: "Boys, let's be serious, here comes a fool." The distance that Israel has traveled since those days may be gauged by the answer that a very high personage in the Israeli Knesset (Parliament) gave to an interpellation on the moral condition of the civil service: "There is not more corruption in our government circles than in those of old established countries." The record does not state whether the answer was applauded as testimony to Israel's moral normalcy. A high official informed me that the criminal rate in Israel is about the same as in London; which was not bad, he felt, in view of the enormous influx of primitive and maladjusted elements. He may be right. But government circles contain very few indeed of the newcomers; and if the old-timers who are supposed to lift the newcomers to their own higher level are dragged down instead, and if the subject is dismissed complacently or with a jest by an Israeli leader, I doubt whether Bialik would be pleased to hear his quip repeated in support.

I would like to anticipate the charge of "impossibilism" and "perfectionism." I never believed that there would arise in Palestine a Jewish homeland composed of saints, intellectuals, idealists, and prigs. But when I used to think of Jews once more building their own cities in Palestine, I prayed that they would be free from the mob spirit. Our kibbutzim were something unique in the modern world; could not our cities achieve a certain distinction, too?

It was the high intellectual life and the liberal-labor earnestness of our cities which kept the mob spirit in check. There was much reading, arguing, and thinking in leisure hours. Twenty years ago the cities were already big enough to breed mobs, but they did not. They were, however, acquiring their distinctive characters. Tel Aviv was the turbulent all-Jewish city, restless and nervous and noisy, the city of the *am peziza*, the St. Vitus folk. Jewish Jerusalem, with its medieval pietism of the *Meah Shearim*, and its staid new quarters of Rehaviah and Talpiot, was a little pompous. It was conscious of its proximity to the sanctity of Mount Moriah and the sanctimoniousness of British officialdom. Jewish Haifa was already the city of the heavy-industry workers, the new type of Jewish proletariat, the in-being or to-be artificers in steel, glass, and cement. There were more beards and earlocks and caftans and creased trousers on the streets of Jerusalem; in the sloping streets of Haifa there were sturdier walkers; the Tel Aviv crowds poured through its streets like blood through the veins of a feverish patient. There were poor quarters in the cities, and well-to-do quarters, there were snobberies and slums; we had the beginnings of luxury shops, and flash hotels, and the toadying to easy spenders which these bring with them. But the accretions of newcomers, even during the Hitler immigration following 1933, did not overwhelm the steadying base. A modesty of bearing, an awareness of *noblesse oblige,* reflected a sense of responsibility to the ancient Jewish name and the new Jewish effort.

Two symbols have forced themselves on my attention for the measurement of the spirit of a place: cafés and political elections. Their use and abuse is peculiarly instructive.

There are few things more pleasant than a neighborhood café, in which acquaintanceships and friendships are maintained outside the intimacy—reserved for the few—of the home itself. It is in fact the periphery or spill-over of the home; a relief from its tyrannous affections; for some, a substitute for it. I am always attracted to such places, which are open house for the locality. Good conversation may be found here, and gossip, without the embarrassment of compulsory return visits. It is, in other words, a highly civilized social institution. But I am repelled and frightened by the blare and glare of the huge cafés, the mob-cafés, which spring up in big cities and are astonishingly alike all over the world: the same nauseating music, the same unheeded babble, the same conjuror-waiters, harried, hostile, obsequious, and tip-absorbing, the same atmosphere of unsuccessful distraction and unrestful stupor. I have the feeling that if I sat down in such a café in Cairo, or Buenos Aires, or Shanghai, or Rome, or on the sea front of Tel Aviv, and addressed myself to a stranger in a language he did not know, we should get along excellently, for he would not listen, and would not suspect that the noises I was making would be unintelligible to him if he could hear them. Now one might interpret this as showing that the big café is the common meeting-ground of strangers, the genuine internationalizing institution. But if it is such, it plays its role at the expense of character and intelligence. There is only a simulacrum of understanding; it stands in the same relation to sympathy (fellow-feeling) as indifference does to tolerance. It is the mob.

But in this sense it is true that the city mob is the most international of phenomena, the most leveling, the most uniform in its manifestations. The animal roar of a Communist mob in Red Square and of a democratic mob in Times Square has the same note, the same ferocious bliss of the raped personality. The centuries make no difference, either. I am sure that the hordes of the Circus Maximus and the Colosseum of ancient Rome were the same composite monsters as our own. And when I attended mass meetings of the political parties in the last Israeli elections, when I stood in the streets of Tel Aviv to watch the passing by of political demonstrations, I recognized the ancient and ubiquitous abomination of civilization, the challenge of the cities, which I hoped we might avoid in the Jewish homeland.

But if a stampede immigration was unavoidable—as it in fact was—the challenge of the mob had to come, and no one can be blamed. Those, however, can be blamed who, instead of exerting themselves to meet it, or at least acknowledging it as a painful setback, respond with a mixture of complacency and exhaustion: "Why should we be better than other peoples? Why should our electioneering be on a higher level? Why shouldn't we have our big, vulgar cafés, and our quota of murderers, rapists, burglars, and narcotics dealers? It's all in the game."

It is not only in Israel that one hears this kind of witty, worldly talk. It is current in American Zionism too. One would think that character is a luxury, that the moral quality of Zionism had been the forgivable wild oats of our youth, and we must now settle down sensibly to the indecencies of maturity.

IV

There are certain aptitudes that it is a distinction to possess, but no defect to lack; as for instance a taste for mathematics. There are other aptitudes which it is a defect to lack, but no distinction to possess. Such is the courage to defend oneself when attacked. It should be regarded as normal equipment in the normal person.

Glorification of the ability to fight awakens the desire to exercise it or see it in action. The Shomrim who were the forerunners of the Haganah, and the Haganah itself, were least concerned to demonstrate their physical courage and prowess. And until the rise of the terrorist movement against the British occupation, there was little talk of "the fighting Jew"; and even then much less than since the war with the Arab States. The "fighting Jew" did not want to be known as such, and the repulsive killer-literature of the Sternist terrorists was regarded as something pathological. The best fighting was done by men averse to fighting and contemptuous of the cult of it. (The Sternists and Irgunists were quite as courageous individually, but they were of distinctly inferior military quality.) But the justest of wars corrupts the justest fighters. When in due course the Palmach (the special troops drawn largely from the youth of the pacifist settlements) began to sing about themselves: "*Anu anu ha-Palmach*—We are, we are the Palmach," one got a sinking feeling at the stomach: "Oh God, there's that Thing again."

Since the victory over the Arab States it has gone much further, and the government has given to the most important national celebrations, like Independence Day and the bringing to Israel of the body of Theodore Herzl, an excessively militarist character. A strong, well-trained, well-equipped army is a life-and-death necessity for Israel; the financial burden, the dislocation of the routine of young lives must be endured; and one must perhaps even suffer the humiliation of not knowing, in a democratic country, what is being done with an indeterminate but large proportion of the national income. If these concessions to necessity, and the memory of the unbelievable victory that saved the young state from complete destruction, combine to overwhelm the traditional pacifism of Jews, some effort, should, again, be made to counteract them. No such effort is made. And here, perhaps as much as anywhere else in the present condition of Zionism, Weizmann's influence is most sorely missed.

In partial self-exoneration for this development, Israeli leaders have much to say about the army as an educational institution, and the extraordinary job it is doing with young men and women from very primitive countries. I have heard old-time labor leaders, too, praise the army as the "maker of Israeli citizens." No doubt there are thousands of illiterate and helpless immigrants who are learning the rudiments of hygiene, physical self-respect, discipline, a trade, and Hebrew, in the Israeli army. We must be grimly satisfied that such an army exists, and can perform this useful service; for, given the staggering difficulties that the immigration created, no other instrument could have fulfilled this function. But to talk for that reason of the army as a "maker of citizens" is a pitiful betrayal of standards.

Such talk is heard very frequently in Nazi-Fascist and Communist countries; much less frequently, heaven be thanked, in democratic countries. And this is in the nature of things. There is no way of changing the basically totalitarian character of an army; all of its internal relationships contradict the methods and purposes of a democracy. The herd living, the compulsory intimacy, the rigid hierarchy, the mass manipulation of minds, the excessive cultivation of pure reflex action, the suppression of individual responsibility outside of small prescribed areas, the dedication of all effort to effectiveness in combat—these constitute an ordeal bravely undertaken by normal people under intolerable duress. It is a sad but unavoidable circumstance that large numbers of Israeli immigrants must learn to brush their teeth, bathe regularly, walk properly, speak the language of the country, and use a spade or awl, in such a setting. Why must it be exalted into a great affirmation? And why must the army be obtruded with such emphasis on the public attention, an incitement to the mob spirit?

Admiration of men as fighters is an easily inflammable, easily extinguishable sentiment. When it flashes up it devours all other aspects of the admired men, when it subsides it leaves a moral blank. The periodic whipping up of such admiration is a mortally dangerous practice. It creates a habit, a flight from introspection, a substitute for public spirit and social conscience. Between the fits of adulation the fighting man becomes an object of indifference, but the damage to the conscience has been done.

The central Israel celebrations, those proclaiming the essential character of the state, should be weighted with other than military symbols. If military parades are needed in order to impress the Arabs and the rest of the world, let other occasions be chosen. Or is it supposed that by associating the army with Israel's special sanctities a fighting spirit is infused into the people?

It is very probable that the best fighter is the infuriated pacifist, and this holds of the people as well as of the individual. Arguing this out with a high Israeli officer—who did not wholly disagree with me—I cited the Hasideans, under Judas Maccabeus, and Woodrow Wilson, who had coined the daring phrase "too proud to fight," and indulged America's pacifist temper to the breaking-point, thereby stoking up the irresistible fury of an outraged non-militaristic people. I also offered in that conversation a vivid recollection of my own, now thirty-five years old, regarding the military value of the militarist spirit.

At Camp Upton where I received my training, there were thousands of boys from the East Side of New York. Many of them had only a rudimentary knowledge of English. I must have shown an unholy aptitude for spit-and-polish soldiering, for I was detailed to help in the training of two squads of recent immigrants, teaching them the commands in English and explaining the meaning in Yiddish. A man called Strauss, who still haunts me in dreams, was the bane of my brief instructor's career. In the most approved drill-ground manner I bellowed at the slouching recruits, in Yiddish, something like the following: "At the command *atten-shun!* pull yourselves up straight, throw back your shoulders, tighten your buttocks, throw out your feet at an angle of forty-five degrees— *Atten-shun!*" Wholly unimpressed, Strauss said, mildly: "Looka here, Samuel, what's all this monkey business for? I've been standing on

my feet for twenty-five years, and don't remember ever
falling down. If you'll stop making those noises, and give
me a gun, I will go out and kill Germans."

As far as I remember, Strauss and his companions never
became ornaments of the parade ground. It was not merely
that they found it difficult to march in step and put a snap
into their "Present hharrrms!" When they managed it they
made you aware of an incongruity, a foolishness, an irrelevance in the act, as related to the business of fighting.
But there was a large group of these same East Side boys
who fought in the Whittlesey battalion of Argonne fame.

V

There is an almost mathematical relation between the
deterioration of public morality and the surrender to mob
psychology. Flag-waving and military parades and patriotic
ranting always go hand in hand with low standards of
thought, behavior, and aspiration. And it is the city multitude that tempts the leader to turn mis-leader. The infection spreads from the city to the countryside. The glorification by Israel and by world Jewry of the fighting ability
of the settlements has helped to undermine their moral
standing, which was based on other criteria. If the kibbutzim and moshavim are, despite their excellent record
in the War of Independence—and in previous crises, too,
for that matter—the least militaristic part of the country,
it is in no wise due to the Jewish public in Israel and
America.

The glorification of the army is part of this feverish
hankering for "normality," and for the promiscuous approval that it seeks. The point is well brought out—perhaps unintentionally—in Koestler's pro-terrorist novel of
Palestine, *Thieves in the Night.* The "Jewish" motivation
of his hero is the need to belong, irrespective of standards;

to be accepted, no matter on what level; to be "one of them," whoever "they" may be. And the feeling that in having established their fighting qualities the Jews of Israel have won approval for themselves and for all other Jews on the level of the common denominator (the pistol, the "Esperanto" of mankind, as Koestler calls it), is encouraged and exploited both in Israel and in American Jewry. The leaders of public opinion can now shout that "we belong."

To what we belong, and with what effect on us, seems to be irrelevant.

VI

Nevertheless the effects on us are serious, for they penetrate to the foundation of the Jewish being. I shall speak here only of one—the encouragement, in the youth of Israel (but also in sections of the older generation) of contempt for the passivity of Jews under persecution during their long exile; of contempt, therefore, for the whole millennial episode of the Exile; and occasionally for the six million who were done to death in Hitler's Europe, with only an occasional burst of retaliation or self-defense, as in the revolt of the Warsaw ghetto.

The survival of the Jews across eighteen centuries and more of exile and persecution is one of the wonders of history. It might have been merely a curiosity if that which survived had been a kind of indestructible crustacean, a sluggish, scarce-living organism under an unbreakable carapace. It is a wonderful thing, instead, because instead of minimum sensitivity there was a high maximum. From generation to generation the organism transmitted a persistent and adaptable spiritual vitality; and the creation of the Jewish State is almost without point except against the background of the millennial survival.

The technique of that survival—and this is putting it rather crassly—was a bitter determination not to take up an impossible and cowardly challenge, not to court "a glorious death" in an exhibition of the boxing-ring concept of manliness; but to endure, if necessary, a death in life for the sake of a certain commitment that it was impossible to repudiate. This is not to imply that all Jews were heroes of the spirit; and not even that the heroes of the spirit were always at peace with their own determination. They knew the meaning of "pride" and "honor" in the ordinary, worthless, worldly sense, too, and had enough of the pagan and animal in them to hanker for vindication on that level; therein, perhaps, lies the essence of the sacrifice, for had they been entirely above or below that level they would have suffered only in the body. They did, in fact, suffer in the spirit; they were scarred. But the performance remains, unique in human experience.

Thomas Mann has crystallized this phase of the Jewish Exile in the section of *Joseph and His Brothers* subtitled "Eliphaz." Adapting for his purpose an ancient *midrash,* he describes Jacob flying from the vengeance of the warrior boy, Eliphaz, son of brother Esau, who had just been swindled out of the blessing. He describes the humiliation of Jacob, who would simply have been committing suicide if he had stood up to the youth "like a man."

What happened then had touched Jacob's pride and honour more sorely than anything else in all his life; it was calculated to undermine and would have undermined forever the dignity and self-confidence of another man. He was obliged—if he wanted to live, and that he did at all costs; not, we must remember, out of common cowardice but because he was consecrated, because the promise and the blessing handed down from Abraham lay upon him—to try to soften by en-

treaties the heart of this lad, his nephew, so much
younger than himself, so much lower in station, who
in the heat of his anger already and more than once
had lifted the sword above his head; to reach him
through self-abasement and tears and flatteries,
through whining appeals to his magnanimity, with a
thousand pleas and excuses. . . .

He escaped with his life, and with that alone, placating
Eliphaz with all his possessions. And Thomas Mann goes
on:

He had saved his life, his precious, covenanted life,
for God and the future—what were gold and cornelian
set against that? For life is all; and young Eliphaz had
been even more brilliantly swindled than his parent
—but at what a price! Above and beyond the valua-
bles it had meant the loss of the man's whole honour;
for how could one be more shamed than Jacob was,
having bowed his head in the dust before a stripling,
whining, his face smeared with dust and tears? And
then? What had happened straightway after the degradation?

There happened the dream of the ladders reaching from
earth to heaven, and the ascending and descending angels.
"Then truly his head was lifted up from every ignominy,
even to the countenance of the Most High, wherein
mingled all of the royal and of the divine which his soul
had ever compassed in its imaginings; which that soul,
then, humbled, yet smiling privily in its abasement, erected
for its own strengthening and consolation in the space of
its dream."

It is odd that a German should understand, and the
Israeli youth should not.

CHAPTER XI

Histadrut

I

Aɴʏ attempt to understand the workers' movement of Israel—here I include the land settlements—as a purely economic phenomenon must end in confusion. Is the Histadrut—the Israel Federation of Labor—a labor union? Certainly; as much so as the T.U.C. of England, the C.G.T. of France, and the A.F. of L. and the C.I.O. of America; and, in proportion to population, much stronger than any of these. But I have never heard of a trade union anywhere else in the world which was concerned, as Histadrut was, with training workers abroad and bringing them into the country; and which made this strategy, apparently so harmful to the home labor market, a cardinal principle. This paradox alone must suffice to set Histadrut apart in the history of world labor movements, and should make students of the subject alert to unexpected values. But there are other features of Histadrut, not quite so startling in a trade union, which nevertheless in Israel, and as part of the dynamics of the country, must also be approached with special insights.

As the Federation of Trade Unions Histadrut represents labor in balance against capital. As the Chevrat Ovdim, or Worker's Company, it is both the owner of large enterprises and a federation of co-operatives and semi-co-operatives. There are also combinations of Histadrut (or rather Chevrat Ovdim) ownership in partnership with private capital; and in all of its forms Histadrut is concerned with the development of the country, the increase of its population, and the fulfillment of the Zionist purpose. I shall mention the four principle forms of Histadrut enterprise which modify its character as a purely labor-defending agency:

(1) Straight co-operatives, owned by their workers. Of these the kibbutzim and moshavim are of course the outstanding examples. (But these do not own their land, which is leased to them by the Jewish National Fund, the property of the Jewish people.) In the cities, building and transport co-operatives were created, embodying the same basic principles as the kibbutzim and moshavim, that is to say, all hired labor was precluded.

(2) Workers' co-operatives in partnership with Histadrut. These are owned jointly by the co-operative members and the Histadrut. Histadrut holds 51 per cent of the shares. In these, hired labor is permitted, but the surplus value of such labor is turned over to Histadrut, which uses it to expand the co-operative and increase its own shares.

(3) Enterprises owned by the Histadrut as a whole (that is, by the Chevrat Ovdim) and not by the workers in them. These are comprised by the great combine called Solel Boneh (Pave and Build).

(4) Enterprises owned in partnership by Solel Boneh and private capital.

A member of the Histadrut is automatically a member of Chevrat Ovdim. He is therefore a part owner of the largest group of enterprises in the country, with a turnover of over fifty million pounds, comprising fifteen per cent of the country's industries. If you were to ask him what he gets out of it, he would be puzzled for an answer. In a direct way, he certainly gets nothing. Solel Boneh does not distribute dividends to its owners, for it is not a profit-making concern. Perhaps it helps to set a higher standard of employer-employee relationships. On the other hand if the energy spent on Solel Boneh were directed into purely trade-union activities, the results might even be better for the workers. I have heard it argued cogently that workers hamper themselves in negotiations with employers when they create a confusion of functions by themselves becoming employers.

If it was ever a dream of the Histadrut that by a mixture of self-labor co-operatives and Histadrut-owned enterprises the workers might in time extend their ownership over most of the country, that dream is gone—as completely as the dream of the kibbutzim and moshavim that they might in time draw in all agricultural production. I gather from Histadrut leaders and not unfriendly private capitalists that the Solel Boneh enterprises have about reached the limit of their capacity for the foreseeable future. Unfriendly capitalists—in the majority—and general public opinion would have it that Solel Boneh is already too large —a deterrent to private investment, or even, it is said, "an octopus" strangling the spirit of initiative in the country. I ought to add that the greatest hostility came from the smallest capitalists; and in general, the same holds for hostility to the Histadrut.

The position is quite unique, the result of a unique history of development. The labor leaders of Israel are of course the founders and leading spirits of the Histadrut. They have also become the governmental leaders, though they naturally do not hold posts simultaneously in government and Histadrut. So far we have a parallel with the British Labour Movement when it came into office. But the British Trades Union Congress does not own, under another name, fifteen per cent of the country's industries. Thus, on the surface, the situation in Israel has something irregular about it. Here is a government that, though a coalition, is largely controlled by men who have spent their lives building up the Histadrut, and are among the "owners" of the vast Solel Boneh enterprises. What chance has private initiative? Are not these men dedicated to the task of transforming Israel into a purely socialist country? And even if they want to be fair to capital, provisionally, on temporary grounds, are they capable of it?

Here is a summary of the views I have canvassed. First comes the curious fact that top industrialists, if they have criticized Solel Boneh to me, have done so with detailed reference to certain mistakes, and not as a matter of basic disagreement. On the question whether the government had discriminated against private capital in favor of Histadrut enterprises, their answers were guarded. Yes, managers of Histadrut enterprises obviously had the inside track to high government officials by way of personal contacts. But the high government officials are—the critics conceded—grimly concerned with the encouragement of import of private capital. Solel Boneh, though it is strongest in a key industry, building, nevertheless is only fifteen per cent of the country's industry. There are branches that Solel Boneh has not touched. On the whole, Solel Boneh is not a deterrent to private enterprise. Besides, it has been a great builder of the country on its own account.

As against this, executives of Solel Boneh have complained to me that labor comrades of the Histadrut, once in the government, lean over backwards to favor private capital in areas where it competes with Solel Boneh. There were hair-raising stories of sudden government orders to Solel Boneh to suspend negotiations and cancel plans for a new enterprise because a capitalist had suddenly appeared on the scene, and had expressed interest in a similar enterprise: the upshot being that Solel Boneh yielded the ground and the capitalist did not ultimately occupy it.

One listens to all these views, makes notes, tries to construct an objective picture. There is no doubt about the sincerity of the Solel Boneh officials. There is no doubt, either, regarding the sincerity of the large number of smaller capitalists who think of Histadrut and Solel Boneh as obstacles in the way of Israel's economic development. But it would need equipment, knowledge, and time not at my disposal to render an "objective" judgment; and who knows what these objective judgments are worth? A recent impartial committee of investigation exonerated Solel Boneh, to the satisfaction of its friends and the knowing skepticism of its enemies.

Uninformed sincerity holds out the hope that the problem can be straightened out by honest effort. It is not so with strategic prejudice and doctrinaire deafness. There are reactionary groups in Israel and among American Zionists for whom the discrediting of Solel Boneh is a psychological necessity and/or a political fundamental. There are also Jews who are in the uncomfortable position of having to explain why they are not investing capital in Israel; or—the cases are fewer—must find a scapegoat for the failure of an enterprise, which may have been due to bad luck or inefficiency. There are also those who want Israel to offer them profit opportunities that they will not obtain in other foreign countries. And of course there are those who have a genuine grievance (who has not, anywhere?) against the delays and confusions of government offices, and attribute part of them to anti-capitalist policy.

At the bottom of the list, but perhaps not least important in the mischievous effect they produce on the public mind, are the obnoxious boys who are an inevitable part of the stampede immigration, the seekers of a fast dollar or pound, the prehensile profiteers. These are men whose natural milieu of operation is the area of crisis and constriction. They are pulled in by the smell of distress; and wherever the law is likely to break under the pressures of want, they will be found, sniffing the air like jackals. I listened with a sour smile when the chief of police in Israel told me how he had assigned two men to keep an eye on a famous international Jewish swindler who suddenly sought asylum in Israel, and was filled with benevolent intentions toward its economy. Fortunately this one was famous enough to attract attention. The less illustrious came and went. Like all get-rich-quick operators they look on a constructive enterprise as a relapse into barbarism, a chore for suckers and the feeble-minded generally. Hard work, except when it is done to avoid hard work, they regard as one of the ills that flesh is heir to by an almost universal allergy that they alone have escaped. They are poles apart from the decent, older middle class and entrepreneurs of Israeli Jewry, and the serious newcomers; but they have done a good deal to lower the morale of both—and of the attitude of capital toward labor. And having for the most part failed to make a killing in Israel, they do their best to spread the impression that the government and Solel Boneh are in a conspiracy to discourage the entry of capital into Israel, or else to confiscate whatever enters despite their vigilance.

These people merit, as parasites at large, and as particular pests in Israel, more extensive treatment than I can give them here. I have met a few of them in the hotels in Israel, and they have approached me in other countries. For patriotism and high Jewish sentiment they have not— by their own account—their equals anywhere in the world; and their lamentations over the suicidal anti-capitalist bias of the Israeli government (at least, until the time of the new coalition), the narrow selfishness of the working class of Israel, and the constructive opportunities that they have not been permitted to develop, constitute a new branch of

Jewish literature, or rather oral folklore. They must not be confused with the more or less innocent victims of their propaganda, and the definitely less innocent exploiters of it. And here I willingly take my leave of this subject.

II

A knowledge of the history of Histadrut and its enterprises, of the role they have played in the national struggle, is essential to an understanding of their value and prospects. It is simply no use sending into the country, for a survey of the problem, an economist, no matter how well-trained in his craft, unless he is Jewish-historically minded. Perhaps also metaphysically minded. The drives that brought the Jewish workers to Israel and wove the patterns of their achievements cannot, to begin with, be resolved along the co-ordinates of the class struggle; they were as complex, as powerful, and as folkloristic as those of the land Chalutzim. Many of the city workers passed through kibbutzim in training periods of varying duration. Like the kibbutzniks, they were not simply individuals in search of a livelihood; or simply Jews in search of security; or simply socialists creating a new order. They were perhaps more than anything else the composite drive of Judaism for survival, Judaism being for them a way of life socially, culturally, and ethically. It may be said that Histadrut set out to create a new Jewish history; the scene of its operations was to be Palestine, the time the present; its distinguishing force was drawn from the Jewish past, its influence was to be felt upon the Jewish future everywhere.

Histadrut was therefore a state-creator. That is why immigration into Palestine was fundamental to its program. It wanted a dynamic immigration—the kind that leads to more immigration, and not the kind that leads to a static condition. It wanted workers and creative capitalists. It was afraid of the in-betweens, people with a few hundred pounds, a few thousand dollars, who said: "That's enough to make a living with; if there are a hundred shops, there's room for one more." Workers had to be trained—and Histadrut did it, both in the Diaspora and in Palestine. But capitalists were harder to come by—and Histadrut set about the development of its own enterprises.

As a state-creator Histadrut was concerned with culture, welfare, morale; that is, with matters like the theater, books, medical care, civics, and the revival of Hebrew. Its buying and selling co-operatives, which served the land settlements and the cities, its workers' co-operatives, its Solel Boneh enterprises, were interpenetrated therefore with an all-round sense of state-creating responsibility.

This responsibility brought it into conflict with the British administration, which was in any case uneasy about a local working-class movement of such high calibre. The Histadrut was, as an organized body, the most effective of Jewish Palestine's political forces. It was the matrix of the Haganah, which was the deciding factor in the struggle for independence. It is very revealing that during this struggle the British were more concerned to break the power of the Jewish Agency—the controller of Haganah—than that of the terrorists. The development of Histadrut must always be seen in the light of its nationalist functions. The old harmony between "general Zionists" and "labor Zionists," of which Weizmann can be regarded as the symbol, was partly rooted in an appreciation of these functions.

III

Appreciation came easily when the function was obvious. Sometimes it was more than that—it was spectacular. Histadrut, which always saw eye to eye with Weizmann on the subject of "dynamic immigration," stopped asking questions—as of course everyone else did—when it was a straightforward matter of saving Jewish lives. The Hitler persecution wiped out all distinctions, worker, capitalist, middleman, parasite, trained, untrained, Zionist, anti-Zionist, assimilationist, apostatizing, liberal, reactionary—the words lost meaning. In the horrible struggle with the Mandatory Government to bring refugees illegally into Palestine—especially from 1936 to 1948—the Histadrut and its affiliates did unforgettable work. Theirs were the refugee ships that again and again broke the British blockade. Theirs were the agents who spread a network of rescue—pitifully ragged and inadequate—over the European countries. Theirs were the "Lighterage Companies" and "Chandler's Companies" which served Haifa harbor and played a deadly cat-and-mouse game with the British authorities, loyal to them during the war in the overriding purpose of defeating Germany, deceiving and defeating them in the matter of sneaking refugees into Palestine. (This was the meaning of ben Gurion's brilliant slogan, launched at the Zionist Congress that took place on the eve of the Second World War: "We will fight Germany as if there were no White Paper, we will fight the White Paper as if there were no war.") I have called these activities spectacular, which would imply that the British authorities too must have been aware of them. They were; sometimes they could not crush them, and resigned themselves to paying this price for Jewish help in defeating Germany (the only help they got in the Near East); sometimes they did not have the heart to carry out to the last consequences the inhuman—and unprofitable—policy of Arab appeasement. Certainly the general population was aware of them. "Everybody" knew who was organizing the boats, the night encounters on the shore, the flights of the landed refugees into the interior: it was the Histadrut, through Solel

Boneh affiliates and Haganah. Similarly, "everyone" knew that nobody else could or would do it. The terrorist organizations had not the means, and they had to concentrate on seeming to be important rather than on being important.

This was a great episode in the history of Histadrut; it ended, naturally, with the establishment of the Jewish State. Immigration at once became the business of the government of Israel. So did Jewish self-defense. Haganah was transformed into the army of Israel. Thus two exciting and challenging functions disappeared from the *raisons d'être* of Histadrut. This was not all. Under the Mandatory Government Histadrut's effort to create a model social system had derived a particular zest from its nationalist-liberationist character. The opposition, or lethargy, or indifference, or colonial-mindedness of British officials was an additional spur to Histadrut. With the coming of Jewish statehood, social legislation become the concern of a Jewish government that drew away from Histadrut a large part of its leadership. Thus its role was narrowed, its incentive diminished, and its top manpower depleted simultaneously. We shall see that there is a tremendous amount of work still left to it; but like the Zionist movement as a whole Histadrut has entered the phase of the long and unspectacular chores that do not radiate their own morale.

IV

Time has been at work on the Histadrut not less than on the kibbutzim, and the excitements of great challenges and achievements have not been enough to sustain the initial inspiration. A very human picture emerges, a checkerwork of successes and failures. In the midst of idealistic and heroic effort in one direction, there is defection in another. We have a striking instance in the record of the transport co-operatives. In periods of national stress truck and taxi drivers displayed a spirit of responsibility and courage which set the poets singing and the public cheering. During the Arab rebellion of 1936-9, when roads were mined and the hills enfolding them were infested with snipers, the drivers kept communications open at the cost of many lives. They played a similar role in the turbulent days of the liberation. There was never a question about it; they accepted the assignment tacitly. But throughout it all they were also building up a monopoly, and the socialist prohibition against the use of hired labor simply went by the board. They became, that is, not co-operatives but capitalist owners of a key industry—and they proceeded to abuse their position with a high-handedness which would not have been tolerated from an openly and officially capitalist body.

They avoided a natural increase of their co-operatives by putting the entrance cost beyond the reach of a worker, and their use of hired labor enabled them to meet part of the increased demand for their service. But only a part. They paid themselves high wages and bonuses with funds that should have gone into the purchase of new equipment. They built themselves, to the north of Tel Aviv, a driver's quarter with some of the handsomest houses in Israel—and it was impossible to do this without a good deal of black-marketeering in building material. Meanwhile the public is wretchedly served. There would have been a crisis in transportation anyhow, with the flood of immigration; the ruthlessness of the drivers' co-operatives exacerbated it enormously. Bus travel in Israel, in and between cities, is a brutal experience. The situation has of course stimulated the Jewish sense of humor. I stood in a long line at the central bus station of Tel Aviv, with a ticket for Jerusalem; before I gave up in despair and found a taxi, I shuffled past a pillar to which someone had fastened a newspaper cartoon the caption of which was the immemorial exile prayer of the Jews: *"L'shanah habaah b'yerushalayim*—Next year in Jerusalem."

Why has Histadrut continued the membership of the bus drivers' co-operatives? Why has it not made an example of them? To this question I obtained no clear answers. Such a move had been on foot, some Histadrut leaders told me. In the end it was decided to retain them if certain concessions were obtained—by which time all the damage had been done. Was it the percentage of profit which goes from the co-operatives into the funds of the Histadrut? No, they said. That didn't amount to much. Was it political timidity? Not that, either. It simply was not considered good policy to rush to extremes. The drivers' co-operatives had a noble record; they weren't all as bad as they were painted. The worst abuses were being eliminated; and so forth, and so forth. I drew the conclusion that the reasons were neither financial nor political, but moral. The Histadrut leadership had not the standing, the authority, to take the drastic and necessary step.

The transport co-operatives are an instance of organized abuse of the workers' powers. Not organized, more pervasive, in the aggregate more substantial, are abuses by individual members of Histadrut, by independent artisans, plumbers, plasterers, masons, carpenters, by doctors (not those in the health system of Histadrut), lawyers, dentists, and by members of other liberal professions, members or non-members. Here we have systematic and sustained two-way black-marketeering; in the matter of income, and in the matter of expenditures; all apart from the concomitant evasion of taxes. The aristocracy of labor is a danger to the country's economy and a drag on its morale. Particularly disturbing is the fact that this aristocracy is of necessity composed almost exclusively of old-timers, who came to the country as idealists, and have given up their ideals.

Thus, besides over-earning and over-spending, they emphasize something that resembles racial distinctions. For they are all "white" Jews, Westerners. The "colored" Jews, the recent arrivals from Oriental countries, see none of their own kind among the privileged; and they ascribe this not to the handicaps that they share in part with recent arrivals from the West, but to the color bar. I would emphasize the words "in part." There is in fact a color bar, the result largely of strangeness. It is strengthened by the aristocracy of Israel's labor.

Histadrut cannot be held as responsible for the large number of individual delinquencies among members as it can for the delinquency of a public body affiliated with it. It would be enormously difficult to set up a control machinery. Nevertheless a negative moral effect on Histadrut flows from the inescapable fact that a substantial proportion of its membership (it is estimated at five or six per cent) is anti-social; and what is worst, the delinquents are not the newcomers who have to be taught the principles of Histadrut responsibility, but veterans who have forgotten them.

In saying that the reasons for Histadrut's failure to meet honestly the impudent challenge of the transport co-operatives were of a moral order, I did not mean to exclude the political factor. I meant rather to subordinate the political to the moral. The problems of Histadrut, like those of the kibbutzim, can be roughly classified as the organic, or innate, or inevitable, and the fortuitous and unforeseeable. But there is a continuous interplay. Fortuitous and unforeseeable in Histadrut's history were both the stampede immigration into Israel and the world-wide East-West split, with its local effects. The composition of Histadrut puts it preponderantly—like the land settlements, grouping together kibbutzim and moshavim—into the anti-Communist world front. There is, however, a solid minority belonging to the pro-Communist world front. Just as the kibbutzniks in the divided kibbutzim were subjected to the relentless pressure of pro-Communist groups, so that every development, every minor move, took on extraneous meaning irrelevant to its own merits, so the leadership of Histadrut had to gauge its decisions with reference to the Mapai (anti-Communist) and Mapam (pro-Communist) balance. There was some talk in Israel of a breakup of the Histadrut into two separate organizations, one affiliated with Mapai, one with Mapam. (I am ignoring the existence of a splinter group of Nationalist Workers.) It has not come to anything; and now, after the Prague trial and the case of the doctors, is not likely to. But it indicated dangerous possibilities. A stern policy on the part of Histadrut toward delinquent co-operatives and profiteering workers—the latter are numbered in the thousands—would have created just the kind of turmoil that makes pro-Communists happy.

The new situation, which has made possible at long last the government coalition between labor and the center, also makes possible a raising of Histadrut standards without the old fear that the pro-Communists will exploit it. Even so, Histadrut morale must be higher than it is today before the sanitation can be begun. But that, I am afraid, almost begs the question; for Histadrut morale can only be raised by a crusade which would of itself do much of the sanitation and therefore remove much of the problem.

V

Black marketeer co-operatives and workers are not the only ticklish issue. Histadrut, not being an ordinary trade union, and still being strongly aware of its state-creating role, worries about the production standards of Israel's workers. A great many of them are not putting their backs

179

into their jobs. Now job security has been one of the primary concerns of Histadrut, which is an excellent thing. But nothing is so good that it carries an automatic safeguard against its abuse. The capitalists friendliest to Histadrut—they are genuinely friendly—complain sharply that Histadrut over-protects its members. It is next to impossible to fire a worker for laziness, or chronic incompetence, or willful negligence. In private talks with me Histadrut leaders have admitted the justice of the complaint, just as some of them have admitted that the offending transport co-operatives should have been thrown out. With enormous difficulty Histadrut yielded here and there on the principle of *kablanut,* or piecework, introducing at least the incentive of reward where it could not apply the deterrent of punishment. But the problem is still largely unsolved, and it is one of the most serious facing the country.

Here too the historical development of the Israel working class, and Histadrut's role in it, belong to the present picture. The worker-pioneers of thirty and forty and fifty years ago brought with them a religion of labor. *Kibbush avodah* was a mighty slogan—the conquest of work, meaning the transformation of Jewish middlemen into laborers; meaning also the conquest of every type of physical task necessary for the building of the country, from the draining of swamps and laying of roads to the literal building of cities and the feeding of them from Jewish produce. They were willing and devoted workers, and zealous apostles of labor. They had their songs, their philosopher, their propaganda: "Work will rescue us from every disaster." There is unfortunately a difference between the sincerest belief in the nobility and the salutary results of work, and an actual liking for one's job. One can go far with the first, but the second is more reliable, and the second has not developed as it should have.

Side by side with the religion of labor another influence came in with the worker-pioneers—a type of socialism which taught that it is a form of social morality to extract from an employer the maximum of pay in return for the minimum of effort; that one must avoid as far as possible anything which will benefit the employer class. This influence never got the upper hand, for it was held in check by the state-building consciousness of the workers. But it still represents today the dominant attitude of the Mapam. Therefore, when it is a question of spurring on the workers to greater productivity the old, easily-formulated, catchy appeal is heard: "Why should you sweat your years out, and shorten your life, to fatten your employer?" And Mapam springs forward as the sole protector of the working classes, in distinction to those American-imperialism-inspired reactionaries, those betrayers of Israeli's workers (and of the Korean masses)—the Mapai-minded majority that still controls the Histadrut.

Again the block seems to be political; and in an important sense it is. But again it is the moral question that underlies it.

VI

Most of us have struggled with the question: "Does history produce leaders, or do leaders make history?" and if we have reached a conclusion one way or the other it is usually out of exhaustion. The interplay of influence between Israel's workers and their leaders could easily become, to very little purpose, an exercise in this question; it is better to stay for the time being within the limits of observable fact. It is a fact—at any rate I am convinced of it from observation and inquiry—that Israeli labor leaders are dissatisfied with the attitude of many workers toward their jobs; they are convinced that the incentive motive—a system of rewards and of penalties—should play a larger role in the factories. It is also a fact that they talk like this far more freely in private than in the hearing of their constituencies; and when it comes to the problem of engaging the unions and the worker-manager production committees to act against malingerers and loafers on the job, the labor leaders are exceedingly wary.

"Labor leaders" here means the whole body of leadership, whether the individuals are technically Histadrut executives, or members of the government, or theoreticians, or policy-makers, or writers. All are caught in the complex web of habit and power and the effect of time on the personality. Labor leadership is not the simple face-to-face relationship of the old days; it is big-time stuff, with mass meetings, newspapers, committees, interdepartmental conferences, political calculations. And labor leaders are important men, with their cars, prestige, secretaries, public statements, followers. There are delegations to foreign countries, reports to conventions. Labor leaders who have passed into the government are international figures, and their names appear in the Sunday *New York Times* crossword puzzles. Such positions are acquired by ability and hard work, and part of the hard work consists in winning recognition for one's ability. With recognition comes a special kind of self-recognition, the feeling of indispensability, the conviction that loss of office would be a public more than a personal calamity; and what makes this last conviction so insidious is the fact that, objectively, one does believe it sometimes of others, and therefore one may also believe it of oneself. And therefore, again, one must weigh such questions as: "Will the over-all welfare of the labor cause gain or lose if I keep quiet on this or that abuse or error, and also keep my job? Suppose I come out in open opposition to this or that policy demanded by the head of the government, and lose my job without changing the policy, what good will I have done? I shall do my protesting within, as far as I can, without depriving the country of my services." So here we are, back at the old game, the very old game. We are in politics. That is to say, Mapai is in politics, and very much so. And the fact that everyone else is also in politics is perhaps a mitigation of Mapai's comparative guilt but no consolation to the general public.

I suppose that it is not worse than in many other respectable countries, just as the proportion of corruption in the government is not higher than in many old and well-established governments. But that is no reason for thinking that nothing can or should be done about it; and least of all should we relinquish the belief that we can and should and must be a special case.

VII

There are plenty of able men and hard workers in the labor leadership, and Histadrut has enormous tasks to perform, above and beyond those of the orthodox trade union, which still give it a place of unique importance in the evolving life of the Jewish State. If it has lost two of its most exciting functions—illegal immigration and Haganah —it has retained from its long state-building history machinery and experiences which are irreplaceable. It may decide to restrict itself still further, but it can never become an ordinary worker-employer regulator.

Solel Boneh is perhaps the most difficult question for Histadrut. Its great record was not built merely on underground activities. It was an industrial pioneer in areas —literal and figurative—which private capital would not approach. It can still take risks which private capital should not take. It is, in fact, pioneering today, in the Negev, on a vast scale. But in the leadership of Solel Boneh the suggestion has been offered that the entire group of industries should be nationalized, and Histadrut relieved of the responsibility for this area of production.

Histadrut has between 450,000 and 500,000 member "owners" of Solel Boneh. The workers in the various enterprises of Solel Boneh number about 40,000. Neither the 450,000 owners nor the 40,000 workers have anything of importance to say about the conduct of Solel Boneh as a business. It is the management, and the management alone, that makes the decisions. As a purely practical matter, the 450,000 owners can no more decide Solel Boneh policies than the 1,000,000 owners can decide the policies of the A.T. and T. And since the workers in the enterprises are merely wage-earners, and not owners, as in a co-operative, they are excluded from the direction of affairs, except to the extent that management-worker production committees have, as in private enterprises, some say in the handling of minor problems. Interestingly enough, management-worker committees in Solel Boneh are not doing noticeably better than in private enterprise. The gap between worker and management is just as wide; and here as in private enterprise one hardly ever finds representatives drawn from the "colored" Jews.

Here is the curious situation: a number of able men, the management of Solel Boneh, are directing a vast enterprise in a spirit of liberal capitalism. These men have few successors. For not only have many of the ablest veterans of Histadrut been drawn away into government service, but the young people, too, on whom the veterans counted for the continuation of the work, are now attracted to government posts. And so the worker-owned "industrial empire," which the workers do not own or profit from, but which has been a contribution to the development of the state as a whole, is liable to become a drain on the workers' movement, a heritage of unrewarding responsibility from a period whose patterns are dissolving. If Solel Boneh profits only the nation at large, let the nation take it over.

That which Histadrut has retained from its long history of state-building makes it the most important civic instrument in Israel. With all the derelictions noted, Histadrut incorporates a powerful creative tradition which gives its institutions a greater total value than the sum of the separate parts. The Kupat Cholim—the health insurance and health service of the Histadrut, with its network of hospitals, clinics, and dispensaries—covers about two thirds of the Israeli population. This too may some day be taken over by the state. What cannot as easily be taken over is the propagation of the social outlook that accompanied, and still accompanies, the system. That it has been the creation of the workers, an expression of their sense of social responsibility, means as much for working-class morale as the medical service itself means to working-class health. The cultural tradition of Histadrut, and the institutions through which it has grown up constitute an unequaled opportunity for the special service of assimilating the masses of newcomers. It is better able than any other instrument to combine the trade-school atmosphere with that of the cultural school. For its beginnings were rooted in that symbiosis of occupational rehabilitation and cultural regeneration which was the essence of Zionism.

It is a very different atmosphere indeed in which Histadrut must now operate, and there is a tragic difference between the levels. It is not occupied mainly with intellectual comrades, moral equals, willing pioneers, eager to be integrated with the land. It is dealing instead with the masses of refugees who are strangers to any notion of organized social obligation. And it must fight against two adverse forces. For in the factories, both of private industry and of Solel Boneh, new workers—now varying between thirty and seventy per cent of the total—pull down the social idealism, as well as the productive skill, of the old. If the newcomers learn quickly the meaning of trade unionism—so necessary a part of civic education generally—in the crudest terms, they cannot learn so easily the peculiar meaning of Histadrut. Actually the Histadrut workers in this field must content themselves with the most elementary lessons, with children's Hebrew, with inculcation of the first perceptions of privileges and obligations, with the meaning and function of a newspaper, with the awakening of a sense of belonging to the new community and the new country, with a bit of folk music and folk dancing. And how to pass from this to the higher values, and when, is a problem not yet solved; nor will it be solved without much trial and error, and the passing of time.

That Histadrut must continue to receive special support in the discharge of functions it is peculiarly fitted to fulfill is, I believe, obvious. That it is suffering from the general decline in morale, and in Zionist "charge," is equally obvious. Less obvious is the nature of the change in outlook that must be wrought in the whole Zionist movement, and therefore in labor Zionism, before we can hope to reverse the trend. At this I have already hinted more than once, and I will return to it in more detail.

CHAPTER XII

"I Choose to Believe"

❀

I

I HAVE heard men with economic training argue their heads off about Israel's economic prospects, and come out of the argument with their opposing views unchanged. I have also watched, over the years, the evolution—if it can be called that—of opinion in writers who have consistently held that "it can't be done." "It" kept changing over the years, but the "can't be done" was a constant. "It" was the creation of a Jewish farming class; or the revival of the Hebrew language; or the achievement of independence—or another of a dozen things. Now "it" is the economic stabilization of Israel.

Opinions do change, of course, but rarely as the result of mere discussion. A good argument will give a man an excuse for changing his mind—but he heard the same argument a dozen times before, without effect. If it takes effect now, it is for reasons outside of itself.

A fascinating example, or series of examples, is to be found in the book *The God that Failed,* in which a number of ex-Communists, or ex-pro-Communists, tell us why, or rather how (or, still more exactly, neither why nor how) they lost their Communist faith. They do not add a single new argument to the familiar armory of anti-Communist literature; they could just as well have left the Communist movement years before they did, or never joined at all; and even the plea "I had to see for myself" is irrelevant, because they always saw what they chose to see. (In passing, the title, which blames the "God" instead of the dupes, is a characteristically dishonest one.)

You may choose what to see in Israel; or you may make the attempt to see everything, still without being sure that you haven't exercised unconscious choice. I do not pretend to have made that attempt; long residence in Palestine, frequent visits of two, three, four months' duration to Israel, are not enough. Perhaps continuous residence there is not enough either. I have made, I think, the attempt to see both negative and the affirmative forces at work in the country; but I have always chosen to believe that "it" can be done.

II

Everywhere, a feverish activity, and evidences of production. Year after year, as I return, new districts spring up; spartan little settlements on plains, on hilltops, in valleys; new suburbs and housing developments; new stretches of green where the year before I saw only burnt soil; new roads, with double rows of new-planted trees; gardens flourish around prefabricated houses; buses and trucks flash along the roads, which widen and lengthen from year to year; streets are cluttered with drainpipes, smoke belches from factory chimneys, there is a rushing and shouting and furious gesticulation.

So much for one set of impressions. Another set issues from closer inspection. Workmanship is inferior. Doors jam and windows rattle; waiters are absent-minded or intrusive; taxi drivers are mannerless; carpenters, plumbers, and mechanics have a mysterious relationship to time and an all too tangible one to money; clerks in stores are somehow unable to focus; they are bafflingly incurious about a customer's needs, they regard a sale as something thrust upon them. If you happen to have a telephone, you must learn a new technique: when it rings, pick it up, say: "*Ta-oot*—Wrong number," and put it down briskly. In four cases out of five it will not ring again; but if it does ring again, you may pick it up and listen, because now the chances are even that it is for you. A call to a point fifteen miles away will take up to half an hour, beyond that anything between an hour and two, even with the imperative and expensive "*Dahoof*—Urgent." A letter from Tel Aviv to Jerusalem—an hour's distance by car—will usually be delivered within forty-eight hours, but sometimes takes three days. Of the inspired inefficiency of government offices I will not speak.

You go on collecting these contradictory impressions, and you let them affect you according to your temperament, mood, and basic belief. Or you stand aloof from impressions, distrustfully, and ask for statistics.

Statistics, alas, also lead to opposing conclusions in opposed minds. There are striking increases in housing, agriculture, industry, consumption of electricity. But there is a relative decrease as against the sudden rise in population. On the other hand, production is not supposed to keep pace with a rapid populational increase—certainly not when a country has doubled its population in three years. And the circumstances are peculiar, in fact, unique.

There is a vast gap between imports and exports, the former exceeding the latter by six to one, or two to three hundred million dollars a year. But a new developing country always needs large credits. It depends, therefore, on the country's natural resources—among which is the resourcefulness of the inhabitants.

Well, then, we have the sulphates and the copper and the other metals of the Negev; the chemicals of the Dead

Sea; the orange industry, which the war all but destroyed and which we are restoring—all foreign-currency earners. If the maximum is extracted from the soil for home consumption, if the tourist trade is intelligently nursed, if consumption is held down, and imports restricted as far as possible to capital goods and materials to be processed for export, then, in five, six, seven, perhaps ten years at the outside, the country can certainly balance its budget. As this objective is approached, the country will be helped along by German reparations, American grants-in-aid, investments from abroad, loans, including the sale of Israeli bonds, and the voluntary offerings of world Jewry. And there is the prospect of oil. It makes sense.

Yes, but, says the negative: what of the things you have described, poor production, bad workmanship, decline of morale, the inability to manage a tiny telephone system and a county-size postal organization; what about governmental inefficiency?

To which the positive replies: We must not forget the peculiar, the unique circumstances. How fast should the Jews have been able to set up efficient government services after taking over in 1948? A minority in the country up to the last days of the Mandate, they had even less than their proportionate numbers in government services—post, telegraph, telephone, immigration, customs, treasury; their "army" was illegal; they had no experience in official diplomacy. The British withdrew under circumstances that of themselves were sufficiently conducive to chaos; embittered by their defeat in the nasty struggle, they did what they could to make confusion worse confounded. Overlapping with their withdrawal—in 1948—came the Arab invasions, which cost the lives of over five thousand young Israelis. And overlapping with the war came the immigration flood, with consequences I have already referred to. Bearing all this in mind, by what standard is it expected

190

that a letter from Rehobot to Jerusalem should be delivered in one day, or two days, or three? By what standard can we speak of incompetence if the overloaded, semi-obsolete telephone system, managed by a national staff scrabbled together in the last four years gives us only one quarter or one tenth of the service we are accustomed to in America? How much more efficient ought the departments of immigration, taxation, commerce and industry to be? And why?

There is no intelligent answer to these questions. One can plausibly argue that all things considered the Israelis have done astoundingly well. Moreover, the dissatisfactions I voice, for others as well as for myself, do not hinge on the alarmist question: "Do you think Israel can make it—that is, survive, become self-supporting?" That the achievement should have been brought so far only to collapse on the physical plane is for me outside reasonable probability. I have watched too long, seen too many vicissitudes, to be shaken. But there is such a thing as mediocre and sloppy survival, getting by, and there is such a thing as creditable and inspiring survival. And the decline in morale means a too ready acceptance of the first. The survival itself is not in question.

III

At the beginning of my last stay, in the spring of 1952, Israel was in the midst of one of its periodic financial crises. There were dark mutterings: "This is it. In two months we shall have no oil, no grain." As usual the government, on the verge of bankruptcy, pulled solvency out of a conjurer's hat. And the public smiled, a trifle nervously: "Just propaganda. *They* won't let us go bankrupt"—"they" meaning world Jewry, the Western powers, Providence.

But I also heard serious and responsible Israelis say in private: "A good dose of bankruptcy is just what the country needs to wake it up: suspension of payments on public debts; cutting off of all credits abroad; reduction of all purchases, even the most necessary, like fuel and food, to cash in hand. Then they'll know where they stand." These talkers were more than half serious, and, as I believe, wholly wrong. Nothing good would have come of such shock treatment. Perhaps they knew it, and it was not a question of making the public understand where the country stood economically. For sometimes we would talk of the probability—a quite good one—of striking oil, perhaps in large quantities; then I would sometimes see a flicker of anxiety succeed the flash of hope: oil! Affluence, easy money, a repetition of the immigration stampede, a swamping of the last citadels of the old spirit, those remainders of the hard-won forms and disciplines of the classic days.

I could not get from economists and businessmen a coherent estimate of the savings to be made by lowering still further the standard of living; and there was much divergence on the areas of application. Apart from possible effects on the standard of production—itself a difficult subject—it is affirmed and denied that any considerable portion of the national bill can be cut down. It is generally agreed that the Israelis can do with less clothing. Food is very debatable ground. Travel and holidays are also debatable—though less so. It is a majority opinion, however, that the Israelis see too many cinemas, read too many newspapers, enjoy too many services. If one tries to get at the figures involved in the total of these uneven complaints one remains unimpressed.

More drastic, less debatable, is the suggestion that all living accommodations should be frozen for the next few years. Let the *maabarot* (the transition shanty towns) stay as they are; let no more dwellings be put up, no cinemas, synagogues, meeting-halls, cafés, etc. Let building be restricted to productive structures, industrial plants, offices. I have heard this suggestion more than once and it certainly is not debatable in the sense that a great deal of money could be "saved." Its practicability is, however, very dubious. Another suggestion is that the army be cut by one third or even one half. That, for the time being, is the most debatable of all the suggestions.

It would seem, then, that the answer lies in increased production rather than in diminished consumption, although the latter cannot be wholly ignored. But increased production depends not only on development of resources and encouragement of investment; it depends on morale; and morale is also involved in the acceptance of a lowered standard of living. Morale, in turn, will never—certainly not in Israel, perhaps nowhere else, either—depend exclusively on carrot and stick, on material reward and penalty, on promise and threat, whether these are applied to the individual or to the community. You cannot terrify a community into vigorous exertion; if you point to a mortal threat, you must also indicate, beyond the threat, something more than mere physical survival and security. Neither can you inspire a community to vigorous exertion by the mere promise of physical reward; beyond the physical reward you must indicate something more than the physical. As with the community, so with the individual. It is of the essence of Israel's confusion that physical threat and physical promise are being overemphasized (they do have their proper emphasis in a sensible appraisal) as correctives in the difficulties of the present phase. It was not physical threat and promise which characterized the highest moral moments of Zionism.

In the absence of the larger ideal, in the almost exclusive focus of attention on the physical, mutual recrimination sharpens, and the objective evaluation of physical factors becomes impossible. Private cars roll along the roads in the thousand, sometimes giving a lift, sometimes not. Some of the cars are out on business, many are not. In expensive cafés and restaurants the well-to-do eat and drink well; some are tourists bringing in foreign currency; some— most—are Israelis finding relief from the monotony and drudgery of home cooking. Many obtain meat meals without points—black market. The people in the cafés are of course better dressed than the workers; the women have expensive beauty parlors to cater to them. And in working-class circles they tell me: "There's where our foreign currency goes." When you are sitting in the simple, austere home of a working-class family, you understand only too well.

But you will also sit, sometimes, in the not austere but by no means luxurious home of middle-class friends, and they will remind you of the expensive homes of the bus drivers; of the carpenters and plumbers and plasterers whose income is double that of your host, and no income tax; of the costly services that the kibbutzim have developed for themselves.

Each side minimizes its own misdemeanors, exaggerates those of the other. The middle class tells me that if you were to take *all* private cars off the road, you would save less than one per cent of the fuel bill. Also: "If you were to crack down on the black-marketeer diners in the restaurants you would save an insignificant portion of the food bill. *But*—those tens of thousands of workers forever rushing around on jaunts, those thousands of aristocrats of labor. . . . That is what retards the country's economic stabilization. . . ."

Sometimes, again—this usually after they have had their fling at the other side—my hosts would be willing to concede a degree of shortcoming on their own. I asked

several well-to-do Israeli householders whether they could
not manage on less, could not, for the next few years, set
an example. The almost uniform answer has been: "We
lack leadership." Of the admission made by labor leaders,
that they lack the standing to bear down on labor's abuses,
I have already spoken. These confessional moods, on either
side, are however mixed with general self-exculpations.
"We've been living an abnormal life for more than a decade and a half. Since the Arab rebellion of 1936 it has been
one trial after another. The Arab rebellion, with its constant pressure on our nerves, its toll of lives, lasted practically until the beginning of the war in 1939. Just before
the war came the White Paper, which was an attempt to
crush the Zionist hope. During the war we fought on the
Allied side, and at the same time carried on an underground struggle with the British to bring in refugees.
When the war ended for others, we had our own war with
England's Labour government. And when England went,
we had our war with the Arabs. Then came the stampede
of refugees. Well, you can take just so much and no more.
We've got to relax a little."

You cannot argue with such a statement. Exhortation
from an outsider is mere impudence; and even from an
insider it is pretty futile. In any case, the large argument,
the argument that is concerned with the historic destiny
and meaning of Israel, is not along these lines. It may very
well be asked whether this is a time for "large argument"
and talk about "historic destiny," when it is a question of
persuading Israelis to eat less and work more, and non-
Israelis to donate more and invest more. I would answer
that in the long run there is a functional relationship
between the two frames of reference. It is impossible not
to be concerned about conditions in Israel; it would be
heartless, as well as cowardly, to discourage participation
in its economic reconstruction; but it *is* possible to say at

the same time: "This excessive, if natural worry over the day's problems, this concentration on the immediate, obstructs even its own purpose. I choose to believe that under any circumstances short of a world cataclysm the State of Israel, with all its defects, divisions, frictions, will pull through into stability. But the level and character of that stability will depend on something other than economic factors; it will depend on the restoration of some of the original insights that accompanied the beginnings of our work. For though it is true that much has happened that we could not foresee or provide against—'we didn't plan it this way'—we can still refuse to be swamped by accident. Besides, within the area of our free will too, we fell short of our principles, and we must not yield to the last weakness of declaring ourselves blameless."

CHAPTER XIII

The Sundering

❀

I

I SAT with a dozen Israeli leaders of public opinion—members of the Knesset (Parliament), journalists, academicians—and listened to a long and earnest discussion of one of Israel's most urgent needs—reinforcements from the Western lands of freedom; and in particular from the foremost of them, the greatest reservoir of Jewish manpower, America.

It was a bewildering thing: out of five million American Jews not five hundred a year were inspired to throw in their lot with this miracle of the ages, the reborn Jewish State. A trickle of youngsters had joined the pioneers; a handful of businessmen had transferred their activities. There were a few thousand visitors every year, tens of millions of dollars were contributed to the funds, tens of millions invested in the bonds, countless meetings were held in America, conventions and conferences passed laudatory resolutions—but of a moderately large movement toward the land, no sign. And many factors called imperatively for Western immigration. There were needed: the leaven of a voluntary as offset to the vast refugee influx; the skills of the West to instruct the instructors of the primitive masses of the East; the moral declaration, to Israel and to the world, that the reborn

Jewish State was something more than an assembly of refugees. And as much as anything else there was needed a counteraction to the threat of Levantinization.

For two long sessions they discussed the reasons for the failure. They suggested that Israel had not been presented to American Jewry as it should have been; the miracle had been diluted in transmission; the Jewish intellectuals of America had been neglected; in the constant—and under-standable—solicitation of gift money and investments for Israel the solicitation of personal commitment had gone by default. A renewal of effort must be undertaken; the teachers of American Jewry, the leaders of its public opinion, had to be convened, mobilized, thrown into action. The full meaning of Israel had to be conveyed to the American Jewish youth. . . .

The longer I listened the clearer it became to me that I was looking into the heart of one of the great deviations in Zionism. These highly intelligent men were concerned with a single idea: the development of Israel. They thought of Jews everywhere else in the world as material for Israel, *and as nothing else.* The central Jewish problem everywhere, as they saw it, was the creation of a will to migrate to Israel. They were grateful, of course, for financial and political aid. But for the sake of those Jews —in America and elsewhere—and not only for the sake of Israel, Jewish education and indoctrination had to point in one direction, migration to the Jewish State.

Not once in the long discussions was it remotely suggested that American Jewry had a destiny, too; that these five million Jews would not dissolve without having made a distinctive contribution to Jewish history comparable with that of Babylonian Jewry, or Spanish and Russian Jewries; that for a long time to come there would be two great Jewries, Israel and America, with complementary roles; that it was for Israeli Jewry to be concerned with

American Jewry as a continuing and evolving force. And naturally it could occur to no one that this summary dismissal of a great Jewry from the stage of history was itself a symptom of a dimmed inspiration from which no effective appeal could issue.

II

One met it everywhere; sometimes tactfully implied, sometimes flung down bluntly; sometimes as expostulation, sometimes as warning. It might be:

"Why are you American Jews going through the motions of building seminaries, synagogues, schools, centers, universities? Don't you realize that you are assimilating so fast that unless you send us your best today, even they will be lost tomorrow?"

Or else:

"Can you, after what has happened in the last fifteen years, continue calmly with far-reaching plans for yourselves and your children and your grandchildren? Even if we don't accept the extreme view, if we don't talk of a second Hitler episode, this time *not* in Germany, hasn't the first one left you shaken? Isn't it enough for you that the very question should exist? Can you be content to suffer, for the foreseeable future, the equivocal status that attaches to the very word 'Jew'? Can you remain in the midst of the world that even witnessed—let us not say participated in, let us forget the failure to protest—that even witnessed the degradation of the Jewish name and identity?"

But Mapam and Hashomer Hatzair do accept the extreme view. They *know* America is going fascist. They *know* that the fate of European Jewry awaits American Jewry. The quality of their conviction about that which is going to happen almost puts the event in the irrevocable past. "Columbus discovered America, Napoleon lost the battle of Waterloo, America is going fascist and will massacre the Jews. Let them get out: it's now or never."

Which Jews? The five million of them? Practically. How can we get five million, or even two million Jews into Israel in the next ten or fifteen years? When you ask this question you are answered in proverbs and allusions: "Where there's a will there's a way." "We've done the impossible before."

In one manner or another, on one level or another, whether in warning or expostulation, they were all writing off American Jewry, consigning it to history's rubbish heap.

III

This negativism toward world Jewry, this tacit assumption that world Jewry is done for, physically or morally, or both, expresses itself differently on the different levels; and with every group it has its special mixture of motivations.

The leaders of public opinion whose conferences I attended were of middle age or beyond. All had been born outside Israel. They had been in the country anywhere from fifteen to fifty years, years of intense experience which had re-centered their personalities. They were passionately concerned with the urgent problem of immigration from the free West. They could not understand this massive reluctance on the part of Western Jewry. It was so obvious to them that Israel alone mattered to the Jewish people and that Israel alone could be relied on, that they blamed themselves for not being able to make it clear to others. They were moreover under harassing pressure. Israel *needs* Western Jews and needs them now; and it is every man's illusion that his need ought to create someone's willingness to help him. Therefore they could not think of a destiny for American Jewry. It was an interference; at best a dangerous delay in their planning, at worst a total negation of their faith. So the discussions went on, intelligent, impatient, and baffled.

The young people in Israel, native born or childhood immigrants, take a simpler view. In their eyes it is evidence of delinquency and decay that an American Jew should not want to settle in Israel. The "exile" is a uniformly disgraceful thing, in principle if not in actuality. One country may be tolerant of Jews, another may practice discrimination, a third may massacre them; the degree does not affect the quality—it is all *galut,* exile. And Jews who do not want to leave the Exile when they can, hardly deserve to be received when they must. For these youngsters the notion of a positive destiny for American or any other Diaspora Jewry is not even intelligible. For them no Exilic Jewry of the past has had a destiny. The two thousand years of Jewish experience between the crushing of Bar Kochba and the creation of the Republic of Israel were a disreputable episode called "Exile." Jews could not be blamed too much for enduring it when there was no alternative. But that they should choose its continuation now, with freedom theirs for the asking. . . . Again one does not raise the question: "What would you do if all free Jews wanted to come to little Israel?" The fact is, very few of them do. Therefore they are not really Jews any more; the Exile has turned them into something neither Jew nor gentile.

No distinction is made between gradations of Jewish self-identification, of Jewish knowledge, sympathy, co-operation. Now it is quite true that there are hundreds of thousands of Jews, in America and elsewhere, who are neither Jews nor gentiles. But there are hundreds of thousands of Jews who cling to part of their heritage, and hundreds of thousands more who are conscious if imperfect carriers of the Jewish life-view. To the young Israeli these gradations are irrelevant in the face of a refusal to migrate into the Jewish State. He would even say that a pretension to Jewish loyalty, or Jewish learning, whether of a religious or cultural tinge, only makes the case worse. Of course it is good to have Jews throughout the world helping the Jewish State with funds and political influence; but such help would not be necessary if the immigration into Israel did not consist entirely of penniless and broken refugees —that is, if the immigration contained a fair proportion of the Jews of the free and affluent West. So even the philanthropic Jews are only buying themselves out from their primary duty; and their contributions to Israel are bribes to their own conscience. And in any case: if it is a question of philanthropy, the Jews of America are getting away with mere money contributions, while the Jews of Israel must submit to a long regime of the most rigorous austerity—and the end not yet in sight—in order to make room for the newcomers. And again if it is a question of philanthropy, why are the Jews of Israel more responsible for the threatened Jews of Irak and the Yemen, and the ruined survivors of Europe, than are the Jews of America?

IV

Sense and nonsense are closely interwoven in all of these views. It is true that the miracle of the reborn Jewish State has not been presented to American and other Western Jewries as it should have been. But that it can be presented as it were from the outside, by enthusiasm, by propaganda, by dramatization, is not true. Such appeals have their place and purpose, but their limitations must be understood. The deeper effect of the rebirth of Israel must work itself out with the simultaneous acquisition, by American Jewry, of its own character, its regionalist form of Judaism. Until that has happened—and it is now in process—personal commitments to Israel, migration, pioneering, will be minimal and symbolic.

It is true that assimilation is at work in American Jewry. But it is equally true that there is a profoundly significant recoil from assimilation. There is a falling away; but there is also a reconcentration.

It is true that even in America and England the word "Jew" still touches off equivocal reactions. But the very heart of the Jewish problem, as it interlocks today with the world problem, is precisely the distinction between the free and totalitarian worlds which the blanket warning ignores. To a tired or confused mind one may appeal easily with these phrases: "The Jews of America feel safe? Well, so did the Jews of Germany. These think that America is 'different'? That's what the others thought about Germany." Thence one deduces: "Because the Jews of Germany were so tragically deceived, the Jews of America will also be tragically deceived." The conclusion ignores the fundamental fact that such a deception implies a world collapse, a world in total ruin. An America thus totalitarian-fascist-minded must meet a totalitarian-Communist-minded Russia in a head-on collision that will obliterate the Jewish problem together with all other human problems.

Something more is implied, of course: namely, that in so far as it relates to Jewish survival, the struggle between East and West is meaningless! The West will go fascist and exterminate the Jews; the East is communistic, and in communistic countries there is no reason why Jews should go on existing as a separate people. Such is Mapam's analysis of "fact," though it repudiates the implication of indifference, insisting that it is better—as it is indeed inevitable —that the East should triumph. Yet the amoral implication is unavoidable: in the most fateful decision which has ever faced the human species, Judaism apparently has no stake.

The inexorable unveiling of the anti-Semitic motif in leftist totalitarianism will perhaps introduce new verbalisms into Mapam and Hashomor Hatzair propaganda. Mapam's warnings of American Jewry's impending extermination were muted even before the Prague trials. Some time ago I pointed out to Mapam leaders in Israel that their emissaries to America were defeating their own purposes; looking for pioneers, and for communal encouragement of pioneering to Israel, they developed the theme of America as the graveyard of five million Jews. "You cannot," I said, "move a community to great action by playing its funeral march." The Mapam leaders admitted the pedagogic error, and assured me that it had been corrected. But the fundamental view had not changed. The tactical readjustment on the American scene has had no effect on the general propagandistic strategy. Mapam still concentrates on the death-sentence that American fascism has pronounced against American Jewry. It forced itself on me that this furious concentration on America's fascist and anti-Semitic role was a trick to deflect attention from the condition of two to three million Jews behind the Iron Curtain. Screaming about five million American Jews, Mapam wanted to deafen us to the muted cry of the Jews who were agonizing under the pressure of leftist forcible assimilation. And whatever the new mythology, one certainty remains: for Mapam too (and for its own special reasons), all of Jewry's future is contracted to the confines of Israel; no framework of reference projects the attention of Israeli Jewry to values other than those it possesses at the moment.

V

Sometimes the nonsense is precipitated out in a heap, and appropriated by a special group. Then we perceive a definitely pathological condition. Such a group, styling itself "the Canaanites," issues a weekly publication called *Aleph*. Their cry is: "What does our government mean by flooding the country with a rabble of refugees who carry the name of Jews? Who is this mob that assumes the right —in which our corrupt officials, for reasons of their own, concur—on the basis of a fiction of kinship, to crowd out the natives? What special business is it of ours that persons listed as 'Jews'—whatever that means—are persecuted somewhere? Many are persecuted in this bad world, but no one asks us to surrender our land, our character, our future, to their need. Much less do we concede their *right* to this territory, or even their right to associate their identity with ours."

In this "Canaanitism" there are overtones of neo-paganism reminiscent of the German hankering for the ancient gods when Ludendorff and Baldur von Schirach were representative figures. But here the gods are the Baalim of pre-Judaic Canaan; and one even hears rumors of rites celebrated in "groves and high places," after the manner denounced by the Hebrew Prophets thousands of years ago.

This is going native with a vengeance. "The Canaanites" are not, as might be supposed, eighth- or ninth-generation Palestinians. They are the sons and daughters of immigrants. And *they* see themselves as autochthones. *They* are the Canaanites. To them even the refugees whom Moses brought into the country would therefore count as foreigners. Nay, Abraham himself would be an intruder, in flight from Nimrod's religious intolerance. It is all completely mad, of course; and it is confined to an esoteric coterie—the circulation of *Aleph* is five hundred at most.

Perhaps there is in it a certain amount of pose. Nevertheless to this, as to all other pathological social phenomena, there is a wider background of susceptibility. Even before the creation of the State of Israel we already had youth associations with names like *Yelide Aretz*—Native Sons. They had their social philosophy—invariably reactionary —and their special attitude toward immigrants, even such as came from choice, and not under compulsion. With these "Mayflower" Jews Zionism had climaxed as a slightly comical, slightly sinister local chauvinism from which world Jewry was completely excluded.

A phrase in wide currency among the youth of Israel today is *"Al tekashkesh Tzionut"* which, colloquialism for colloquialism, means: "Don't give me that Zionist claptrap." That Zionist claptrap! If it referred to the windy speeches of Zionist orators, to pretentious idealism and political bombast, it would be a healthy sign. But it refers to something else, namely, to the unity of world Jewry, to the Jewish State as an organic part of the Jewish ideal, as the effort of the Jewish part of the Jewish people to renew itself. It is an intolerant assertion that the Jewish State is a thing in itself, self-justified, self-explanatory; it is a demand not to be burdened with Jewish history and tradition and larger significances.

It will do us no good to address reproaches and pleas to the youth of Israel; it does not merit the first, will not respond to the second. Its character is sound; if its views are narrow the blame belongs elsewhere: in part to the violence of the struggle it has sustained, in part to the false values that we of the older generation introduced into its education. To some extent its touchy spiritual isolationism is the passing reflex action of recent excitements; where it is deeper it calls for long-range revaluation of Zionist concepts.

This sundering from Diaspora Jewry, this severance of life-transmitting connections, is a pervasive thing. I have already made reference to it in speaking of the kibbutzim (Chapters Six and Seven); but it is characteristic of Israel as a whole.

It may be defined as the collapse of Zionist perspective. As the range of their responsiveness shrinks, as the seven or eight thousand square miles of their homeland assert a more and more exclusive dominion over their spirit, the Israelis find it progressively harder to lift themselves to new efforts of creation and endurance. There is interaction, of course; the more exhausted they become, the harder it is to push back the limits of perspective. However we apportion the causes, this fact remains central: the Jewish State as a thing in itself, self-justified, self-explanatory, has not the power to move tens of thousands of people to great creative action. And again we may put it conversely: when the renewal of Zionist action will come, it will be accompanied by a re-establishment of the connections, an expansion of responsiveness.

For a Jewish State as thing in itself is not a Jewish concept at all. It was not so to the teachers of antiquity, who have left their denunciations of it—and of those Jews who nourished it—as the classic and imperishable "literature" of Judaism. It was not so throughout the Jewish Exile; and, in spite of aberrations, it was not so in the time of classic Zionism. Israel's turning away from world Jewry is a turning away from the Prophetic subordination of statism to the Idea that transcends the state. It is therefore a turning away from the sources of Jewish strength. There is a pathetic struggle of self-contradiction in the search of Israeli leaders for a return to the old standards of Zionist idealism within Israel; they have narrowed the vision and expect a wider response; they call on the people to lift itself up but they offer only the restricted horizon which is visible five feet from ground level.

I have repeatedly used the phrases "isolation from world Jewry," "sundering from world Jewry." But I must also emphasize again the paradoxical fact that no other Jewish community is as sensitive as the Israeli to attacks on other Jewish communities. Leaving out the "Canaanites," whom I cannot understand except as unhinged people whom one studies for their condition, not their views; leaving out the penumbra of sympathizers with them; allowing also for the subdued feeling that Jews who suffer in countries which they could have left for Israel deserve their suffering; taking it all in all, Israeli Jewry responds more swiftly, more instinctively, more profoundly, than any other community to manifestations of anti-Semitism anywhere in the world. And yet the response does not disturb the conviction that world Judaism has—and perhaps *ought* to have—no future. Which is the more significant, the more enduring, the sensitivity or the conviction? The answer is not analytical but dynamic; for neither the splitting up of world Jewry, nor its reunification, is an inevitability. The issue waits on developments that self-criticism, understanding, and foresight will help us to control.

VI

The sundering from world Jewry and world Judaism has another aspect, having to do with time rather than space. Israel is cut off from the past. This will be an astounding assertion to many; for if Israel is anything at all, it is—one would insist—the most remarkable historic instance of the past made present. But it is necessary to point out that while this is a correct description of classic Zionism, it need not be one of Israel.

Less than a decade ago—but the war had kept me away from Israel for some years prior to that—I wrote, in *Harvest in the Desert:*

For the children [who would grow up in the Jewish homeland] Hebrew would be natural in a profound sense. The land into which they would be born had acquired its imperishable name through Hebrew-speaking men and women. The language was one with the land, if we think of that land not merely as random territory but as the theatre of the unique utterances of the Bible. Hebrew *could* not be a secondary language to the new generation, if the bond between it and the land was to be enduring. And it turned out as the Zionists had planned. The associations which to me, for instance, are a cultural acquisition, are to the children of the Emek, the Valley of Jezreel, an immediate experience. I have seen little tots come out of the kindergartens of Nahalal and Ain Charod and Bet Alpha to play in the morning sun, and they have looked up at Mount Gilboa, or at the Carmel range, or at the hills of southern Galilee; and I have heard them clamor, as children do everywhere, for a story. What better stories could their teacher tell them than the one about King Saul and Jonathan and David and the wars against the Philistines (and there was Mount Gilboa, where Saul and Jonathan were killed, right before them); and the one about Elijah and the prophets of Baal and the wicked King Ahab (and there on the other side was Mount Carmel, where the contest took place between Elijah and the false prophets); and the one about the Prophet Jeremiah, trailing through this very valley after the Jewish prisoners being carried into the Babylonian captivity; and all of it told in the language of the record, in Hebrew. The triple cord of people, land, and language was woven into their minds, and a triple cord shall not easily be broken. To these children the Bible is not only sacred; it is the source of their first awareness of their childhood surroundings.

It sounded reasonable and compelling to me ten years ago, and yet its implication is—as I now perceive—only a dangerous half-truth. To begin with, I was at fault in belittling "the associations which are a cultural acquisition." If we think of "cultural acquisition" in the all important sense of transmitted tradition, father-to-son bond, continuity of spiritual identity, we are close to a definition of civilization itself. Land and language and peoplehood lose their meaning without the fourth strand; it is a quadruple, not a triple cord; and the fourth strand is time.

In the old days, before the embitterment of our relations with the Arabs, I used to go to Palestine by way of Egypt; and I would break the journey there to linger for a few days in the museum of Cairo or at Mena House opposite the pyramids. I never ceased to marvel at the discontinuity of Egyptian life. Records and remains and monuments which attracted visitors from every part of the world were without meaning to the local population. There was simply no connection between the glories of the Pharaonic ages and the spirit of the Egyptian people. There was a reason, of course. It is not the same people; it is not the same language. The Egyptian is an Arab; his roots are in another world; his presence in the land of the Pharaohs is pure accident. There is no lever that, resting on the fulcrum of a common tradition, can enable the past to lift up the present.

But in later years I made my visits to Palestine and Israel via Rome and Athens; and I lingered at these stations, too; particularly at the first, for the sake of a Renaissance novel I was planning. Here the languages of past and present have much in common; one passes easily from Italian to Latin, while there is no passage from Arabic to Coptic. There is a strong strain of the Italian peoples of the Imperial time in the modern Italians, despite intervening admixtures. Moreover, Italian schoolchildren study the history of Imperial Rome as their own history; the monuments of the splendid past are more numerous than those of ancient Egypt; its literature, unlike that of the ancient Egyptians, is copious and fascinating, a universal cultural necessity. But between the Rome of Augustus and Marcus Aurelius, of Virgil and Tacitus, and the Rome that swarmed about me, there was no living connection; they were as far from each other as the magnificence of the Foro Romano and the forum of Trajan, at which the ruins hinted, is from the Corso and the Palazzo di Justitia. The Fascist evocation of ancestral greatness was a windy futility. The people I talked to, even the cultivated, did not feel a continuity between themselves and a far-off exalted past. The tumultuous Roman streets and squares stand away from the reminders of antique achievement which are inescapably imbedded in them almost as if actively disclaiming kinship.

Even more striking is the sense of discontinuity in Athens. I remember how I stood in the bow of the ship approaching the Piræus, and saw for the first time the Parthenon and the Lycabettus towering over the still-concealed inland city. I thought of Athenians of old returning from a journey, and of ancient Romans making their pilgrimage to the birthplace of Western civilization; and I thought how they, too, must have caught the first glimpse of their destination in these landmarks. But passing through the streets of Athens to the Acropolis, I asked myself how it was possible for these descendants—partial at least—of the most gifted people of antiquity, perhaps the most gifted of all history, to be so indifferent to the suggestion of these memorials. It was the question that Byron asked in "The Isles of Greece"; and thousands of others have asked it, too. For though there is much boasting in modern Athens about a glorious past, there is no organic nexus between the glory and its panegyrists. Yet they speak Greek, and are a people, and have inherited the land.

True, their Greek (I am told) is remoter from Plato's than our modern Hebrew is from Isaiah's; as remote as the Italian of modern Rome from the Latin of Virgil. But the triple cord is there, land, people, language; even if the last is slightly frayed. What, then, is lacking?

I can see now that there is lacking the bond of the intermediate generations. There is no channel of filial communication. The fourth strand has been snapped and cannot be rewoven. The past is a legend, not a reality, because the sons did not receive from the fathers the heritage of the grandfathers.

VII

These are the two dangers and frustrations in Israel at the present time; the sundering from world Jewry, and the concomitant sundering from historic Jewry, which can make of Gilboa and Carmel legends, instead of living realities.

Partly because they are crushed by burdens that we of the wealthy West do not lighten as we should, partly because of the cyclical decline that characterizes all creative movements, partly because we have committed errors— some yet to be discussed—the Israelis no longer feel themselves to be, as once they did, the expression of the latent will and destiny of the whole Jewish people. Their struggles take place on the limited stage of contemporary Israel.

No tide of historic and world-wide significance, the lift of the Jewish people in time and space, carries them today. It may be a cruel thing to suggest, and yet it thrusts itself on the mind, that their special sensitivity with regard to oppression of Jews everywhere is in part a reflex of the feeling: "That human material belongs to us." It is Israel that is wounded and threatened with loss; Israel, and not the Jewish people at large. And so, as they struggle with their moral problems, of discipline, of production, of over-consumption, of doctrinaire rigidity, they become more and more intent on their own salvation, and move toward the isolation that is the the enemy of salvation.

To most of the internal problems of Israel there are no purely technical answers. Neither will answers come from party programs strategically reformulated. But while technical programs are being carried out, as they must be, both Israel and world Jewry must turn back to the sources of Zionist strength, to the vision which made the Jewish homeland an instrument, not an end. Even the discovery of good technical ideas depends on mood, and the change of mood now needed must have a common source and purpose in Israeli and world Jewry.

CHAPTER XIV

Tug of War

❀

I

ZIONISM and the Jewish homeland in the making did not become, among American Jews, anything like the educative force that I—and others—hoped for. The reasons fall into the familiar pattern; some of them were outside our control; for others we are responsible.

Forty years ago the movement had its strongest support among the Yiddish-speaking and foreign-born. But even among these it was a minority movement, being *as a movement,* weaker than the socialist non-Zionist and anti-Zionist movements. The words are italicized because movements are themselves minority phenomena. As a representative force, however, Zionism was more significant by far; it had the same relationship to the American semi-ghetto as to the Manchester semi-ghetto of my childhood. Among the English-speaking and American-born, Zionism was a minority within a minority; for only a minority of native American Jewry was concerned with Jewish matters, and within that minority the Zionists were a minority. Here they were not even representative; the generation that Zionism would serve was yet to be born.

The Yiddish-speaking, Jewish-trained core of the Zionist movement was by no means elite through and through, either. The divisions I have described in Chapter Two

("Refuge or Renaissance?") extended into it. Herzl's faith in the *Judennot,* the misery of the Jews, as a redemptive force, was shared by thousands of Yiddish-speaking Zionists; in their Zionism flickered up, now and again, glimpses of affirmation; but fundamentally it was a wailful kind of Zionism; its hymn was *"Eli, Eli,"* not *"Hatikvah."* Thus even within Yiddish-speaking, Hebrew-tinged Zionism there was a tug of war between mendicancy and Messianism as opposing concepts of Jewish dynamism.

II

The First World War increased that inner tension. A great philanthropic activity developed in American Jewry during and after the war in behalf of the ruined Jewish communities of eastern Europe. This was not a partisan enterprise; it enrolled Zionists, non-Zionists, and anti-Zionists. But it had a peculiar partisan effect on the Zionist movement. It strengthened the mendicant aspect of Zionism.

In that great philanthropic action the Americanized non-Zionists and anti-Zionists, though numerically weaker, were far stronger financially. They were also troubled by inner insecurity. Their impulse to help needy Jews in other countries was spontaneous and honest; they had, however, to take the maximum safeguards against being misunderstood by their Christian fellow-citizens. They wanted everyone to know that this was purely philanthropic action; that it did not imply a special and compromising bond with subjects or citizens of foreign countries. Even when Americanized Jews like Louis Marshal fought at the Versailles Peace Conference for the political minority-rights of Polish Jews, it meant no more than, let us say, England's efforts on behalf of Rumanian Jews at the Congress of Berlin. Feeding the hungry, clothing the naked, safeguarding the political rights of the defenseless —it was all straightforward humanitarianism; the Jewish side of it was ostensibly incidental.

I have spoken, in Chapter Two, of "the exile psychology that it was the business of Zionism to cure." Part of that psychology found expression in the philanthropist (as distinguished from the materialist, or idealist) interpretation of history. The long exile life of the Jewish people had developed in it its special technique of public action. The collection box was the foundation of our domestic and foreign policy. It was our army, our navy, and our State Department. We relieved the needy in our communities, we ransomed captives, we bought ourselves out—when we could—from the clutches of tyrants, on the proceeds of the charity appeal. Fight we could not, except to commit suicide: but we committed suicide only at the stake, proclaiming, till the last moment, the unity of God. Thus the management of our affairs was accompanied by a perpetual weeping at the front doors of the Jewish rich and at the back doors of the gentile powerful; and when part of the Jewish people was stirred by the call to rebuild a Jewish homeland, there were some who, in the new movement, the renaissance movement, retained the habitual attitude of mendicancy. They wanted to weep their way to a Jewish State.

Then, after the First World War, Zionists found themselves in double competition with non-Zionists and anti-Zionists. There was the purely philanthropic activity of the relief campaigns, in which Zionists were as zealous as the rest. There was also the rebuiding of the Jewish homeland, to which Zionists were compelled to give an additional philanthropic twist because that was the prevalent tone of Jewish public-spiritedness. The creative, redemptive, curative, and spiritual side of Zionism was correspondingly weakened.

III

The building of the Jewish homeland had to be financed entirely by our voluntary contributions. There were no grants-in-aid from America, no loans from international banks in those days. All that the Balfour Declaration and the Mandate gave us was the precarious right to pay our way. Everyone, including Weizmann, was pulled into the fund-raising campaigns; and these were, as they are till this day, mixtures of public spirit, imaginative kindness, publicity-hunting, social pressure, cajolery, professional slickness, sentimentality, Jewish loyalty, high-pressure salesmanship, advertising stunts, and nostalgic echoes of forgotten pieties. It was and is a perpetual tug of war between educational effort and surrender to techniques.

In the early nineteen twenties I accompanied Weizmann to dozens of banquets and mass and group meetings, taking notes that I afterwards worked up into a small volume of his addresses. I have never known him to stoop to tearfulness or rabble-rousing. He was always concerned with the dignity of his subject and the intellectual needs of his audiences. So were the top-level delegates who accompanied him, or alternated with him—Shmarya Levin, Chaim Nachman Bialik, Leo Motzkin, and others. The leaders of American Zionism were on the whole equally understanding. But neither they, nor the visitors, could stand up to the tide of lachrymosity.

Weizmann suffered during these campaigns. When he speaks in his autobiography of the "weary months of travel and disappointment" for which the clustered village lights of the Emek were his reward, he means the money-raising side of the work. For he was not averse to traveling and teaching. He loved both the people and people. The disappointment lay partly in the slowness of the response, partly in the moral damage that the movement suffered in the campaigns. Often he had to negotiate with unpleasant persons, or, in exchange for a probable donation to the funds, cater to someone's social snobbery by dining in his home. More than once he delivered his part of the agreement, only to be bilked by the party of the second part. There would be no donation—or only a derisory one. He would sometimes take me along to such social events, hoping I would deflect part of the pressure. He would say: "Come, take a stroll with me this evening along the *Via Dolorosa*." And he would ask me to acknowledge the "returns" from such a stroll with: "Maurice, write him a letter from the bottom of my heart."

His patience was a wondrous thing to see. He remained courteous and good-humored in circumstances which froze me into speechlessness. Once a host who celebrated the honor of Weizmann's presence in his home with more than he could carry threw his arms round him at parting, and wept: "Dr. Weizmann, call me Nat." The words sounded vaguely Hebrew, something like *"Kol Minat,"* and puzzled Weizmann until I deciphered them for him on the way home. Thereafter *"Kol Minat"* was a password between us.

Dictating his autobiography long, long after, he remembered those incidents with a shudder, and in the first draft expressed himself freely about them. When I read it back and we had talked it over, he toned the expressions down. But his resentment had very little to do with personal distaste. He was concerned with the harm done to the movement by the general atmosphere and manner of the fund-raising campaigns.

Long experience with campaign rallies and dinners has left me unshakably convinced that sob appeals do no good on the spot in financial terms, and much harm in the long run from every other point of view. It is destructive of public morale—because it is a continuous degradation of the public intelligence—to subject audiences to the fund-rais-

ing banquets of Zionists and other causes, at which the
stereotyped meal closes with the stereotyped appeal. The
phrases have become nauseatingly impotent; indeed, their
impotence is an offense to the subject matter. "Our unfortunate brethren," and "the hungry little ones," and
"the weeping mothers," and "the homeless and the persecuted"; also, by way of balance: "You who live in a land of
plenty . . ." and: "You who have escaped these horrors
and enjoy the freedom and security of America . . ." over
and over and over again, till the most inarticulate member
of the community could utter them with the same ineffec-
tiveness. One might defend the practice after a fashion if
the feelings of the audience were harrowed, but that precisely is what they are not. The technique of the good meal
(sometimes accompanied by entertainment!) and the tear-
ful appeal puts one in mind of the old Yiddish story of the
returned traveler at his first family reunion. Sitting at the
well-laden table, together with friends and relatives, he is
informed by degrees of the losses that had occurred
throughout his long absence, during which, it appears, no
news had reached him from his community. "We want you
to know, Reb Chayim," says one relative, gently, "that
your friend Reb Shachna is now a sleeper in the dust." The
returned traveler goes on eating stolidly. After a pause another relative, using the same kind of high circumlocution,
adds: "And your brother-in-law of the nearby community,
Reb Ziesel, is also now in the True World." Reb Chayim
continues to plow through his food. A third relative tries
his hand, amid the shocked incomprehension of the rest.
"And your sister's son, the promising student, also sleeps in
the Eternal House." No sign from Reb Chayim. Finally
someone bursts out: "Man! Has your heart turned to
stone?" Whereupon Reb Chayim answers, with his mouth
full: "Wait till I've finished the meal. I will then let out a
wail of lamentation which will startle the whole city."

The truth was and is that the guests at the dinners I am describing know what they are there for; and they have more or less decided what they are going to donate. Their presence itself is an admission of commitment and obligation; their awareness of obligation may be mixed with other factors, less edifying; but the speeches do nothing to improve the pattern of motivation. Or to increase the yield.

An impressive, intelligent chairman, a well-organized crew on the floor, solid advance preparation, both of initial gifts and of attendance, can make a considerable difference in the amount obtained at the function. A good, sensible speech helps a little toward the immediate objective; a poor speech can do some harm. But one cannot make a good, sensible speech by reverting to the wretched formulas of destitution, which by repetition have become weaker than the emotion already felt by the audience. The real business of the main speakers is, I believe, the strengthening of the permanent background of a movement. Of course, where a movement does not exist, where it is a repetition of charitable appeal year after year, the problem is of another kind.

You cannot do much with one address. But there have been tens of thousands of addresses in the last thirty or forty years. Not all of them have been delivered at fundraising functions, and not all of them have been "tearjerkers." There has been some decent exposition on a level worthy of the subject; there have occasionally been interesting, instructive, and heartening pictures of Israeli effort. But even when the occasion permitted such luxury, there has been far too much intrusion of the "two thousand years of homelessness" theme. One would think that in these two thousand years the Jewish people had produced nothing but elegies and martyrologies, whereas it is the astonishing fact that books like *The Rod of Judah* and

The Valley of Weeping, memorials of massacres, are quite exceptional. The immense mass of literature which the Jews have produced in the sixty generations of exile concentrates on their intellectual, spiritual, and religious problems.

It is true that we did not have enough speakers of intelligence and ability to go round; but we did not use properly those that we had, and, what is therefore natural, we made no effort to develop a new generation of speakers and teachers. We founded no Zionist seminaries, we supported no superior publications, nurtured no writers by providing them with an outlet, conducted no consistent campaign of popular education. We had not, in this country, the equivalent of Achad Ha-Am's famous society of the Bnai Moshe. And so till this day action for Israel is afflicted with the old curse of mendicancy. And the power of bad habit was marvelously illustrated during the three- or four-year period 1946–9, when American Jewry was in a fever of excitement over Israel's destiny. The community was stirred to its uttermost depths by the struggle for independence, and by the triumphant outcome. During that period American Jewry was a captive audience. Moreover, it had been touched to a rare sensitivity. It was begging to be allowed to donate money; and it would have listened with gratitude to the kind of addresses which should have accompanied the extraordinary situation. In short, it was as ready to take as to give, to be redeemed as to redeem. What it got was largely the familiar combination of stunt and lamentation, alternating now with a complementary mob appeal: Jewish jingoism, mass rancor that, in revulsion from the horror of the Hitler massacres, found unworthy relief in admiration of the Palestinian terrorists. The opportunity was muffed.

Again it was not simply a shortage of teachers. It was a failure in American Zionist leadership.

IV

"Shortsightedness," Zionists will admit; and they have their excuses. From the beginning Palestine was in chronic need of funds, and getting them absorbed all energies. The Chalutzim of the nineteen twenties starved; we had to buy our land square foot by square foot; there came the crisis of 1926–7, when Jews fled from the bread lines and soup kitchens and the dole, and more left Palestine than entered; 1929 brought the great riots, followed not long after by the beginnings of the Hitler pressure. And so on until the outbreak of the war. "Perhaps we should, in spite of everything, have diverted some of the funds and energies to the education of the Jewish community. We admit we were shortsighted."

But this shortsightedness was a secondary effect. As there was one tug of war in Zionism between mendicancy and Messianism, so there was one between two theories of timing.

It was generally understood that a Jewish homeland, once created, would automatically reorientate large numbers of American Jews toward the Jewish values they were abandoning. The sooner the homeland was created, then, the sooner would the beneficial spiritual results flow from it. We assumed tacitly that Jews settling in Palestine naturally constituted a Jewish Palestine, that is, a homeland incorporating our universal Jewishness, and sensitive to historic and world Judaism. The assumption was based largely on the extraordinarily high character of the men and women who actually went to Palestine, and therefore it was reasonable at the time. But it was shortsighted. We were mentally lazy. Of our two big tasks, cultivating the Jewish renaissance among ourselves, and pushing the work in Palestine, the second was the less difficult. Also we permitted ourselves another assumption. We said that merely helping to get Jews into Palestine, and settling them there, was a spiritually regenerative activity. The upshot was that we rationalized away the need for educative work; in the tug of war between continuous education and practical or technical effort, the second carried the day.

There was a Zionist minority which held that with the creation of the Jewish homeland Judaism throughout the rest of the world would become devoid of meaning. But it was not a powerful minority. It made no inroads on the dominant doctrine that the Jewish homeland would automatically, as well as programmatically, radiate a spiritual influence on world Jewry, this being, indeed, of the essence of its existence. It was the majority that, of its own accord, unled by a minority, acted contrary to its own doctrine.

In its neglect of what used to be called *Gegenwartsarbeit* (working with and for the existing Jewish communities), in its self-defeating concentration on technical reconstruction (to which it was increasingly urged, we must remember, by tragic circumstances), the Zionist movement distorted, also, the interpretation of the Exile. The consequence was an astonishing contradiction of utterance. On the one hand we said that the creation of a Jewish homeland would add dignity and content to Jewish life everywhere. On the other hand, when we spoke of the Chalutzim, and of all those that went to build Palestine, we would by contrast depict the life of Jews outside of Palestine as being, in its nature, irremediably debased. We did not quite mean it. We had in fact the picture of a realizable ideal of American Jewish life, a dignified and creative life. We spoke that way out of admiration of the Chalutzim, out of propagandist exaggeration, out of traditions carried over from past humiliations, out of a present frustration (the nonexistence, as yet, of a Jewish homeland), out of a feeling of guilt that we had chosen the easier way, and out of irri-

223

tation with our opponents, whose timidity about Jewish
and Zionistic values was a debasement of both Judaism and
Americanism. We carried over into our extramural utterances our intramural Yiddish self-criticisms, which have
always been hyperbolic.

I repeat that we did not quite mean it; but its effects on
the nascent Jewish homeland were bad. We encouraged
within Palestine a superior attitude toward Jews outside of
it, which became most manifest in the young generation.
We watched without protest, we even tacitly concurred
in the growth of a spirit, especially in the schools, which
reflected all of our own exaggerated negations of Jewish
life outside of Palestine. This has contributed greatly to
the fission of world Jewry. The youth of Israel has been
poisoned against Judaism outside of Israel. Its contempt for
Jews who will not come to Israel, its rejection of a possible
Judaism anywhere but within the confines of the country,
is one of the failures of the Zionist movement. The older
generation in Israel has been pulled along in the process;
and, as I have shown, the most thoughtful veteran Israelis,
the immigrants of twenty, thirty, forty, fifty years ago, cannot bring themselves to think of American Jewry as having
a right to a regionalist destiny.

It should be added that the veteran Israeli leaders are
almost without exception of European origin. They have
not got the feel of American Jewish life.

V

There was still another tug of war in the Zionist
movement, on the subject of "Jewish nationalism." I have
already noted that as applied to the original concept of
Zionism it is a misleading term, and we used it for want of
a better. "Nationalism" is a specifically non-Jewish term.

It has to do with forms and content arising out of Western political and economic developments from which the Jews were excluded. Pathological nationalism, or jingoism, was not a Jewish sin; we had, in its place, the sin of spiritual pride, which is as bad but quite different. We certainly did not want to have both sins, and we fought against the importation into our renaissance and our emergent homeland of the European-historic and non-Jewish spirit of nationalism. Our group consciousness has crystallized from of old around an idea and a moral condition. Judaism did not emerge from our historical condition; it was imposed on our condition. Abraham went out of Ur Kasdim to found a people on a preconceived program. Moses promulgated the laws before we had the land, and possession of the latter dependent on obedience to the former. Such, at least, was our belief and our folklore, which, if they were inaccurate as record, were not the less potent as molders of our character.

Zionism was not born of nationalistic complexes, but of the older, more permanent Jewish spirit. It wanted a homeland around which to re-crystallize the Jewish spirit under modern conditions. It accepted the inevitable conditions attached to the enterprise, political action, organization of self-defense, a certain degree of independence—but only in so far as these conditions were inevitable. The instruments were not goods in themselves.

A minority, of which I have already spoken, saw the instruments as goods in themselves. There were Zionists to whom the possession of a Jewish flag, the existence of a Jewish army, the recognition of a Jewish government, were the substance of Jewish fulfillment. To have these things meant being Jewish; to indulge the emotions around the contemplation of these things was, in their eyes, "to feel Jewish," and to be free.

This interpretation of Zionism we did resist successfully

for a long time, and the resistance found its most useful and effective expression in the personality of Weizmann. I wish to emphasize the word "personality" here. Not simply what he said and did, but what he was, the effect of his presence, his pattern of reactions, gave forcefulness to our view of Jewish purpose. He incorporated a humor, a tolerance, an ironical but not hostile penetration to the heart of things, which bespoke the antiquity and experience of his people. He was skilled in the ways of the world, he was worldly, and yet he seemed always to be hinting: "All is vanity, except goodness and honesty and the right life."

Being what he was, he irritated those who wanted to compensate for Jewish disabilities by imitating the trumpery aspects of political independence. I think that when he was negotiating with the reluctant, semi-assimilated German-Jewish leaders in America for their financial support, he puzzled them by his failure to talk Jewish jingo nationalism. Not that they would have been won over to it (that took place among large numbers of them only when the Jewish State was established), but they would have found it intelligible. The Jewish perception of moral essentials, trained by centuries of exile, was difficult for them. And this Jewish perception of moral essentials, heightened by our exile life, this special quality that the Jewish exile should bring into the Jewish State, is in danger, is being specifically rejected by the youth of Israel. They have been conditioned against the ancient wisdom of Exilic Judaism because they have heard only of its external squalor.

Perhaps I shall help the reader to understand the significance of Weizmann's personality in this connection, the symbolism of the man, if I describe a little incident that is deeply engraved in my memory.

I once sat through a conference that he held in a New

York hotel suite with two Englishmen of high position. The subject matter was Palestine's "absorptive capacity," that everlasting bone of contention between the Zionists and the British even in the "good" old days. Weizmann was explaining, as he had done elsewhere a hundred times, that the economic absorptive capacity of a new country was a thing created, not found or waited for; and in part it was created by the act of absorption. The Englishmen defended the static view, in line with the policy of their government. But I remember that I was not interested in the discussion itself, too familiar as it was, but in the atmosphere.

There was about Weizmann, as he pressed his thesis, an ease, a kingly patience, a magnificence of bearing, which almost transformed the conference into an audience. One might have said that here were two rather awkward and confused ghetto Jews explaining themselves somewhat uneasily to a brilliant English aristocrat. What gave the whole performance its particular flavor was the fact that the note of excessive formality was introduced by the Englishmen. I think they were not wholly at ease because they were quite aware of having the weaker side of the argument. Their Oxfordian English was thrown in as a counterweight, so to speak, to the lightness of their defense. Weizmann's English, which was rich, idiomatic, and ingenious, but adorned by occasional foreignisms, and delivered with a slight Russian accent, seemed, as against this, to bring out the irresistibility of his view. Beyond this, Weizmann was a very brilliant debater and—as all his students at Manchester University remembered—a wonderful expositor. The Englishmen represented power; theirs was the Mandatory Government of Palestine; theirs were army and navy and international status. Weizmann represented the idea. And since discussion meant idea, he was master of the situation.

When the conference was over Weizmann escorted his visitors to the door, closed it behind them, turned round to me, put his finger to his nose, looked at me steadily for a few seconds, and said, in Yiddish: "Fooled them, what?"

He did not mean that he had said anything dishonest, attempted a deception of any kind. Nor that he had taken advantage of them intellectually. He meant that he had outdone them at their own style; he had shown himself to the manner born, when he really was not. But wasn't he? Perhaps more so than they. Or did he mean that he found the whole business a bit silly. But it wasn't silly at all. It was necessary business. And he had enjoyed transacting it. After long reflection I find that I don't know what he really meant.

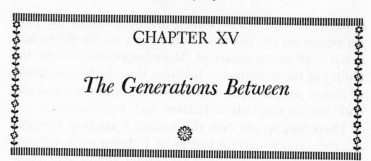

CHAPTER XV

The Generations Between

❀

I

WEIZMANN was fond of quoting a Yiddish proverb: "What your wisdom won't do, time will." It may be interpreted variously. "Things work themselves out, whether you understand them or not; you can only hasten or retard the process." Or: "Don't despair of human stupidity; Providence has limited its powers." Or, again: "Human wisdom is not a substitute for history." I think of this last interpretation in connection with the failure of Zionism to take hold of American Jewry thirty and twenty years ago, and with its failure to deliver the right message today.

Nine tenths of American Jewry goes back less than three generations, and an American Jewish community, with a specifically American complexion, is only just emerging. The process might have been hastened or retarded—certain events, as we shall see, did hasten it—but by how much it is impossible to say. Things had to work themselves out.

The American-born Jewish youth that I met here on my arrival, forty years ago, was impatient with Judaism, with tradition, with everything reminiscent of the Old World. It is often said that the general drift toward assimilation characterizing that period resulted from the early economic struggle. Parents had no time or strength left for the Jewish education of children. This is part of the truth, but it has been overemphasized. More important was the inability of the parents—an inability that lay in the nature of things, and for which there was no cure—to show the children the synthesis of Judaism and Americanism.

There was, in any case, the natural struggle of the generations; and its terrain had to be Judaism itself, because here the struggle acquired maximum significance. The children asserted their independence most effectively by rejecting the Jewish heritage; they did this naturally, and in a sense unconscious of the underlying motive. Even where no tension existed, where family harmony prevailed—and it often did—Judaism was instinctively equated by the children with foreignness. Parents might be loved, their Judaism respected even to the point of imitation; nevertheless, America did not know, could not know, what Judaism was. Judaism did not belong to the scene. Putting anti-Semitism on one side, considering only America the free, the liberal, the friendly, the hospitable, the young generation felt it was a sort of imposition, or let us say an incongruity, to bring into the open the exotic collection of beliefs, practices, and memories which were an integral part of the alienness of the parents.

So at best young people looked on the Jewishness of their parents as a harmless oddity, and when they spoke about it "to the outside" they put on a friendly, supplicatory smile, and invited all good people to share their own understanding. They liked books about Jews written in that spirit, and they created the legend of the adorable comicality of the ghetto. This is the literature of the cute and lovable little Jews whose attractiveness is concealed from an impatient world by the irrelevance of a beard and of unfamiliarity with sport. It is a literature of evasion, of shamefacedness, of suppression. It is an attempt to smile an identity out of existence, and to explain one's origins good-humoredly as trivial and irrelevant. The invitation to "understanding" is a lie; it is really a plea for ignorance and forbearance.

On lovers of this literature portrayals like Fagin, or Shylock, or Isaac of York produce a specially painful impression. It is not playing the game. "Here we are," they say, inwardly, "doing our best to shake off this Jewish business by a gentleman's agreement, for the common benefit of Jew and gentile, and instead of helping us . . ."

The literature of the quaint Jew connects here and there with the Jewish literature of self-hatred; very often Jewish critics label as covertly and unconsciously anti-Semitic some of those apparently harmless Jewish "character" studies, usually by Jews, full of mispronounced English, low cleverness, and viscous sentimentality, which appear first in serial form in one of the "better" magazines. The criticism is sound, but as it needs a lot of explaining it is generally misunderstood.

II

The foregoing applies to the majority of the younger Jewish generation twenty and thirty years ago. The "intellectual" minority had its own assimilative formula, in which the key word was not Americanism but rationalism. However, in the strangest way it was a mob rationalism. This phrase may offend at first sight, so I must ask for a little patience. There is such a thing as the rationalist mob, the group which is intoxicated with the feeling of its exclusive and impregnable possession of the total truth of universal process on the logical or rather technical level. I say deliberately "intoxicated," because that describes the public mood of organized rationalists. The Western intellectuals of the twenties and thirties formed a kind of new church, and its revivalist affairs, called conferences, though they used the terminology of reason, were as opaquely and impenetrably emotional as those of a Chassidic or Southern Baptist jamboree. The emotions cultivated were pride and intolerance.

In a book called *King Mob,* published in 1930, I wrote: "If the rationalist Mob stops short as a rule this side of violence, it is perhaps because of its physical weakness. But in Russia—the scene of the first State attempt at organized rationalism—this is no longer true. The suppression of religion is a correct copy of the classic persecutions. That its tortures stress the psychological rather than the physical sensitivities of its victims is only an indication of its superior refinement and skill." I cannot help recalling with what a feeling of hopelessness I wrote this passage, aware that practically every intellectual chancing across it would dismiss it contemptuously with: "Obscurantist, reactionary jackass!" (The higher reaches of leftist Billingsgate had not yet been developed.)

Taking the two together—the unintelligent Americanism of the many, the insolent rationalism of the minority —it was hard going for Jewish and Zionist educational work.

III

One is tempted to say that the creation of the Jewish State was for many anti-Zionists what the Hitler-Stalin pact was for many pro-Communists—the collapse of a world. The impossible had happened! A revision of fundamentals was in order.

The parallel is instructive, but should not be overworked. American Jewish life was running its own course. Somewhat more than a decade ago I began to observe an

interesting change in the attitude of the "young people"—
no longer so young—whose attention I had solicited in
vain fifteen and twenty years before; and a still more interesting phenomenon—you could not call it a change—
in the generation that was crowding them. I had exceptional opportunities for observation. I traveled each year
through almost every part of the country, and as free-lance
lecturer met between sixty and ninety audiences, to whose
questions I paid considerably more attention than they to
my answers. Between lectures I was "entertained," and I
managed quite early to establish a reputation for un-
sociability by choosing my own company—the people from
whom I could learn what was going on. Pursuing my own
education while trying to contribute to theirs, I learned
from the Jews of America a new application of the proverb: "What your wisdom won't do, time will."

My audiences grew younger as I grew older, and the
questions that were addressed to me after the lectures took
on a different character. Apart from the usual proportion
of silly ones, generally asked by exhibitionists, they fell
into two classes: questions put direct, and questions the
answers to which were for a third (and absent) party. The
second class was more revealing, because it arose from discussions in the home and community. If the lecture was
not on a literary subject, or purely informational, but addressed to fundamentals of Judaism, I might be asked:
"Why do we need Judaism in America?" Or: "Why do we
Jews have to go on being different?" Coming from older
people, twenty years ago and more, the questions often
meant: "How shall I answer my son or my daughter?" For
it was evident that the questioner was not troubled on his
own account. Or it might be: "How can you be a Zionist
and a one-hundred-per-cent American?" Sometimes this
type of question was direct, coming at first hand; the questioners would then be of the younger generation, and they

had come to my lectures not as sympathizers with Jewish causes, but as critics. All these questions can be subsumed under a class: "*Why* should I be a Jew?" The interesting change is in the incidence of a new question: "*How* can I be a Jew?" One might say that the new question is the historically reorientated form of the old one.

Queerly enough, the new question too has a secondary character, and again it is the younger generation that is behind it. But now the parents are themselves fairly young, in the late twenties and early thirties; and they are not asking me for a formula with which to counter the arguments of a rebellious younger generation. They are asking me, instead, how they can contrive to give their children a Jewish education.

I cannot help being deeply moved by the manifestations of this change, and I am confronted by them more and more frequently. In every part of the country there are springing up new Jewish congregations formed by a younger generation—usually in the suburbs of larger cities—that is alarmed for the spiritual future of its children. From Long Island, in New York, to the San Fernando Valley in California, they start away from old attitudes of scorn, or indifference; and what adds a special pathos to their awakening is, precisely, their anxiety for the young; it is almost as if they gave up hope of a satisfactory personal reorientation, or as if they sought it only through their children.

IV

A generation or two had to pass before the change could work itself out, and it might have taken longer but for the double shock—the horror of the Hitler episode and the miracle of the Jewish State. The feeling of Americanism, of belonging, had to become tacit, implying an affirmative condition without reference to an older generation. There was no more struggle, no need to reject Judaism for purposes of self-assertion. Rejection was replaced by nostalgia.

This was not all. It began to dawn on the Americanized generation that this heritage that they had spurned was apparently a remarkable thing, held in respect by the majority of decent people. The Judaism of the older generations had, therefore, not been a picturesque and trivial incidental of their foreignness; that was only part of the form, and even there a revaluation was necessary. Judaism was, it now appeared, a component of civilization. It belonged.

More followed. When the struggle between the generations died, it left a void; the nostalgia was accompanied by a hunger. It was most definitely a religious hunger, a search for meaning outside the rationalist frame of reference, and outside material and social satisfactions. There was—with rare exceptions—no thought of satisfying the hunger in another than the Jewish religion. The new generation felt that permanent Judaism alone could satisfy the hunger, having a peculiar nutritive relationship to its psychic metabolism.

The roles played by Hitlerism and by the birth of the Jewish State must be seen in two settings; the first is the immediate and emotional; the second, which includes the role of communism, is the historical.

Nazi anti-Semitism set up a tremendous ferment in American Jewry. I am, however, strongly convinced that by itself it would have had only a negative and retarding effect on the Judaizing process here described. If it had not been followed by the miracle of the Jewish State, the rage, pity, humiliation, and rancor awakened by Hitlerism would have held up rather than encouraged the process of the generations. It was the double shock that had the creative effect.

As long as the democracies were in retreat before Hitlerism and Fascism, the Jews everywhere had the status of pariahs. In Germany and German-occupied territories that status was formal and legal; in the democratic countries it was psychological. Jews could not make the proper, unfrustrated protest against the abomination of Hitlerism because it appeared that they were the only interested parties; they would be—and they were—accused of warmongering. They were expected to perish quietly for the sake of world peace. When it was at last revealed that the Jews had been only the preliminary objectives before the universal attack on the world's freedom, their status improved. But it was a consolation that came too late and meant too little. It was a tactical change; it was not a change of heart or principle.

Had this been the final picture after the victory of the democracies, something like a trauma would have resulted for the Jewish psyche. But there followed the astounding, for the world at large, as for many Jews, totally unpredictable birth of the Jewish State. Now this was not primarily a political event; the political side of it is almost trivial in world terms; it was a psychological, moral, proto-religious event. It was, for an instant of insight, a vast dislocation of perspective. The Jewish people, which in the decline of the democracies had fallen to the nadir of human status, rose after the victory of the democracies to an eminence of accomplishment which could not be matched in history.

We can easily take the thing apart. We can show—I have in fact shown—the imperfections of the Jewish role in the accomplishment; we can show the hesitancies, reluctances, obstructions—I have shown some of them—on the side of the democracies. A totalitarian power had to contribute its support, on a miscalculation. But it is our business to see the forest as well as the trees. And I have no doubt that if we went into the heavenly kitchen of miracles we would be quite astonished by the confusions and cross-purposes among the multiplicity of angelic cooks. Or, to speak somewhat technically, we must not be guilty of the genetic fallacy, and equate a phenomenon *as such* with the sum of its causes. The Jewish State, with all the mistakes that went into it, with all the mistakes which we will yet put into it and derive from it, cannot, as a historic incident, be analyzed into a triviality.

It can decline into one. It can, as a continuing reality, lose touch with the inspirational fact of its birth. But that does not affect the miracle itself. The Americanized generations of which I am speaking were startled into a new thoughtfulness. Their dawning perception of something remarkable in the Jewish heritage found here moments of confirmation. Particularly relevant was the contrast between the utter abasement of the Hitler time and the lifting up in the universally applauded emergence of the Jewish State. There was in it also something deeply folkloristic which many did not identify—namely, the ancient prophecy of apocalyptic destruction preceding redemption; but among orthodox Jews this fulfillment was widely discussed.

V

These young parents whom I now see by the thousands in my audiences were never drawn toward Judaism by argument. Only reality touched them. In other words, it seems that the only effective "argument" was—the creation of the Jewish State. And until it was created, educational work was futile, and always would have been.

But we shall never know; for no real, large-scale educational effort was ever launched. And today the same old dilemma faces us, in another form. The Jews of Israel—or those of them who express views on this subject—now assert that there is only one test of Jewishness, and that is the readiness to migrate without compulsion into the Jewish State. The new insights and sensitivities which the new generations of Americanized Jews have won are declared to be meaningless unless they lead to migration into Israel. All or nothing, is the cry, and no time to be lost. "Either stop pretending to be Jews, or accept the consequences and become Israelis."

But it is only asking for trouble to be so categorical and abrupt. The awakening American Jewish generation wants guidance, not dictation, and is offended to be told that these stirrings of the spirit are, Jewishly speaking, nothing more than silly self-deceptions. With all its admiration for what the Israelis have done it just cannot jump out of its skin, that is, out of its own evolutionary setting.

Israel's rejection of American Jews is of course not as violent in practice as in theory. Their help is wanted, and passionately solicited, *quand même*. But even when the rejection is softened, even where it is admitted that American Jews have, as American Jews, souls to be saved, the attitude is, once more: "Let us get past the present crisis; let us see the state definitely stabilized; give us these six, seven, ten years of practical help, and then we will be able to turn our attention to your problems."

Even as short-range strategy this formula is shortsighted. The creative effect of the state is dissipating; the exclusive help on technical assistance leads to forms of appeal which are anti-educational. And the generation of the great teachers, those who were able to combine practical appeal with spiritual content, is gone.

In speaking of the re-Judaizing generation in America I am anxious not to exaggerate. It is a minority, but I believe it to be the dynamic minority in Jewish life. In its relation to American Jewry as a whole it makes me think of Zionism fifty years ago in its relation to the Jewish masses of Europe. But there is a considerable difference in our favor. This pre-renaissance phenomenon in American Jewry does not look quite so forlorn, so utterly at odds with all appearances of objective reality, as Zionism did at the turn of the century.

I know: there are vast areas of the Jewish population to which the matters discussed in this book are perfectly meaningless. There are Jews who never see the inside of a synagogue or temple, never attend a Jewish meeting, have never been members of a Jewish organization, have never contributed to any Jewish cause, not even to a simple Jewish philanthropy; Jews who, if they do any reading, will avoid Jewish books, and whose homes will be devoid of a single Jewish cultural symbol. There are Jews still floundering in the psychic insecurities of a vanished epoch, feverishly proclaiming their superior Americanism; there are Christian Science Jews and Ethical Culture Jews; there are hangovers from the Jewish socialist anti-Zionism of a generation ago; and of course there are Jewish intellectuals and careerists and golf-club aspirants. Those who judge quantitatively rather than qualitatively, statically rather than dynamically, will easily reach the conclusion I have often heard expressed in Israel: "American Judaism has no future." Reaching this conclusion, they will naturally act so as to make it come true. That is, they will continue in their Jewish inactivity.

Even among the "active" Jews there are discouraging elements. There are Jews who do not deny their Jewish obligations, but have no faith in a Jewish future. They mean well, but work in a defeatist spirit. They are to be found among Zionists who empty Zionism of all spiritual content; they appeal to the most superficial and most spectacular features of the practical enterprise; they bespeak for it the kind of applause that tickles the spectator at a football game or a boxing match; and they are generous and self-sacrificing. They are, in fact, extremely helpful in one way, destructive in another. They have to be taught —and they have to be kept out of the leadership.

Admitting all this, the difference between the Jewish content of American-born Jews of today and of those of thirty and forty years ago bespeaks a profound historic change. Judging forty years ago by the attitudes of American-born Jews, one might plausibly have said: "Judaism will decline more or less as the use of Yiddish declines." Such a prophecy would have proven false. Nor have the practical pressures of Zionist work and Israel's need everywhere crowded out the affirmation of American Judaism.

In relation to the generation of American Jews here being discussed it is Hadassah, the Women's Zionist Organization, which has drawn the necessary conclusions and accepted the consequent responsibilities. This remarkable organization, with its three hundred thousand members, is worth an extensive study as a sociological phenomenon. It has rescued tens of thousands of Jewish women from the futilities and vacuities of the middle-class pattern of recent times. It has managed to combine action for Israel with programmatic concern for the educational tasks of American Jewish life; it has kept clear of the kind of mob-Zionism which came to terms with terrorism in Israel, which plays up to a non-Jewish nationalist spirit, and which was easily deflected into anti-labor attitudes. Hadassah's leadership challenged the Israeli assumption of exclusive Jewishness not simply in words, but by acting on the tacit assumption that American Judaism is a force in its own right, even if today largely latent. It is therefore natural that the young mothers who are making the return —for the sake of the children, and for their own sake— should be found here in large numbers.

In saying that the dynamic minority of American Jews stands today where the Zionists stood fifty years ago, I did not wish to imply that another fifty years must pass before American Jewry finds itself, before it creates its own forms, before the present fumbling at elementary education changes into a rich cultural curriculum, before the unifying force of world Zionism makes itself felt, before a stream of pioneers sets in from America to Israel. No one can guess how long that will take. But it is certain that we must first go through a thorough re-examination of the Jewish position, and that some important views must be formulated as being common to American and Israeli Jewries.

CHAPTER XVI

A New Perspective

❀

I

I F THE Israelis have not got the feel of American Jewish life, it cannot be said either that American Jews understand what is behind their own feelings. They have always laid claim to a special love of America; for they have so often known—at first hand if they are immigrants, in family history if they are native-born—the meaning of tyranny, oppression, and discrimination. They therefore appreciate freedom with a lyric freshness that even the non-Jewish immigrant has never experienced, let alone the non-Jewish native-born American, who takes his freedom for granted. On this issue the generations agree; or if they differ, it is to concede a superior sensitivity to the parents and grandparents. But in this special Jewish love, of either degree, there is something that none of the generations quite understands, a something that is only now becoming apparent to the intelligence, long after it has been apprehended by instinct. And Israeli Jews must now adjust all Jewish evaluation to this new perception, not less than American Jews.

II

First let it be set down that if America had not been wide open to the Jews of Europe between 1880 and 1921, there would be practically no Jewish people today. America was of course wide open before the first date, and partially open after the second, but those forty years were the crucial period for the Jewish people. Other Western countries were only partially open; some of them had no room for large numbers, others were not as eager as America; some closed their doors (England, for instance, in 1904) sooner than America. The tremendous fact remains that but for America the Jews of Europe would have remained substantially where they were, to be physically annihilated by the totalitarianism of the right, or forced into assimilation—that is, spiritually annihilated—by totalitarianism of the left.

Let us now consider more closely the relationship of Jewry to what is called the East-West struggle. This struggle is the present phase of the crisis in our civilization, which quivers between two alternatives: the first is a continuation of the long difficult upward path, past human error and ill will and inertia, toward a life conceived as having divine intentions; the second is an abrupt and furious denial of the existence of any such path; the first acknowledges sin and blunders about in the search for the cure; the second knows neither sin nor salvation, and abandons man to the managerial rage of man. We are now accustomed to the idea that the second alternative shows two façades, that of the right and that of the left, always, however, keeping its identity unimpaired. But the supreme confirmation of this truth, which should indeed have led to an earlier and clearer perception of it, is the fate of the Jewish people.

It was, as I have pointed out, from leftist totalitarianism that the Jewish people received the first staggering blow, with the loss to Communist dehumanization of its most richly Jewish segment. I was foolish enough to believe for a time that this act of spiritual genocide was incidental to the general brutality of Russian Communism, it was part of the over-all campaign against religion. I should have known that in time the Communists would single out the Jews just as the Nazis did. I believed, and still believe, that the Nazis concentrated such an insane hatred on the Jew because *their* attack on Christianity was concealed; therefore they took it out on the people that had produced Christ. Thence I reasoned wrongly that the Communists, being open in their attack on Christianity, would place no special emphasis on the Jew. Moreover, the Communists did not operate with the racial myth; therefore they would not regard the Jews as "incurably" anti-Communist. Russian Jewry, then, was doomed to spiritual extinction, but there would be no physical holocaust. Such, I repeat, was my belief at one time, and I was grateful for small mercies. Such is no longer my belief; and I expressed my change of view long before the Prague trials and the case of the doctors.

But that horrible incident, or series of incidents, has left an unforgettable impression. For a time it looked as though the Jews were about to be denounced as a sort of incurable kulak class, with all the consequences that such a denunciation would entail. And the danger of such a denunciation is not wholly past, for under totalitarian government no accusation or retraction has to stay put. At this writing we are still waiting to hear an admission that the Prague trials were as anti-Semitic in their purpose as the case of the doctors is acknowledged to have been. We are also waiting for an admission that leading up to these incidents was a long history of oppression which felt a special challenge in the "cosmopolitanism" of the Jews, that is, in the identification of the word "Jew" with the universal brotherhood of man.

A communism cleansed by such retractions—in deed as well as word—may be approaching. The word "communism" is now perhaps ready to take on new and humane connotations; Russia is perhaps beginning the retreat—which must surely come sooner or later, if the democracies stand firm—from totalitarianism. If so, we are in a new phase of the vast struggle for the world's democratization, and if in the recoil from the last forty years Russia takes a leading role, the prospect lies before us of a far greater advance in human freedom than was made even in the nineteenth century between Napoleon's proto-World War, and World War One. But until this is completely manifest, my text must stand as it is; after that only the tense need be changed.

III

Second let it be noted that the extinction of the Jewish people by totalitarianism was not to be a simple "historic necessity." By no means. It was intended to stand up forever after as a stern act of justice, the execution of a criminal by an outraged humanity. Realists will tell me that whether a vanished people leaves behind it an honored or a wounded name is really of no importance, to the vanished people above all. But perhaps even a realist will concede that the falsification of history, the erection of a lie as one of the pillars of human "self-knowledge," is itself a criminal act. Or perhaps he will, as a "real" realist, refuse to talk this language, and assert that whatever serves the state (in the view of the masters of the state) is history, truth and untruth being themselves sentimental objectivisms, probably the result of Jewish infection. However that may be, we know that while a man lives he cannot bear the thought of being slandered after his death, especially by his murderer. And so it is with a people. Moreover, the execution of the Jewish people could not have been quite complete; there would have been left small communities here and there, tainted survivors, reminders of that epidemic called Judaism which was one of the misfortunes of the bad old days. America saved the Jewish name from infamy as it saved the Jewish people from extinction.

This is part of the general truth that America has so far saved democracy for the world—a truth that it is easy to deride because while the democratic idea has survived, it has not triumphed. Of late, since it became necessary to range Germany among the checks on Russia, we have been hearing much of America's mistake in entering the First World War, and in helping to crush the old, pre-Nazi type of German imperialism. It is assumed that Nazism was preponderantly the result of the German defeat of 1918, and of a vindictive and "doctrinaire" or "moralizing" peace. That mistakes were made and crimes committed at Versailles can be granted without argument. But I have always believed that a triumphant German imperialism, after World War One, fresh, arrogant, ascendant, as contrasted with an old British imperialism, mellowing and even decaying, would have been a bad setback to human hopes. It is also clear to me that American victory in that war was as essential to humanity's progress as was the victory of the Maccabees over the Seleucids. When I spoke in Chapter Two of the change in my attitude toward the First World War, after my arrival in America, I am referring in part to this perception.

IV

It goes without saying that there would have been no Israel, either, if Jewry had not been saved by America. The creation of an American Jewry of these dimensions was an absolute prerequisite to the creation of the Jewish State. Historically speaking, Israel is the child of America not less than of the Jewish people and England.

But the extent of America's help is not appreciated. We know of course that the mere existence of American Jewry encouraged England to initiate the plan of a Jewish homeland; we know that the continuous expressions of interest and benevolence which came from leading Americans had a deterrent effect on England when she wanted to retract; we remember also the role America played in precipitating the last stages; we also think of the funds contributed by American Jewry, and, latterly, of American grants-in-aid and credits. What we do not understand and appreciate is America's role *as the providential selective factor* in the creation of the Jewish State.

Even if the Turkish government had been ready to admit into Palestine tens of thousands of Jews annually between 1880 and 1914, an indiscriminate influx of refugees would have been fatal to Zionism in those formative years. No firm foundations would have been laid for a Jewish State. As it was, because America was open, Palestine drew to itself only those Zionists who were psychologically ready for the revolutionary task. They were hand-picked, then and in the following two decades, by the historic set-up.

Not less remarkable than this subtle co-operation has been American generosity of spirit toward the pioneering question for Israel. Some thousands of Jews have left the America that saved them, and have migrated to the Jewish homeland. We speak hopefully of the time when thousands more will be ready to emulate them. Not one responsible and respected American has cited this as ingratitude. Jews have been unworthily apprehensive of such a reproach. America has not begrudged us the manpower we have wanted to withdraw into Israel.

V

We must step back for an even larger perspective to get the full meaning of America in Jewish history. Throughout the ages Jewish survival was made possible only by the fragmentation of the world. Persecution alternated with relaxation in most lands, and there was never a concerted, universal attempt made on the Jews. If the world could not unite for good, it could not unite for evil either. There were always high-pressure and low-pressure areas. Before Babylon became uninhabitable for us, Spain opened her doors; when the Crusades sent an anti-Jewish wave through western Europe, eastern Europe was still comparatively safe; when Spain turned upon us, there were Holland and the Levant. But when in modern times central and eastern Europe threatened our largest communities, the world stage was being set for the first all-human struggle. There was no alternative to America!

Today's world dualism is the obvious prelude to world unification, which will ensue only if there is no third World War. But a third World War—in the cataclysmic sense usually attached to the words—seems to me to be extremely improbable now; and will become more so as democracy clarifies the issues to itself, and in that clarification shakes the pathological self-confidence of totalitarianism. It is the characteristic of totalitarianism that it hypnotizes before it attacks; and as part of the world was hypnotized by rightist totalitarianism, so part of it was hypnotized by leftist totalitarianism. I am not referring now to Communists and to fellow-travelers, but to persons who have always been sharply anti-Communist (myself, for instance) and who nevertheless have confused Communist denunciations of capitalist evil—Marx will never be surpassed on that subject—with some sort of good will toward its victims. The exploitation of a grievance in a bid for power has of course nothing to do with good will. I am referring also to persons who have believed that communism was an attempt, however twisted from its purpose, to correct capitalism, whereas in truth communism is capitalism gone mad, become all-powerful and therefore all-corrupt in the person of the state. Only a hypnotic condition can concede to communism the slightest moral advantage over Nazism or Fascism, and that hypnotic condition was part of the general moral decline in the democracies which I discussed in connection with Israel.

I hold it to be a favorable augury that as America takes the lead in democratic self-recovery, it also becomes the locale of a Jewish self-recovery, while it is the chief support of a Jewish State. The first Bill of Rights known to the record was formulated, in terms that can never become obsolete, within the Jewish people, placing upon it a peculiar responsibility. We are beginning to acknowledge that responsibility again, as always imperfectly, amidst confusion, and yet unmistakably; and the interweave between American and Jewish destiny is of the stuff of humanity's purpose.

I have used the word miracle in speaking of the rebirth of a Jewish State. Actually there is only one universal and all-embracing miracle, and that is the existence of meaning in human affairs. Whatever helps us to catch a glimpse of such meaning is so to speak a secondary miracle; and in this sense the word must be applied to the co-operation of America and Jewry.

VI

This miracle too can be picked to pieces. Expanding capitalist America wanted a larger population. Greedy railroad barons and ruthless shipping companies prospered for half a century on the flood of immigrants—among whom there happened to be more than two million Jews. Then, settled in large cities, in strategic voting centers, the Jews were able to maneuver American public opinion, or American politicians, into support of a Zionist policy. This, more or less, is the "real and complete" story of the co-operation of America and Jewry.

Is it? If the real and complete history of human relations consists of a tabulation of economic motives then neither human relations nor economic motives are worth discussing; they are both reflex actions. All books, all ideas, all exhortations, all propaganda—everything is a queer shadow-world that the "real" world ignores, knows nothing about. But nobody believes this, not even the people who say they do, because if they really believed it they would not bother to say it. Actually the statement of this belief is meaningless; it is a childish intellectual self-teasing, like: "I have never told the truth in all my life; I am not telling it even in this statement." And when grownups tease themselves like that they are victims of a complicated infantilism; it is a form of flight from adult spiritual responsibility.

The three dimensions of human behavior, the well-meant, the ill-meant, and the un-meant, expand and shrink in our sight according to our mood. Sometimes we say: "That there should be *any* goodness in the world is the only significant thing." Sometimes: "The little bit of goodness I see is insignificant." Sometimes: "For tailless monkeys we are rather intelligent, aren't we?" And sometimes: "We are nothing but tailless monkeys." None of the statements is wrong; and none is meaningful. We can say: "The American spirit of freedom was exploited by greedy men who profited from immigration." Or: "Greed made America look like a land of refuge." Or: "Response to economic factors was everything, greed and liberty are epiphenomenal." Again the statements are neither wrong nor meaningful. We can describe a human being "perfectly" in electro-chemical terms to the same futile effect. America in the world's history, America the actual in the present condition of humanity, is not to be analyzed away into dimensions. It is to be felt in an act of faith which extends beyond America.

In my first draft of this passage I added to the end of the foregoing paragraph "into God's purpose." I am nearer to my meaning when I say: "That act of faith *is* God's purpose."

VII

I have just said: "A third World War—in the cataclysmic sense usually attached to the words—seems to me to be extremely improbable now; and will become more so as democracy clarifies the issue to itself." Improbable does not mean impossible; and I do not think that it argues lack of faith to admit the possibility of the world's self-destruction. On the contrary, if either peace or war were inevitable and calculable, faith would have no function. Nor is faith an intuitive foreknowledge that if we ourselves do the right thing, everything will come out right in the end. Faith is rather an intuitive perception that the essence of being human is our commitment to the right, regardless of consequences. In other words, faith is not a means to an end: it is an end and a means simultaneously; to the extent that we have faith, things have in fact come out right; and if we have lost faith, they have come out badly, whether or not there is a third World War. For, losing faith, we could simply surrender to evil without a struggle, and this would as surely end our civilization for the foreseeable future as would our physical destruction. It would be self-destruction by compact rather than by combat.

I repeat, then, that a third World War becomes more and more improbable as democracy clarifies the issue to itself. But the avoidance of a third World War is not enough. It is possible to lose a peace without fighting a war. Therefore when I speak of world survival I go beyond the physical meaning to the moral; I am concerned with the survival of the humanity of mankind.

When I think of America and Jewry, of America and Israel, my mind goes back more than a hundred generations to a point that is nearer to the beginning of history than to us. It was about then—counting more than thirty years to a generation—that the Jewish idea of humanity crystallized in its earliest form; and it occupies more than half of the interval between the first surmisable historic date and the present. It has persisted under its own name, and with its special purpose, into this present crisis of man's last choice—which, indeed, it foretold. It will perish if the world perishes; it will survive if the world survives; and world survival depends on the moral strength of America. Thus it comes about that Jewry and Judaism have a relationship of destiny to America that they have never had to any other land. Let Jewry understand this, in Israel and everywhere else.

CHAPTER XVII

America and Anti-Semitism

❀

I

As far back as I can remember, I have distinguished between two kinds of anti-Semitism. The first is a dislike of Jews as persons; the second is a hatred of the concept, Jew. The first—which I shall call anti-Jewishness—presupposes some contact with Jews; the second is folkloristic and does not depend on contact with Jews. Anti-Jewishness is the universal crime—common among Jews too—of group prejudice; anti-Semitism is a special disease of the Western [1] mind, and is the concealed rejection of the Jewish moral concept through the open rejection of the Jew as concept. Anti-Jewishness and anti-Semitism frequently overlap; they are nevertheless distinguishable. Anti-Jewishness is a normal sickness, anti-Semitism is abnormal.

Anti-Jewishness and anti-Semitism in America are in substance very much what they are elsewhere. They are subject to fluctuations of the public mind; they are affected by economic conditions; they are fostered by special types and special interests. But because of America's fateful role in world affairs they have here a special meaning.

II

There are countries with a democratic tradition not inferior to America's; big ones, like England and France, lit-

[1] Here again I include Russia.

tle ones like Switzerland and Norway and Sweden and Denmark. Among them England alone has played a world role comparable with America's, but hers did not coincide with a universal crisis. Thus the contending influences of America and Russia in the world today have no parallels in the past. This is a situation that suits Communist Russia admirably, and creates no moral problems for her. It creates many for America.

It is an unsettling dilemma—one that does not exist for Russia—to be as powerful as we are, and at the same time the leader of world democracy. We fall into the error of believing that we are the most democratic country in the world. Of course in a sense we really are; for if we multiply democratic charge by mass of country or power we have the largest momentum. But that is not what we mean. We mean that we have the highest democratic charge; and what is more, we assert that we have acquired our power primarily by being democratic; it is the reward of our democratic competence and our democratic merit.

Actually America rose to power through a combination of luck, competence, and merit—in that order. In the exercise of her power she must reverse the order of those factors, and this calls for an unparalleled moral effort.

We must make the effort partly for our own sake, because our character is our destiny; and partly for the sake of others, although in the end this too is for our own sake. We are being watched more intently than any other country has ever been watched before, and though it sounds fatuous to talk about setting an example, we have been placed in a position that leaves us no alternative. We are in fact setting one even when we refuse to do so—but then it is in a negative sense: we are merely "making an exhibition of ourselves."

One way of refusing is by taking up a cynical attitude, saying: "Every country watches us primarily from its par-

ticular angle of interest; there is no moral judgment." This
is a partial truth. Certain of our actions will always be
praised or condemned by others merely as their interests
are affected. But for every country the majority of our actions have no obvious relation to its interests. Making all
allowance for indifference, distortion, and prejudice, we
do in the end accumulate credits and demerits roughly according to our deserts. It is for instance widely held that
we are given to spasms of violence. This is roughly true.
As against this we have captured the imagination of the
world with the figure of Abraham Lincoln; and we have
done this because we have made him the mirror of our
moral aspirations.

III

I have said that anti-Jewishness presupposes some contact with Jews, while anti-Semitism does not. The contact
may be at second or even at third hand, but actual Jews
figure in it somewhere. A group dislike is the projection
of an unpleasant contact with some members of a class into
the whole class; and group dislikes are anti-democratic
simply because they don't give the individual a chance.
The individual is in fact obliterated, and with him the
basis of democracy.

(We should note in passing that war is profoundly anti-
democratic for the above reason; and wars are justifiable
only as a last desperate and dangerous appeal from something even more anti-democratic.)

Every manifestation of group dislike in America is a
blow to the morale of world democracy. The denial of
rights to Negroes and Niseis disheartens not only Africans
and Japanese; it weakens the self-confidence of all people
of good will; it sends a vindicating message to all frustrated
apostles of hatred.

But while group dislikes—anti-Jewishness among them —are anti-democratic and immoral, they are not a total uprising against democracy and morality. In each instance the delinquent has a special plea; he has an antipathy to this or that group, for this or that reason, on the basis of this or that experience, his own or another's. He argues about it—untruthfully, of course—in terms of reality. He says—perhaps also thinks—that he is concerned with people.

Anti-Semitism is altogether different. It is a general phenomenon of the Western world, and though it is directed against the Jewish people, it has nothing to do with people. It does not argue in terms of reality. It is obsessed by the fantasy of an ancient and far-flung conspiracy against the Western world. Its theoreticians construct enormously erudite schemata of forces operating across the ages, with the Jew on one side, the Western world on the other. On the popular level these treatises become simple demonology. (Compare for instance Chamberlain's *Grundlagen des Neunzehnten Jahrhunderts* and Rosenberg's *Myth of the Twentieth Century* with the *Protocols of the Elders of Zion* and Hitler's *Mein Kampf*.)

I have written elsewhere:

Anti-Jewishness manifests itself in the readiness to think badly of Jews at large, to believe evil of them, even extreme forms of evil, but always conceivable and as it were reasonable evil. Anti-Semitism manifests itself in unmistakable symptoms of hallucination. Anti-Jewishness is marked by feelings of distaste, distrust and perhaps contempt; anti-Semitism by fear, convulsive horror ("the horrors," in fact) and vast delusions of persecution. Anti-Jewishness goes hand in hand with self-assurance and an at least ostensible conviction of superiority; anti-Semitism betrays a cringing inferiority complex and a haunting, unremitting fear. The cue words for anti-Jewishness are "kike," "sheeny," "swindler," "Ikey-Mo," "ol' clo' man," etc. For anti-Semitism they are "World corruptor," "international plotter," "enemy of civilization."

The only way I can explain this extraordinary phenomenon of anti-Semitism, the only way I can bring into line the political insignificance of the Jewish people and the world volume of the anti-Semitic hallucinations, is to look for the only big thing the Jews have done to the mind of the Western world; and that is, of course, provided it with the material for Christianity. Thus I am led to the inescapable conclusion that anti-Semitism is the pagan identity of Christendom denying the Semitic identity of its Christianity. So while anti-Jewishness is, like anti-Negroism, or anti-Niseiism, an individual immorality, an individual mischief done to democracy, anti-Semitism is the total rejection, made all the more furious and convulsive by its self-deception.

This enormous difference begets another, of equal importance. Mistreatment of Negroes in America, I have said, encourages racial and group hatreds everywhere. But each particular race prejudice has a language of its own; its intelligibility and appeal are restricted. The mutually hostile Sudenten German and the Czech, the Irishman and the Ulsterman, the Armenian and the Turk, form separate and enclosed areas of hatred, which have not a common terminology and legend. Each delinquent is, to be sure, encouraged in his own bad habit by the delinquency of others; but he does not gather material, as it were, for the indulgence of his delinquency. Anti-Semitism is, however, a universal phenomenon in its various degrees. The international encouragement of anti-Semitism is all the easier because it touches a universal chord, and no delinquent is in this case puzzled by the delinquency of others. On the contrary, his encouragement comes from the opposite fact that he thinks every other delinquent has in this instance done right. Outbursts of particular prejudices and dislikes are local; outbursts of anti-Semitism cover large areas, and sometimes are world-wide.

Anti-Semitism is the Esperanto of totalitarianism.

IV

No other single country has ever contained as large a Jewish community as America. Czarist Russia does not count, for it was an empire that included conquered Poland. No other country has played a role equal to America's in rescuing the Jewish people from destruction. And no other country has ever occupied America's strategic position in the history of mankind. These are the three elemental facts against which we have to consider America and anti-Semitism.

Just as there are countries with a democratic tradition not inferior to America's, so there are countries that have had less per capita anti-Semitism than America. But for the sum of the reasons just given none of them could have played the role that destiny may have reserved for America—that of the St. George of the dragon of anti-Semitism.

I shall insist again and again that I do not speak here of anti-Jewishness. In respect of this individual instance of a general evil, we Jews—also guilty in our degree—must suffer with others, and work with others for the abatement of the evil. But anti-Semitism is a deep-rooted perversion of a special kind in the mental structure of Christendom. It is the most malignant of all the folk-complexes of the West, serving as the cover to periodic revulsions from the discipline imposed in the name of Christ. It has done as much harm to the gentile world as to the Jewish, and it is capable of precipitating mass moods peculiarly dangerous in the present crisis.

I know how naïve it sounds to ask for the eradication of so ancient a psychic twist in the Western mind, and one that is so irreplaceably useful to the mechanism of the Godless will. But many naïve hopes will have to be fulfilled if the world is not to destroy itself. Or rather, it will be seen that naïveté is the chronic affliction of those power-minded people who hold to the preposterous belief that they can manage the atomic age as they have "managed" the preceding ages.

Over and over again we are reminded that man's control of nature has wildly outrun his control of self—hence the uniquely explosive tension of our time. Therefore, the admonition continues, either the morality and social intelligence of man will catch up with his scientific ingenuity, or he is done for. And yet very few people are convinced that the species is done for—not even those that pose the apocalyptic alternative. What do they mean, then, when they talk of man catching up with his scientific ingenuity? Do they mean some miraculous organizational gadget which will leave us psychologically pretty much as we are, and save the world without in any way disturbing our routine of hatreds, obsessions, and hallucinations? Admitting that terror alone will keep us out of World War Three for a time, how long do they think that this exhausting and crippling inhibition will serve its purpose? Surely it is they who are simpletons if they can imagine so astounding a thing as the disappearance of major wars —major wars mean world war—without a corresponding revolution in human habits of mind and feeling. And what should such a revolution bring with it if not the cleansing of the West from that furtive anti-Christ complex which expresses itself in anti-Semitism?

It will of course bring much more: a diminution in the irascibilities of groups and peoples; a de-emphasizing of the competitive impulse in the releasing of energies and the provoking of initiative; a shifting of the animal play-impulses toward athletics and away from the dangerous infantilism of mob-sport spectacles; an improvement in the pedagogics of creative self-employment; a displacement of the psychology of: "The more I have the less you can have," by the psychology of: "The more you have the more I can have"; an increasing preference for "being" over "having"; an increasing skill in doing without dominating. I am speaking of the spirit that must inform the new time, and have nothing to say about the organizational forms that must emerge from it and encourage it in continuous interaction; also I have nothing to say in this paragraph about the religious foundation of the change because on that subject I have spread my views throughout the book. All these things must as surely come—if we live —as medicine came to replace the medicine-man, astronomy to replace astrology, chemistry to replace alchemy; must come much faster than they did, under the pressure of the dread realization of our dilemma; must come with the help of conscious and purposive effort, during the period that will witness the recession of the world's totalitarian infection.

Resisting the infection is the first necessity, immunizing ourselves against it the second. As in certain diseases, so here, immunization consists both of the use of anti-bodies and the building up of the health of the organism. I have used various metaphors in speaking of the relation between America and anti-Semitism. I have called anti-Semitism the Esperanto of totalitarianism. Let me now speak of it as a constituent part of the disease of totalitarianism. I have spoken of America as the fated St. George of the dragon of anti-Semitism. Let me now speak of her as the anti-body to the disease.

V

The fact that America was God's instrument for saving Jewry and Judaism places upon her a specific responsibility. She did not seek it? She did not seek world leadership either. Did the Jews seek the Ten Commandments at Sinai? We are free to recognize our responsibilities, not to choose them. The Hebrew saying is: "Virtues beget virtues, sins beget sins." A virtue which begets a sin is a monstrosity. Did America save Jewry in order to persuade it to forget Judaism? That would be like rescuing a drowning man in order to rob him. The whole American complex of development and character commits her to the encouragement of Judaism.

The encouragement of Judaism implies a strengthening of Christianity and a cleansing away of its pagan adulterations. There is enmity between Christendom and Jewry, not between Christianity and Judaism. The doctrinal and theological differences can be fruitful as long as they do not conceal ulterior motives: in Christians the desire to discredit the people of Christ, in Jews the resentments that confuse the crimes of Christians with Christianity.

What is the reciprocal obligation of the Jews? The strengthening of Judaism, and with it the clarification of the anti-Communist Jewish position throughout the world. It is as senseless as it is immoral to speak of Jewish neutrality in the East-West struggle. For beside the perverted spirits that have declared for Communist totalitarianism "on principle," there are Jews who advocate neutrality in the name of "foresight." I stare at these Menachem Mendel

Machiavellis [2]—they are to be found chiefly in Israel's Mapam—and marvel at the ingenuity of the death-wish. What hope for Jewry or Judaism or Israel can they read into Jewish neutrality in the event of Communist victory (bloodless, we must presume) when the most furious pro-communism is of no avail? To what public opinion do they think they would be able to appeal against adverse Communist decisions? But the ecstatic foolishness of these calculations hardly outdoes their griminess. Perhaps a vague excuse is the one-sided recollection of the fact that Russia helped defeat Germany.

It is a redundancy to say "the clarification of the anti-Communist Jewish position" after speaking of "the strengthening of Judaism." But it may serve to emphasize that anti-communism is not a negative activity: it is a cultivation of the forms and attitudes which are conducive to man's freedom. Anti-Communist action as such is pro-phylactic, not curative, necessary, but provisional and of limited range. In the same way the elimination of anti-Semitism is not to be seen primarily as a head-on assault, with Jews themselves acting, so to speak, as the shock-troops. This is an error of perspective cultivated by Jewish defense organizations, which as a rule tend to look upon Judaism as the fighting of anti-Semitism. Their analogues believe that democracy is the fighting of communism. In both instances it is the enemy that is permitted to choose the place and manner of battle, with stultifying conse-quences for the defender.

VI

Let no one read into my words a plea for special treat-ment of Jews and Israel. The first as individuals, the second

[2] I apologize for the obscurity of this reference, but find it too accurate to forgo. Menachem Mendel is Sholem Aleichem's prototype of the com-pletely confused, wild-eyed ne'er-do-well exhibiting a multifarious futility in the business world.

as a political entity, have only the common claim on human consideration. But that Judaism, and the Jewish people as the carrier of it, have an uncommon claim on the world's attention can be denied only by those who ignore four thousand years of history. When Jews give an imitation of modesty by relinquishing the record, they imagine that they are making it easier for the world. If they are, it is in disservice. The line of human growth leads through the laborious conservation and development of the great tradition of which Judaism is the first expression.

CHAPTER XVIII

If Thou Forget Me, O Jerusalem

I

WE WERE brought up in Zionism on two Biblical slogans, one from the Psalms, one from Isaiah: "If I forget thee, O Jerusalem, let my right hand forget its cunning," and: "For from Zion shall go forth the Law, and the word of God from Jerusalem." It did not occur to us that like chemical equations, these were reversible statements: "If thou forget us, O Jerusalem, thy right hand will lose its cunning," and: "Into Zion shall go the Law, and the word of God into Jerusalem."

The error is understandable—the Jewish homeland was still waiting to be built. Today, though the homeland is not complete, the error is no longer condonable. But the two reversed statements must be taken together: if Israel's neglect of world Jewry is her loss, that is because world Jewry has something to teach her; and again I must emphasize American Jewry, world Jewry's continental center.

II

The notion that America will have Jewish values to teach Israel strikes us first as a perversity, for we remember that Israel was created for the conservation of world Judaism. But this impression of perversity arises from not seeing enough of the time pattern. I will illustrate this point with an analogy.

I have referred more than once to the letdown in morale throughout the Western world which has been mirrored in Israel. Yet I have said that a third World War grows more and more improbable "as democracy clarifies the issue to itself and in that clarification shakes the pathological self-confidence of totalitarianism." Is not this a contradiction? Moreover, I have made it evident that I am a leftist in my economic and political views, and I must—and do—consider the recent shift to the right in England and America as a setback to what I hold to be progress. How do I reconcile this with the belief in a general democratic advance?

I believe that we have here an instance of *reculer pour mieux sauter*—the step back preceding the two steps forward. Moreover, just as the stinging defeat of the British Tories after the war was the rebuke for not having recognized totalitarianism when it came from the right, so the defeat of the liberals there and here was the rebuke for not having recognized totalitarianism when it came from the left. Let us further remark that British rightists of today would have been regarded as revolutionaries by their forebears—and for that matter by themselves as they were thirty years ago; and this is almost equally true of most American rightists. When totalitarianism of the left will have ceased to confuse the Western world, when Communists will no longer be able to make life difficult for liberals, the leftist point of view will again be in the ascendant. But it will be a leftism cleansed of its anti-religious rationalism, a leftism that will not ask human beings to believe in a mechanical progress into a soulless mechanical perfection.

The analogy with the Jewish case in America is in the matter of timing. We see here too an instance of *reculer pour mieux sauter.* We did not recognize it as such. Until twelve or fifteen years ago it looked as though Judaism in this country was in rapid dissolution. And even today, when the reaction has set in, and there is a rising will to Judaism, American Judaism has not yet found its form. Nevertheless I believe one can speak of an American Jewry contributing Jewish values to Israel.

III

No one can foretell which particular lessons and encouragements will issue from the interplay between Americanism and Judaism. Only certain probabilities are suggested.

Israel's greatest spiritual danger is that of a real break with the past while boasting of a spurious re-established contact with it. There will be Hebrew, there will be great respect for the Bible as the national saga, there will be everlasting references to the associations of classical places and persons; but all this, I have said, will be remote legend and uncreative sentimentality if there is no middle ground of attachment and transmission, if the grandfathers are not included as well as the ancestors. If the immense and immensely significant two-thousand-year continuity of Jewish life, which—reading backwards—contains Sholem Aleichem, and Volozhin and Zhitomir, and Chassidism, and Troyes and Worms, and Spanish Jewry and Babylonian Jewry, if this continuity ceases to exist for Israel, then her self-identification with the Prophets will be as fictitious as the modern Greek's self-identification with Plato. Diaspora Jewry, American Jewry, must counteract Israel Jewry's growing illusion that it stands before the world as an unmediated self-resurrection of the bi-millennial past.

That reminder in itself is of great corrective value:

"You will not understand yourselves, your problems, your relations to the living world, if you forget that you and we are one. We who remain in the Diaspora gave birth to you. To know who you are, you must know who we are."

The creation of the Jewish State is credited exclusively to the awakening of aptitudes and faculties which are supposed to be alien to Jewish Exile. Only by throwing off completely the Exile psychology are the Jews supposed to have achieved Israel. This is utterly false. There was change, there was revolution; nevertheless Exile psychology played an emormous role in the creation of the Jewish State. It is probable that without our Exile psychology we would not have been able to follow Weizmann for nearly forty years in the wilderness. Without it we would not have had the endurance to resist the maximalists who were always calling for heroic, exhibitionistic, everything-or-nothing, do-or-die decisions. We would not have been imbued with the faith that came from having watched mighty nations playing the role of successful adventurers —and losing.

When American Jewry will come into its own—and this will perhaps coincide with Israel's coming of age—it will produce an outlook and a literature as different from Israel's as, let us say, the Mishnaic was from the Prophetic. We will not feel Israel's temptation to suppress the middle past. We will cultivate the memory of the founding of American Jewry, and of its roots in Europe. Our tradition will cherish the manifold experience of our people and faith in the heart of the Western world; and this will be our contribution to the widening of Israel's horizon, and to the mitigation of her egocentricity.

IV

So far I have spoken, with the utmost brevity, of American Jewry's Jewish role for Israel. American Jewry, and

Diaspora Jewry as a whole, will also play a role as the continuous bringers to Israel of general Western values.

Years ago we used to speak hopefully of the Jewish homeland as a bridge between East and West, meaning between the Christian and the Moslem worlds, in which sense I use the words "East and West" in this section. It was a favorite theme with Weizmann, who won over to the Zionist idea the Emir Feisal, in the days when reason still had a chance. The theme has been drowned out in the last generation, but it will emerge again as surely as the traditional friendship between England and the Jewish people emerged after the long period of strain and bitterness engendered by the struggle round the proclamation of Jewish State. In the meantime Israel itself is in danger of becoming Orientalized —"Levantinized" is the word often used by Israeli leaders —and of forfeiting the role she was expected to play. I have heard this fear expressed in extreme forms privately, by old-time Western Zionists with whom I have visited the settlements of Iraki and Moroccan and Yemenite and Iranian newcomers: "We are done for. We have no future. We will be outbred and forgotten. The Eastern Jews will obliterate us in Israel." And this, as I have mentioned, is one of the reasons for the demand for Western immigration. It is a justified fear, and a doubly justified demand; but even if we were sending five to ten thousand non-refugee Jews annually out of the West into Israel, the need for a powerful bond between Western Jewry and Israel, as a Westernizing and democratizing influence, would not be obviated.

The metaphor of the bridge is somewhat misleading. A bridge is something static for people to pass over. The metaphor inclines us to think of Israel as something planted there to enable East and West to reach one another. But Israel herself needs a bridge. To change metaphors, Israel is not a catalytic agent; Israel is a living organism, which must keep on receiving nourishment from the West and East so that in time she may help nourish the East with Western ideas, and the West with Eastern ideas. Again, if Israel were in healthy balance today, with East and West blending in the right proportions, and if moreover she were sound economically, and all safe militarily, a severance of her ties with Western Jewry would be fatal to her spiritual values; would be fatal also to her Westernizing function.

It will be asked: "Why could not Israel get her Western ideas direct from the Western world at large?" The answer is that the points of view are too disparate; not as disparate, of course, as between the Christian world and the Arabs, but too disparate nevertheless. What the West wants to give the East is dictated by her own interests; not as crassly as in the old colonizing days, and in the days of primitive capitalism; not without a growing perception of mutuality of interests and a common destiny; nevertheless with a bias that is psychologically inescapable, with a feeling of superiority which is a great handicap. If Jerusalem forgets the Western Diaspora, she will neither learn nor teach; she needs to identify herself with the West through Western Jewry.

V

If it is hard to foretell what particular forms American Jewry will develop, it should at least be easy to see what American lessons it can help to transmit now. Easier, certainly; but not altogether easy. For even the American Jew has in relation to Israel the phychological bias of his Americanism.

Let me take as illustration an outstanding American characteristic—the love of *things*. There has perhaps never been another country with such a passion for handling, scrutinizing, manipulating, arranging, investigating, and combining physical objects. It is a healthy and cheerful preoccupation; it indicates an affection for God's creation; we are pleased with what He has given us, interested in the surroundings He has set about us, grateful for the invitation to craftsmanship.

I associate with this delight in doing the American tradition of "service," a tradition that has been abused by hypocrites, and sneered at by satirists, which nevertheless is a deep-rooted sense of responsibility toward a job. Of course this sense exists everywhere in the world. In America it has become a fresh cult, which is practiced with an exuberance and an earnestness all her own.

I sat with an Israeli lamenting with him the absence, in Israel, of precisely this spirit, and he asked me for one or two American examples. Since he had never been in America I had to be graphic and detailed, and for my first example I chose a soda-jerker in a busy drugstore.

A young man stands behind a long counter serving ice-creams, sodas, coffees, hot chocolates, sandwiches, Coca-Colas, Alka-Seltzers, to a rapid succession of customers filing along the row of swivel chairs before him. In front of him to the right, on an elevated glass shelf, he has a pile of plates; to the left a pile of saucers; behind him to the right on an elevated shelf there are rows of glasses, behind him to the left several trays of silver. In front of him, below, are the ice-cream containers, each with its scoop; behind him between the shelves are the coffee urn, the milk dispenser, and the hot water geyser. Halfway up in front are the faucets for various sirups, the shelves of sliced bread, the ranked pats of butter. The young man is in constant motion, a marvel of happy, one may say jolly co-ordination. He reaches with a minimum of gesture, gracefully, effectively, sight unseen, to right and left, in front, behind, half right, half left, north-northeast, north-east by north, northeast by east, southwest by west, all the while receiving and acknowledging orders, carrying on diverse conversations. He snatches up a scoop with a choreographic flourish, deposits the ice-cream in the saucer or the glass, holds the glass with his right hand while he sets the faucet squirt with his left, frees his left hand to bring up a dash of sirup, a pinch of ground nuts, returns to the faucet to change the squirt to a flush, flips back the cover of the ice-cream container, closes the faucet with his left hand after a final squirt, and while he serves the customer with his right, the left manipulates the register for the check, and before the left hand is finished the right is reaching for the next order. As the piles of plates and saucers sink on right and left in front and above, he directs his snatching hands to both sides in shallower and shallower parabolas; and at the exact split second stamps a bell with his foot and sings out to a concealed fellow-prestidigitator: "Hey, Charley, plates! Hey, Charley, saucers, chocolate, vanilla, strawberry, butter, bread!" And the moment the pile on the right or left, behind or in front, shoots up again, the reaching hand reverts to a steeper parabola, all of it without apparent effort, a functional fulfillment, a joyous rhythm. I doubt whether anything quite like this spectacle has been produced elsewhere, by any other civilization.

Now this young American, this soda-jerker, is neither a hunger-driven *Massemensch,* nor a grimly inspired Stakhanovite; nor is he soulful Tolstoian apostle of the dignity of labor. He is a young man taking pleasure in a job, delighting in motion-saving ingenuities, in rapport with his human surroundings. He is American democracy at work—literally, American democracy making a living. If America did not make a living in this way there would be no American democracy.

My Israeli friend was amused at the description. He had not been in America, but he understood, and agreed. He asked: "What is the young man thinking about?"

"Partly of the work itself," I said, "partly of the people he is serving. The background of thought may be about a college education, a career, a girl, a car, a television set, a garage he plans to buy. He calls these his incentives, and to some extent they are. But what carries him, what imparts dash and delight to his rhythmic operation, is the American scene, the American conquest of processes, the promise of the conquest of want."

"You can't import that kind of Americanism into this country," said my friend. "We haven't the rewards for the individual, the scope for the country. The homes, and garages, and television sets, the enormous colored weeklies with seductive four-color pictures of clothes and foods and gadgets and cars—all these are part of America's high spirits. Perhaps in a very remote future a comparable standard can be reached in this country. It does not help us to broadcast such views."

He uncovered with these words the psychological bias, the feeling of superiority, which hampers Americans in their approach to others. I gave him another instance of American democracy at work.

"As you know," I said, "I am a lecturer by profession. I travel thirty or forty thousand miles within the country every year, by train and plane and car. With more than an average share of absent-mindedness, I leave on trains and planes and in hotels more than my share of books, documents, brief-cases, and articles of attire. I have learned to take for granted the return of these articles; I cannot remember offhand a single disappointment. I take it for granted that train-conductors, plane stewardesses, hotel housekeepers, and hotel managers should be concerned with restoring my property to me. They telephone; they wire ahead; they pack and post. It is to them a matter of professional self-fulfillment. They are frustrated if they fail. And it is all done tacitly, with good humor, patience, and persistence. Reward does not figure in it. Democracy, undefined, does."

My friend found this illustration more to his liking. "You of America," he said, "can't teach us Judaism yet. If meanwhile you could teach us something of this respect for the job you will be doing a great thing. We know about it in theory. The Chassidic and other mystics have taught us that the honest devotion of the shoemaker to his last and of the carpenter to his plane is an acceptable form of worship. Unfortunately this truth is now known only to students of mysticism who don't make shoes or chairs."

VI

There are two ways of bringing American democratic productivity into Israel: by training young Israelis here, by sending Americans into Israel. A little of the first is being done, almost nothing of the second. The fault lies on both sides, but more heavily on the American.

The common error has been indicated at the beginning of this chapter and elsewhere—the failure to understand the mutuality of Jewish life in Israel and in America. It was simply taken for granted that American Jewry had nothing to teach Palestinian Jewry, and never would have; it could provide money, political influence, and perhaps a little human material; but in so far as it remained itself it had no spiritual value for Israel.

A community that is given this negative spiritual evaluation, and accepts it, is discouraged in all its other functions. Its morale fails. Pure economic self-interest will bring few Jews from America. Not that there is such a thing as pure economic self-interest; even our selfishness is—fortunately—impure. The failure to infuse into American Zionism the conviction of American Jewry's spiritual future, hence of its spiritual role in the future of Israel, chills the initiative of the community as a whole. In this atmosphere individuals find no promptings. The attitude toward Israel remains one of philanthropy—and collections are falling off; the bonds of the Israeli government meet with psychological rather than prudential resistance; the call to pioneers and to men of affairs, so much needed by Israel, finds no backing in a communal warmth. In part this is due to American Jewry's undeveloped Judaism; but that development itself is delayed by discouragement on the part of Israel; and there would be something more of a response even today if men of affairs did not feel that they are wanted simply as donors, investors, or "spetzes."

The fault lies more with American Jewry because although it is fond of speaking of Israel as an outpost of democracy, it does not accept the implications for itself. American Jewry, with its specific form of Judaism still to find, is the largest Jewish body ever to have lived in a democratic setting. Its spiritual role in Israel's life should be much greater than it is; and its acquiescence in a low spiritual evaluation vis-à-vis Israel results from a mixture of timidity and shortsightedness. American Jewry is the leader of democracy in world Jewry exactly as America is the leader of democracy in the world at large; and like America as a whole, American Jewry does not yet know how to handle the leadership.

CHAPTER XIX

The Democracy of Science

❀

I

O N NOVEMBER 30, 1947, the day following the decision of the United Nations in favor of an independent Jewish State, Weizmann wrote the last chapter of his autobiography. He began thus:

"We must prepare a constitution, set up a government, organize our defences, and begin to reconstruct the Jewish National Home so as to make it capable of absorbing, according to the plan, *some six to eight thousand immigrants a month.*" (My italics.)

In the middle of the chapter we read:

"Palestine will have to produce quality goods; only in this way can it compete with larger and more powerful countries which swamp the market with mass-produced goods. Now the production of quality goods is not merely a matter of skill. It is also based on an honest relationship to the task in hand, on a desire to do justice to the product, to allow only the best to come out of the workshop, and to avoid shoddiness."

We have seen what happened with the immigration policy. Instead of the seventy to a hundred thousand immigrants a year ("a tremendous task," wrote Weizmann, "which represents an increase of over twelve per cent per annum in a community of six hundred and fifty thousand"), Israel absorbed some seven hundred thousand in three years; and this mass production of Israeli citizens made more difficult than ever the creation or maintenance of the spirit of craftsmanship. It was bad as an example, because it did not display "an honest relationship to the task in hand." It did not do justice to the product; it did not avoid, it invited, shoddiness. And it was bad in substance, for inasmuch as it was creating tools for future use, human tools, citizens, it warped future production too.

II

Weizmann approached the problem of craftsmanship from a special point of view—that of the scientist. Science was to him the *summa summarum* of craftsmanship, a thing of character not less than of aptitudes, a builder of men and of a tradition, not less than of knowledge, power, and goods. It is in fact impossible to get a complete picture of Weizmann's attitude toward humanity, and toward the problems of the Jewish people and of Israel, without some knowledge of the organic interfusion of his scientific with his humanistic and Zionist *Weltanschauungen*. Moreover, as the essential Jew who had absorbed the highest values of the West, he represented in person the process of creative Westernization within the Jewish character. To him the bringing of the West to the East was not a phrase or a generalization; it was as clear-cut as a chemistry course. Not for nothing had he been a brilliant university teacher.

He had learned, and he taught, that science, the craft of crafts, is the practice of honesty toward the "thing," thence toward oneself. It is the cultivation in the individual of the capacity to see for himself, to verify for himself, to have an unmediated relationship to the object, and to think things out for himself. It is the satisfaction of a spiritual need that increases with satisfaction, growing by what it feeds on. It is also a harmony of personal and social fulfillments.

Honesty in science and in craftsmanship, in so far as these can be spoken of separately, is an essential ingredient of democracy. This does not mean that a considerable knowledge of scientific data and a high degree of craftsmanship are incompatible with dishonesty, and with enmity toward democracy. Men can turn dishonest on every level of knowledge and ability. It is the continuing spirit that counts. Wherever the spirit is arrested, at whatever point free, happy inquiry ceases, science negates itself and democracy dies.

It is a peculiar intellectual satisfaction to contemplate the consistency of Weizmann's style, remembering that "the style is the man." In the Zionist movement he was forever warning against shoddiness, show, façade, counterfeit or superficial successes. He criticized Herzl for parading sham results; he fought Jabotinsky for striving after them. He refused to equate necessitousness with possibilities. This sobriety of his in Zionism, this patience, this seriousness and reliability, backed by an inflexible will, was the spiritual, political side of his scientific self. For he showed the same craftsmanship in the scientific field. The pressure for quick results *at all costs,* the interpretation of science as nothing more than an instrument of commodity production, he regarded as anti-scientific, and therefore anti-democratic.

III

What Weizmann the scientist feared and hated most is wonderfully illustrated in *The Proceedings of the Lenin Academy of Agricultural Sciences of the U.S.S.R.* (issued in English by the Foreign Language Publishing House of

Moscow, 1949). I cull a number of passages from it to illustrate the consequences to the scientific spirit flowing from dictatorial pressure for results. It is not necessary for the reader to know the difference between the genetic theories of Mendelism-Morganism and Michurinism to grasp the significance for science of the following passages; he need only remember that Michurinism is (or was at the time of the proceedings and of this writing) in favor with the government, and Mendelism-Morganism was not.

(1) "The Mendelists-Morganists of the Soviet Union, though actually fully sharing the principles of Mendelism-Morganism, often conceal them shamefacedly, veil them, conceal their metaphysics and idealism in a verbal shell. They do this because of their fear of being ridiculed by Soviet readers and audiences who are firm in the knowledge that the germs of organisms, or the sex cells, are a result of the vital activity of the parent organism." (Address of T. D. Lysenko, p. 22.)

Whether it is *only* fear of ridicule which haunts certain scientists may be gauged from the following:

(2) "I firmly believe that if we intensify our action upon the adherents of formal, reactionary genetics, *and go about it the right way,* they will undoubtedly 'mutate,' *and do so precisely in the direction we want them to.* . . . It is high time they realized that today our Morganists-Mendelists are making common cause with, and objectively—and in the case of some even subjectively—are forming a bloc with, the international force of bourgeois apologists not only of the immutability of genes but also of the immutability of the capitalist system." (Address of V. A. Shaumyan, pp. 252–3. My italics.)

(3) "Agricultural science must be developed in the way we are bidden to do by the great coryphaeus of science, our teacher and leader, Comrade Stalin." (Address of V. S. Dimitriyev, p. 319.)

(4) "The truth is that it is not a few Michurinists whom the formal geneticists do not like, but our people, our absolutely new working class, our absolutely new Soviet peasantry who resolutely purify science of everything antiquated, everything that is against the interests of the people, everything that is born of servile worship of the bourgeois west. . . ." (Address of A. V. Mikhaelevich, pp. 424–5.)

(5) "I must first of all apologize for having been unable until now to participate in the deliberations of the occasion on account of my health. To tell the truth, I should not be here and speaking now. But the fact is that I have been the subject of so much attention that if I were to remain silent it would probably be misunderstood. I therefore cannot refrain from making some remarks in elucidation *of the charges which have been levelled at me.*

"The first and chief charge is that I believe in autogenesis. It was moreover stated that in this respect I am not a continuer of the line of my teacher, Academician Severtsov. . . .

"I am accused of stressing the indeterminateness of the variability of organisms. . . .

"I have been charged with the view that evolution proceeds in a descending curve, in correspondence with the views of Mendel, Rose, and other bourgeois theoreticians. . . .

"The last accusation—why I do not speak of Michurin or of the achievements of other of our plant breeders." (Address of I. I. Schmalhausen, pp. 488–94. My italics.)

(6) "The Party and the Government are showing paternal concern for the strengthening and development of the Michurin trend in our science. . . . Progressive biological science owes it to the geniuses of mankind, *Lenin* and *Stalin,* that the *teaching of I. V. Michurin has been added to the treasurehouse of our knowledge, has*

become part of the gold fund of science. . . . Long live the party of Lenin and Stalin, which discovered Michurin for the world and created all the conditions for the progress of advanced materialist biology in our country. *Glory to the great friend and protagonist of science, our Leader and teacher, Comrade Stalin!"* (All rise. Prolonged applause. Address of T. D. Lysenko, p. 617.)

(7) "Comrades, late yesterday evening I decided to make this statement. . . . There are moments in a man's life, especially in our historic days, which are to him of profound and crucial moral and political significance. That is what I experienced yesterday and today. The speech I made the day before yesterday was an unhappy one. . . . *It was my last speech from an incorrect biological and ideological standpoint.* . . . *The speech I made the day before yesterday, at the time when the Central Committee had drawn a dividing line between the two trends in biological science, was unworthy of a member of the Communist Party and of a Soviet scientist.* A sleepless night has helped me to think over my behavior. . . . I declare I shall fight—and there are times when I can fight—for the Michurinian biological science. [Prolonged applause.] I am a man of responsibility . . . I therefore consider that it is my moral duty to be a sincere Michurinist, a sincere Soviet biologist. . . ." (Statement by Academician P. M. Zhovovsky at tenth and closing session, pp. 618–19. My italics.)

(8) "When I leave this session, the first thing I must do is not only to revise my attitude toward the new, Michurinian science, but my entire earlier activity. . . . From tomorrow on I shall not only myself, in all my scientific activity, try to emancipate myself from the old reactionary Weissman-Morganian views, *but shall try to reform* and convince all my pupils and comrades.

"There is no denying that this will be an extremely dif-

ficult and painful process." (Statement by A. I. Alikhanian at the tenth and closing session, p. 621. My italics.)

I do not know how many copies of the Proceedings were printed in Russia, and how many of them were read. We do know that the press reported the outlines, with special emphasis on the "confessions." We may be certain that most teachers of biology and agrobiology in the universities and high schools read the précis, and drew their conclusions. Nor, we may be sure, did teachers of other branches of science fail to understand what the government was driving at. What, we must ask, can the effect be on the teaching of science in Russia, on the general educational system, on the capacity for objective thinking, for "an honest relationship to the task in hand"?

The pressure for quick results in science, the grading of scientific value by this single criterion, is not peculiar to communism or fascism. It is a capitalistic practice, too. But only under a totalitarian government does it become the law, with power to punish nonconformity. Only a totalitarian government can declare, in effect: "That theory of genetics is true, and honest, which produces the largest yield of millet, and anyone who denies it is an enemy of the nation and a corrupt person who must be treated accordingly." In the end such laws destroy science, and the harvest too. And even to say: "We have no interest in genetic theories that do not increase our harvests" is—except as a temporary emergency measure—a death-sentence against science.

There is not the slightest danger that a government of this kind will come to power in Israel. Certainly it is disturbing to come across the book published by the press of Hashomer Hatzair, *Lenin and the Physics of the Twentieth Century,* by one M. A. Umailianovsky (I am transliterating and re-translating from the Hebrew), which opens thus: "The physics of the twentieth century, the theories and discoveries of which have initiated a new era, cannot be properly explained and understood save in the light of dialectic materialism and the distinguished philosophic works of V. I. Lenin and J. Stalin." But it is disturbing only because in the kibbutzim of Hashomer Hatzair the young are segregated educationally in a party atmosphere —and the party is the one that published this book. It is one more powerful argument for the unification of Israel's educational system. The danger I am speaking of is, however, quite different. The degradation of science and crafts-manship can result from the mere absence of standards as much as from the imposition of an intellectual dictatorship. A disrespect for quality, in thinking as well as in service, is at bottom a disrespect for human beings, and therefore anti-democratic. Decay is a less spectacular form of destruction, but it is destruction none the less.

The pressure for immediate and spectacular results has always been a threat to solid Zionist achievement and to the molding of the character of the Jewish homeland. Weizmann sought to counter the threat with the double appeal to ancient Jewish tradition and modern Western science, but particularly to the second because it was unfamiliar to his people. He foresaw the dangers of political success before the state was achieved; he worried about the encouragement it would afford pretentiousness and quackery and jingoism; and he sought in science the spiritual technique of a corrective.

IV

It should already be clear that if Weizmann saw the scientific training as a national character builder he cannot have accepted the usual artificial distinction between "pure" and "applied" science. Actually he illustrated in his own life the interplay of the two on the most ordinary common-sense level.

As a young man, teaching biochemistry in Switzerland and in England, he made extra income by the invention of processes in the field of fermentation. As a mature man he achieved economic independence by these and allied discoveries. He could have become very wealthy if he had been so inclined, but he wanted only as much economic independence as would free him for Zionist work.

His scientific services to England in the first World War brought him contacts with statesmen of the first rank. The legend now runs that the Balfour Declaration was his reward for those services. The truth is more complicated —and more instructive. He had met and profoundly impressed Arthur James Balfour long before the First World War, and long before his scientific reputation was established. When war broke out he was systematically cultivating the friendship of influential Englishmen and bespeaking their support for a Jewish homeland. It was only later that he was called into the service of the Admiralty by Winston Churchill. Here, then, is no fairy tale of sudden achievement and Providential reward. Here was patient and assiduous preparation of background; his science and his Zionism played into each other over a stretch of many years. Without the prepared background he might not have been able to turn to Zionist purpose his scientific service to England; without the scientific service he might not have been able to extend the background and make effective use of it at the critical moment. To a thoughtful person there is infinitely greater meaning—and even dramatic appeal—in this picture of slow, persistent, inexorable pursuit of a purpose than in the rather childish fable of the miracle-man. Besides, the actuality is true to Weizmann's character and method, and the fable is not. But in any case we can, with a certain license, speak of the

Balfour Declaration too as a product of applied science.

Between 1921, when he became president of the World Zionist Organization, and 1949, when he became President of the State of Israel, Weizmann was out of office for two periods, 1931–5, and 1946–9. During these intervals of official freedom he concentrated on his scientific contribution; in the first he founded the Daniel Sieff Institute, in the second the Weizmann Institute. I saw very little of the beginnings of the Sieff Institute, but a great deal of the beginning and the development of the Weizmann Institute.

Weizmann had been a leading proponent of the idea of the Hebrew University in Herzl's time; he had laid the foundation stones of its first building in the midst of the First World War, and within sound of enemy guns; he had played his part—in prewar days—in the founding of the Haifa Technikum, which has developed into the magnificent Technion of today. But the Sieff and Weizmann Institutes were his own, personal enterprises, as it were. He poured into them a special devotion and affection. He wanted them to be the mirror of his Science-Zionism, the incorporation of his life's method and style, a restatement of his life's philosophy in the dynamic form of a creative institution.

The Daniel Sieff Institute was founded in 1931 on the initiative of a group of English friends of Weizmann. The Weizmann Institute, with which the Sieff Institute was incorporated, was the gift to Weizmann of a wider group, in which American Jews took the lead. It began with apparent casualness. Asked what kind of "present" he would like for his seventieth birthday—in 1944—Weizmann suggested the addition of a department to the Sieff Institute. Whether this modest proposal masked ambitious hopes that he intended to reveal in due course, I do not know, but Weizmann was always in favor of modest beginnings on which larger achievements could be erected securely. It was, however, not a favorable moment, in his own life, for the launching of a major enterprise calling for his personal supervision. He was still the president of the World Zionist Organization; he was engaged—as he had been in the other war nearly three decades earlier—in scientific work for Britain. He was also shuttling back and forth between England and the United States, interweaving his scientific with his Zionist activity, making use of the contacts created by the first for the furtherance of the second. Possibly he did not foresee an opportunity to do more than improve the modest equipment of the Sieff Institute.

As things turned out, the founding of the Weizmann Institute was in the sum an act of great moral and political significance, which we can appreciate only by recalling the circumstances attending it.

The plans were drawn up in a time of hope; they were executed in a time of desperation. For the year 1944 was bright with promise for the Zionist dream, and the years between 1945 and 1948 were black with England's eclipse of the dream. This miserable interlude, which all of us recall with a shudder, was the time of the anti-British terror, of the impulse to stake the existence of the home-land on the throw of a bomb; it was the time of the rejection of normal values and processes, a time of cynical rage and contempt, a time that left a scar on the physiognomy of the homeland. Still, the great majority of Palestinian Jews supported the steadfast, disciplined, calculated people's resistance directed by the Labor leadership that subsequently became the government; and constructive work went on despite the feverish mood of the country and the provocations of the terrorists. The development of the Weizmann Institute in those years, the actual official opening in 1947, the implied faith both in the future and in the scientific spirit, were the highest symbols of the constructive will in Zionism.

There was something awesome and monumental, too, in the spectacle of the man, Weizmann, his motions already slowed up by age and by failing eyesight, but his mind still combining the vigor of his youth with the farsightedness of a rich maturity, confronting the special challenge. We did not look too far ahead in those days; we certainly did not foresee the republic in its present form; we only knew that if there was hope we should find it still in the example that Weizmann had set and was setting. I think of Weizmann in those years as standing at the peak of his career, embodying an undiscourageable purpose that had about it a suggestion of a nature phenomenon. As an act in itself, the creation of the Weizmann Institute was perhaps the supreme achievement of his life.

V

Those that worked with Weizmann in this creation— laymen as well as scientists—found their minds broadened by the experience; not even the most gifted of his collaborators had his total vision of the form and meaning of the enterprise. For me, completely the layman, and more a close observer than a collaborator, it was an education; it was also a new revelation of Weizmann, the man of style. I had never appreciated to what an extent the human and the technical are interwoven in a scientific center. The human here means surroundings, inspiration, an atmosphere of corporate responsibility, the conscious acceptance of a tradition that is yet to be molded. The grounds of the Weizmann Institute, its residential buildings, its lawns and retreats, were to him equipment in practically the same sense as a mass spectrometer or an ultracentrifuge.

Even visitors had to feel that here was a special place, the exterior of which predisposed the mind to its inner purpose. Charm and neatness become a scientific institute as grace becomes an athlete. Congeniality of physical and human surroundings is a stimulus to mind and will; and Weizmann was fond of quoting the great German chemist Willstetter, who had advised him in the founding of the Sieff Institute: "One good clubhouse is worth two laboratories."

He sought out for the institute good Jews who were good scientists, and he found many. He would settle for a good scientist who was not a good Jew; but he would never accept a good Jew who was not a good scientist. Scientific research means teamwork, and teamwork means fellowship, and fellowship, in turn, implies the social sense. It is difficult to conceive of a good scientist who has no feeling for the organic relationship between his institution and the society in which it functions. The Weizmann Institute came to being in a specific setting; its responsibilities to pure science could only be defined in terms of the setting. The needs of the society, the opportunities afforded by physical surroundings, that is, by natural resources, the suggestions and stimulations which issued from the condition of the society—all these would be reflected in the interests of the true scientist. One might therefore say that Jewishness is irrelevant except in so far as it brings a scientist to the institute.

The social awareness of the scientist, which makes him responsive to his immediate environment, implies also a responsiveness to the world environment of science. The immediate environment, Israel, directs the attention of the Weizmann Institute to problems in geophysics, because of the local search for oil; to problems in the chemistry of proteins, because of the local shortage of meat and the lack of grazing areas; to the problems of plastics, because of the local possibility of providing the relevant raw material; to problems in pharmaceuticals, because of the resources of the Dead Sea; and with these practical problems, and many more of the kind, are bound up allied research departments, mathematics, crystallography, spectrometry, all dovetailing. The world environment directs the attention of the scientists to problems not peculiarly local—the search for the causes of cancer, and its control or cure, the investigation of the behavior of liquified hydrogen near the absolute zero. But the world environment also produces the intellectual climate of the scientific age; and unless the Weizmann Institute is as sensitive to world research as it is to local needs, it must wither into an isolated parochial school.

The delicate balance between applied and pure science is not maintained by formula or program; it is a natural function of the healthy activity of a science center. Sometimes the balance will shift toward the immediately practical; sometimes toward the general theoretical. This is a *human* matter, not an algebraic or philosophical formula. But always there is a balance, that is to say, at no time does one activity overwhelm the other.

And because it is a human matter, because it is a composite of winged mind and earthbound needs, it must be dealt with in a human environment conducive to friendly interchanges.

VI

The Chalutzim of thirty and forty years ago had a general as well as a Jewish fascination for me. I used to say: "So *this* is how man spreads over the earth, overcoming the infertility of the wilderness, making it serve his physical and spiritual needs." The same fascination was attached to the birth of the Sieff and Weizmann Institutes—as they are, indeed, to the other educational centers of Israel. "This is how science pioneers in a new country, this is how the craftsmanship of the knowledge and the management of nature spreads to new areas." There is a far-reaching parallel between the two processes, revealed by questions that were asked about the pioneers, and which were asked about the Weizmann Institute of Science.

In the days of primitive Zionism the Jewish land worker in Palestine was often regarded as an exotic and largely useless romantic. Clever Jews of the Western world, coming into Palestine, should not, it was said, have to revert to peasantry; they should be managers, merchants, organizers. Ordinary laborers could be hired from among the Arabs.

If it was not put into so many words, the philosophy of it was implicit among settlers of fifty and sixty years ago. It did not die easily, either. For in another form it threatened the structure of the Jewish homeland when the entire notion of agriculture was played down in favor of overwhelming urban development.

With regard to the Weizmann Institute I have more than once heard the question: "*Must* we have such a highly developed science center of our own, the best in the entire Near East? Can't we hire our specialists? Can't we import experts?" The same answer applies to the old and the new questioners: "One can hire laborers and import experts. One cannot hire loyalty or import character."

The Hebrew University had its opponents: "It is a luxury that will have to wait." But the Hebrew University had one good argument—Jewish students were excluded from other universities. The technical school of Haifa, like the Hadassah Medical School, also had easier going. The need for local engineers and doctors is obvious. But a science center on the level of the Weizmann Institute . . .

Granted that some of the work would be useful, still, abstract science, problems that had nothing to do with the development of Israel, would have to wait. I used to wonder why the people who had these objections did not also object to rabbis and poets in Palestine as premature indulgences. True, rabbis and poets are less expensive than research workers; but they are so much more numerous.

As with *Chalutziut,* so with science, Weizmann saw the whole, and saw it steadily. He saw the village not simply as the producer of bread; it was the cradle of character. He thought of the research center not simply as an association of specialists, industrially useful and intellectually decorative. He thought of it as character. The spirit of the center was to pervade the whole country. Its sober attitude toward its all-embracing craft, its insistence on standards of performance, its rejection of the showy, the pretentious, and the shoddy, was to affect the schools, and through the schools the coming generations. It was to be a safeguard against Levantinization. In this sense the usefulness of the Institute is irreplaceable, as well as incalculable.

VII

I have spent many happy days at the Weizmann Institute, among its scientists and apparatus. Now and again it has lifted me into a mood like the one I experienced among the young Chalutzim on the shore of western Galilee. Here too an earnest search is in progress; and here too the ends and means are one, the purity of the search is both instrument and purpose. Again, here as there I have had glimpses of the great cycle of time and purpose in which the Zionist movement has its origins and direction.

I have, in these pages, used the juxtaposition "East-

West" in a variety of senses. Sometimes I have meant the Moslem and Christian worlds; sometimes the Occident and Orient generally; sometimes, in the recent and journalistic usage, Russian totalitarianism versus American-led democracy. I speak now of East and West in the sense of Hebrew and Greek.

The story of these ancient strains as they are intertwined in Western civilization is a familiar one. It played a part in fundamental Zionist ideology—that ideology which suffering, need, and shock have thrust so deeply into the background. In a less harassed generation, Zionists who looked on history as an evolving meaning against the background of millennia thought of a third Jewish commonwealth as a reconciliation—"the wisdom of Javan (the Ionian, or Greek) in the tents of Jacob." Weizmann brooded on these far-reaching associations, combining the pensiveness of the philosopher with the alertness of the statesman. He wanted the homeland to fuse the primal moral tradition of the Hebrews with the speculative restlessness of the Greeks. He saw it practically: you could not rebuild Palestine without the combination of faith and science. Beyond the practical, however, or I should say in a larger view of practicality, the reconciliation of Greek and Hebrew, as exemplified in an ideal Jewish homeland, was the next stage in the progress of civilization.

In the creation of the model, or prototype, the Jews of the world, drawing on the best of Western democracy, were to be equal partners with the Jews of the homeland. To this combination Weizmann pointed the way by anticipation; he was himself the symbiosis; he was Zionism in fulfillment.

CHAPTER XX

The Summing Up

❊

I

I wrote the first draft of this book in Israel during the spring and summer of 1952; I wrote the second and last draft in America during the ensuing half year, leaving the opening chapter unchanged, as a memento. In the midst of the re-writing came the news of Weizmann's death, and I suspended the work for a few days in order to rest my mind in the memory of him. It was a kind of informal *shivah*.

I did not keep the house, and sit on a low stool in stockinged feet, according to the traditional prescription. I traveled about my affairs, but most of the time my thoughts were with him, and once again, as in Rechovot, where I watched his house in morning and evening sunlight, I saw my own life enclosed within the span and purpose of his. Once again I felt—and this time more strongly, and as it were by official notification—the closing of an epoch.

As far as we Jews are concerned you might call it the epoch of our last chance. Weizmann's childhood saw the beginning of the great migration to America; in his last years the Jewish State was established. Had these things not been accomplished when they were, they would never have been accomplished at all. We squeezed through into survival by the historical margin of a lifetime.

But it was, in spite of our frightful loss of blood, something more than mere physical survival. What we rescued out of our downgoing in Europe was not simply millions of individuals; we rescued the elements of our ancient peoplehood and the promise of a spiritual continuity. This is what matters, and this is what Weizmann represented.

A figure that recurred persistently to me in my meditations on Weizmann was Jochanan ben Zakkai. This Rabbi, who lived in the time of the second destruction, took thought for the preservation of the spirit of his people, foreseeing that if the Jews relied on force alone, they would vanish from the face of the earth. While the Romans were besieging Jerusalem he founded the academy at Yabneh, and with his name more than any other is associated the system of intellectual and spiritual disciplines which has held the Jewish people together since his day.

Except for the fact that Weizmann had often expressed a preference for ben Zakkai the scholar over bar Kochba the warrior, the recurrence of the parallel was puzzling, until I considered the similarities which the very dissimilarities suggested. Ben Zakkai lived in an epoch when the Jewish State was being dismantled, Weizmann during an epoch when it was being reassembled. Ben Zakkai was the scholar, Weizmann was the man of action. But if it was the Jewish State that was being destroyed in ben Zakkai's time, it was the Jewish people that was being destroyed in Weizmann's. If ben Zakkai was the scholar, his scholarship was the highest statesmanship of the time. If Weizmann was the man of action, his primary concern was with the spirit of his people. Ben Zakkai stole out of besieged Jerusalem and begged the Roman conqueror for the apparently innocuous privilege of opening a school; Weizmann went up to liberated Jerusalem while northern Palestine was still in the enemy's hands, for the apparently useless purpose of laying the foundation stones of the Hebrew University. Neither Titus the destroyer nor Allenby the liberator understood what was afoot. But as Jochanan ben Zakkai was determined that the Jews should not cease to be Jews because they had lost their state, so Weizmann was determined that they should not cease to be Jews because they had regained it.

Ben Zakkai is a mnemonic of history, the symbol of a process. The creation of the disciplines that preserved the Jewish people in exile began before his time, and was completed after him. Other great spirits contributed, and with them masses of the obscure. But tradition rightly focusses attention on ben Zakkai because at the one fitting moment which would never recur again he crystallized the process in the unforgettable act. So with Weizmann: great spirits and obscure masses were the artificers of the Zionism he believed in. He became its symbol because in the crucial epoch his entire life was the process in action.

The difficulty in comparing the dead of long ago with the recently dead lies in the fact that of the recently dead we know only one half of their lives—the half just ended. The other and larger half is yet to be lived, and we have to guess at its length, its weightiness, and its pattern. Strange things can happen. It is impossible to doubt that men whose names are forgotten have been important factors in the shaping of human events. We also know that history and legend seize on certain names and endow them with a lasting force that has nothing to do with what their owners really did; and you may talk and write yourself blue in the face, you will never correct the usurpation. On the other hand there are historical figures who have been successfully "reinterpreted," and henceforth have exercised a different influence, perhaps more in line with what they really were, perhaps not. Of Weizmann we can say that he certainly will not be forgotten; the second half of his life will be very long; it will also be weighty, that is, influential. But we cannot be so sure that his memory will not be distorted, that his name will not be used for purposes he would have rejected. The image which Israel and world Jewry will retain of him a hundred years from now will be the answer to the questions I set out with. The character of the Jewish people will be revealed by what it thinks of Weizmann.

II

I followed all the newspaper reports of the obsequies, and later received many accounts from friends who attended them. These shadows and echoes were my substitute participation in the rituals that channel the grief of personal loss into wider sympathies and deeper understanding.

He was buried with the pomp that befits the head of a state: with lowered flags, and gunfire, and public mourning, and arrayed troops, and processions of ministers and diplomats. The draped catafalque was erected in the garden of his home, below the stone balcony—more rampart than balcony—on which he used to sit, brooding over the green fields of Judea and the desert hills of Trans-Jordan in the distance. Relays of sentinels stood at attention about the catafalque two days and two nights. When the time came to remove the body to the nearby grave among young olive and fruit trees planted for his seventieth and seventy-fifth birthdays, the coffin was borne by eight high officers of the Israeli Defense Force. Three field guns in the nearby wood fired twenty-one salvos in a last salute.

Interwoven with these, the solemn tributes of the modern state, were the immemorial rites and prayers of the Jewish tradition. But in these, too, the remains of Chaim, son of Ozer and Rachel Weizmann, of the village of Motol, in Pinsk, were treated with the high ceremonial reserved for the elect of a free people. By special dispensation a portion of the estate had just been consecrated as his individual House of Life, his cemetery. The military chaplain and a *minyan* of Rabbis had circled it seven times to the accompaniment of the appropriate prayers and the prescribed blasts on the *shofar;* and the farewell prayer at the graveside had closed with these exalted words: "May his soul be bound up in everlasting life with the souls of the Kings of the House of David and the Princes of Israel, the holy and the mighty, until the end of days."

During the time of the lying-in-state there flowed in from the governments of the world, from the friendly, the indifferent, and the hostile alike, the courteous expressions of condolence which are international protocol. About these, as about the grave and moving choreography of the obsequies, there was nothing singular, in view of the dead man's official status, except this: for the first time the minimum of international form, the compulsion of the last propriety, applied automatically to a Jewish as to any other leader. It may not be worth much; but how much labor, how much anguish and frustration has gone into the securing of it! And how much it means, by that token, at least to the recipients.

Two months after Weizmann's death I received the *In Memoriam* volume issued by the government of Israel, and here, in a sampling of the world's press comment, was something more significant than the appropriate symbolism of state funeral rites and international protocol. I was well aware of Weizmann's standing in the world at large; nevertheless I was startled by the reverberations that followed his death—by this renewed demonstration of the disproportion between the apparently limited field of his endeavor and the universal admiration that he had won in it. For he had been concerned with a small people—one might even say with a section of that people—and with a very small territory. In a world of colossi he, who might have allied himself with one of them, had chosen to work in miniature; and lo, in the end, his name towered among the highest. So much was clear from what they wrote about him in New York and Washington, in London, and Ottawa, and Paris, and Buenos Aires, and Copenhagen, and Rome. For these were not merely respectful obituaries of a man of distinction: you would have said that every one of the writers had known at first hand the magic of his greatness; and indeed, many of them had. But the impress he left went beyond the personal and the Jewish. He had managed, in the mysterious fashion of spiritual genius, to irradiate the time with the effect of his presence. "The death of Chaim Weizmann, President of Israel, has removed from our midst one of the titans of this century. . . ." "His moral force was so great and so concentrated . . . that the vast disparity between his gifts and his material power was scarcely felt. . . ." "All people with hopes and dreams in their hearts may say 'Know ye not that there is a prince and a great man fallen this day in Israel. . . .'" There is a lifting of the heart even among strangers in the recollection of this man's life.

I have often wondered at those of my fellow Jews who have turned away from the problems of their people with a shudder of intellectual and spiritual claustrophobia. They have protested that they need, in order to occupy their capacities and satisfy their sense of service, a wider area than we offer. Their protests are often sincere; it is their sense of instrumentality which is at fault. And I too am a victim of this error when I marvel at the contrast between the numerical insignificance of those whom Weizmann gave his life to, and the vastness of the numbers whom he benefitted indirectly. Certainly the world is physically at the mercy of the giant nations; but that is no reason why little nations should not be the matrices of significant movements, and influences, and men.

But not even Weizmann's impact on the world at large gives us the measure of him. It is no small thing to have brought a momentary touch of grandeur into many lives, but this effect was incidental with him. It was not what he was aiming at. Only one thing mattered to him—the destiny of Jewry and Judaism. To the extent that men glimpsed through him the potentialities and hopes of his people, he was glad to have impressed them; but only to that extent. One obituary notice of him says: "His vibrant, eloquent voice, lowered for emphasis, cutting deftly through details to the essential, was one of the greatest one-man propaganda instruments in history." No doubt it was. For that matter the whole of Weizmann was "one of the greatest one-man propaganda instruments in history." But even if we use the word "propaganda" in an honorable sense, this is not the way he wanted to be thought about. He did not want to leave the impression of having left a great impression. He had a more important purpose in mind.

Many reputations are nothing but achievements in reputation; their owners are famous for their fame, and are content to have it so. Weizmann was too profoundly purposive—and ironical—to fall a victim to such vanity. Nor does the description fit his reputation. He took pleasure in his fame—the craftsman's pleasure, in which the instrument and the objective, the means and the end, are harmoniously blended. He wanted the instrument to be identified with the objective, not with the craftsman.

How, then, can we get his true measure? In the last analysis, only by an intimate study of his objective, which was the renewal of Jewry's destiny. This may be asking a great deal, but how do we get an authentic, first-hand picture of any man's intrinsic greatness if not by studying his

subject matter and his relationship to it? Qualified phi-
losophers assure us of Plato's greatness, and mathemati-
cians of Einstein's. We assume the greatness is there, but
we cannot taste it on the palate of understanding without
a knowledge of philosophy and mathematics. We are
moved by hearsay, not by the substance; we are shaken by
the fever of others.

And yet I have just said that many have known the
magic of Weizmann's greatness merely from a meeting
with him; that he irradiated the time with the effect of his
presence; that there is a lifting of the heart even among
strangers in the recollection of this man's life. Is not this
itself intrinsic greatness, irrespective of the particular purpose to which it was harnessed? Yes, it is intrinsic greatness, but not irrespective of the purpose. Those who have
been moved, in personal encounter or through hearsay,
by the personality of Weizmann, are perhaps not aware
that the source of the emotion was not the man, but the
ideal that found perfect expression in him. The first will
speak of his charm, his skill, his aplomb, the irresistible
suggestion of dignity and grace which he made his listeners
share with him; the second will speak with wonder of the
reports given by the first; and both will have something to
say about the spectacular aspects of his career. They will
all be stirred by a sense of the unusual and exalted, and
they will transmit to later times the rumor that becomes
the legend. But the understanding of Weizmann's greatness lies in the knowledge of what he was to the Jewish
people; and that is a long, long story to which this book is
a brief, imperfect, and premature introduction.

I saw many photographs of the lying-in-state, and I
looked longest at those of the plain people who had come
—hundreds of thousands of them—from the cities and villages, from Galilee and the Emek and the Negev, to pay
their last respects; careworn faces and threadbare clothes

and shapeless shoes; old women in kerchiefs, their deep-sunken eyes staring across God knows what vistas of mem· ory at the draped catafalque; workers with stern lips and gnarled hands; professionals with furrowed brows; school-children awed by the solemnity of the surroundings and by the weeping of the grownups. *Amcho*—Thy people. Here was Weizmann's everlasting love, the bedrock of his faith, the object of his sleepless concern, the source of his measureless will power; this was his crushing burden and his never-failing inspiration. He knew thousands of them —but literally thousands—by name and place and personal history; old Chalutzim of Nahalal and Ain Charod, farmers of Rehovoth and Haderah, artisans and laborers of Tel Aviv and Haifa, shopkeepers, doctors, teachers, chauffeurs, men and women of the Haganah, the ultimate substance through which the meaning of Jewish history was to make itself manifest. And not these alone; he knew and loved their like in Johannesburg and Bulawayo, in New York, and Montreal, and San Francisco, in Manchester, London, Paris, Rome. He remembered still others—again by name and personal history—among the millions who had died before or in the great holocaust; out of his childhood in Motol and Pinsk, out of his visits to Warsaw and Bucharest, from countless congresses and conferences and campaigns and committee meetings and mass meetings. He was soaked in the Jewish masses.

He kept his state because that is the way of the world between the representatives of peoples, and he kept it fault-lessly, out of innate kingliness, out of a liking and a capacity for what was becoming and symbolic. He was at home among the great, but the masses were his home. Like a perpetual ambassador he could seldom be in his home, but you had only to see him there to know where his heart was. Not that his kingliness left him even there, but it was a *heimish,* a homey kingliness, which invited love, and trust, and equality.

This invitation went out from him equally to all whom he met, and if it was sometimes abused, it was not by the common people. His simple courtesy was misunderstood by those who had prominence without eminence, and they disliked him because they could not force his intimacy on their level and for their purpose. They wanted servility, not courtesy—the special treatment that would teach others their place. With these Weizmann returned dislike for dislike—with these and with all careerists. He would not toady to them. But neither did he toady to the masses —for he loved them.

There is only one true love—the one that cherishes and encourages, above all other things, the goodness that is in the beloved. Such was Weizmann's love of the Jewish masses. The easygoing and the indulgent (let alone the ambitious) are incapable of true love; their hearts are set on popularity, which is self-love, or self-regarding love. They have their reward, for the masses meet self-regarding love with self-regarding love, to the mutual undoing of the leader and the led.

Weizmann's insistence on Jewish quality was an expression of love, and in this he was authentically Prophetic, however he might differ from the conventional picture of the Prophets themselves. Sometimes we rebelled against the severity of his demands, only to discover later that our own leniency was weakness. The last time I saw him, in the the fall of 1951, I experienced one of these twinges of impatience. I had come back from a tour of the north, the day before my departure for America. I had seen again the outposts in the famous hill country, and I had looked down from the heights of Menara into the Huleh Valley, thirty years ago a waste, now decorated, like a gigantic bowl of earthenware, with the green patterns of our villages. I had looked only at the good, and closed my eyes to dangers. On the ride down from Haifa, along the Sharon Plain, I had thought of the cultivated and intelligent people in the colonies; I had thought of the bright side of the cities, of labor leaders who have a lively interest in music and art and literature, of manufacturers who quote Isaiah and Dostoievsky and Kant, of members of Parliament bristling with Biblical and Talmudic verses; of shopkeepers and workers to whom books and concerts are as necessary as bread; of the groups who will not traffic on the black market, of those who are alien to chauvinistic pride. I thought of the shepherdess, in the Valley of Jezreel who had suffered almost to death in the Maquis, and now writes her French verses while she tends her flocks between Carmel and Gilboa; of volunteers of the Solel Boneh sweating in the copper mines near the Egyptian border paying a regular toll of lives to marauders, and refusing to withdraw. Of all these I thought, and put the rest out of my mind. And late that evening, after I had taken farewell of Weizmann, I strolled through Rechovot. The hot *hamsin* that had tormented us for three days had broken. The air now blew from the sea, cool by comparison, and the town was out. The crowds on the sidewalks and at the sidewalk cafés were lively in a dozen languages, with Hebrew predominating, especially among the young. It was pleasant to mingle with them, be of them. But I was haunted by the recollection of the brooding, failing old man in the wheel chair, and of his ceaseless warnings. I said to myself: "What does he want of this people of Israel? Why is he so despondent about it? Let him rejoice for the remnant that has been saved, according to the promise, and ask nothing but that it live."

But round about midnight, when I had finished my notes for the day, I opened the Bible and almost instinctively turned to the book of Deuteronomy and the story of the last days of Moses; and I marveled again at this picture of the greatest of all human leaders, the most loving and the most farsighted, the most compassionate and the most demanding, whose last words to his people were a balancing of accounts, promise and admonition, blessing and curse, without concession to national conceit and the self-adulation of the mob. He said of himself, just before his death: "I am an hundred and twenty years old this day, I can no more go out and come in." But his spirit was as fresh as when he led Israel out of Egypt, his standards were as high. It is a daring, perhaps a blasphemous comparison, and Weizmann would not have thought of it. Perhaps we may.

III

It was his wish to be buried near his own house, within sight of the institute, that child of his old age. The government honored his wish; moreover it decided to convert the entire area of the estate and the institute into an active and living memorial to be named *Yad Weizmann,* for the cultivation of the arts and sciences. It is a courageous thing, and in the spirit of Weizmann, to find the strength, in the midst of want and danger, for such an enterprise. He was the type whom dead monuments cannot represent; only a center of learning which both symbolizes and realizes his incorporation with the Jewish future could be his proper memorial. But the *Yad Weizmann* will fail of its purpose if it does not become a center of renewal for the whole of world Jewry. The man who lies buried there would not have understood a narrower compass.

INDEX

Achad Ha-Am: as influence in Zionism, 8, 9, 232, 233; and Bnai Moshe, 221
Aleph, 205
America: as savior of Jewry, 242 ff.; role in creation of Israel, 246 ff.; and racial prejudice, 255 ff.; American ideals and Israel, 269 ff.
American Jewry: and Israel, 197 ff.; as seen by Israelis, 197 ff.; recent evolution of, 229 ff.; reaction from assimilation, 232 ff.; attitude toward America, 242 ff.; influence on Israel, 273 ff.; role in Israel, 267 ff.
anti-Semitism: character and sources of, 16, 17, 253 ff.; and Zionism, 38, 39, 56, 57; and Prague trials, 124; and Communism, 243 ff.; and totalitarianism, 204 ff.; in America, 253 ff.
assimilation: in American Jewry, 229 ff.
Arabs: attempt to reach understanding with, 53; their threat to Israel, 55; their refugee problem, 68 ff.
army, Israeli: as educator, 159 ff.

Balfour, Arthur James: meeting with Weizmann, 283
ben Gurion, David: on danger of Levantinization, 68; and *Kibbutz Galuyot*, 69, 70; on liberation struggle, 174
Bialik, Chaim Nachman, 8, 33; and *Oneg Shabbat*, 153; on Jewish criminals, 154; on Book of Jonah, etc., 148–50; on kibbutzim, 150 ff.
Brandeis, Louis D., 6, 32; controversy with Weizmann, 22, 25; views on Zionism, 25 ff.; on kibbutzim, 47
British Labour Party: its Zionist record, 54, 74

"Canaanites," 205 ff.
Cecil, Lord Robert, 17
Chalutzim: ideals and theories of, 35 ff., 82 ff.; and anti-Semitism, 38; as viewed by general Zionists, 48 ff.; function as colonizers, 51–2, 78 ff.
Chalutziut, 37
Chevrat Ovdim, 166 ff.
Chomah u-Migdal, 138

Christianity: relation to Judaism, 16
collectives, *see* kibbutzim
communal meals: costs of, 111 ff.
Communism: effect on Zionism, 57 ff.; effect on captive Jewries, 243 ff.
co-operatives, structure of, 167 ff.
criminality, in Israel, 154 ff.

Dreyfus affair, 28, 29

Feisal, Emir, 53, 268

Gegenwartsarbeit, 223
Gentleman and the Jew, The, 16
God that Failed, The, 187
Great Britain, as Mandatory Power, 54

Hadassah, Women's Zionist Organization, 240
Haganah: as people's resistance, 72 ff.; as forerunner of army, 174
Hashomer Hatzair, 121 ff.; and American Jewry, 199 ff.; and education of young, 281 ff.
Hebrew University: Weizmann's part in, 284
Herzl, Theodore, 19; Weizmann's opposition to, 29 ff.; and Uganda controversy, 29–30; and practical work in Palestine, 31, 32; and the *Judennot*, 215
Hirsch, Baron de, as colonizer, 79
Histadrut: character of, 166 ff.; as state-creator, 172 ff.; in liberation struggle, 173 ff.; successes and failures, 175 ff.; future of, 183 ff.
Hitler, 37; effect on Zionism, 57 ff.

Ichud ha-Kibbutzim, 121 ff.
Israel: relation to American Jewry, 264 ff.
Israelis: views on American Jewry, 238

Jabotinsky, Vladimir: Weizmann's opposition to, 28; as Zionist maximalist, 31, 32
Jewish National Fund, 52

Kattowicz Conference, 52
Kibbutz Artzi, 121
Kibbush avodah, 180
Kibbutz Galuyot, 61 ff., 75, 76

Kibbutz Ha-Meuchad, 121 ff.
kibbutzim: beginnings, 40; early
theories and modifications, 41 ff.;
opposition to, 45–7; social theories and forms, 81 ff.; modifications, 94 ff.; renewed opposition
to, 100 ff.; development and present state, 108 ff.; costs of, 111;
hired workers in, 113 ff.; problems of "surplus value" in, 113 ff.;
and new immigration, 114 ff.; and
Arab labor, 123; and East-West
split, 121 ff., 130 ff.; struggle for
schools in, 127 ff.; and black market, 133; adaptability in past,
136 ff.; makeup of new, 140 ff.; attitudes of young, 141 ff.; variant
form, 144; future of, 133 ff.; proposed liquidation of, 139 ff.
Koestler, Arthur, 162–3
kumsitz, 95 ff.
Kupat Cholim, 185

Levin, Shmarya, 8, 9, 33; on Jewish
racism, 22; and *Oneg Shabbat*,
153
labor leaders, 181 ff.
Lenin Academy of Agricultural Sciences of U.S.S.R., Proceedings of,
277 ff.

Manchester: Rumanian ghetto in,
9
Mann, Thomas, on Jacob and Eli-
phaz, 164–5
Mapam, 121 ff.; and American
Jewry, 199 ff.
Marshal, Louis, 215
Marx, Karl, 36, 37
Michurinism, 277 ff.
militarism, 158 ff., 162 ff.
moshav ovdim: theory and form,
87 ff.; and new immigration, 135
Motzkin, Leo, 33
Mufti of Jerusalem, and uprising of
1936, 137
Mussolini, 37

Nahalal, 87
nationalism: and Zionism, 224 ff.
Ness Zionah, 3, 4
Nordau, Max, 33

Oneg Shabbat, in Tel Aviv, 153

Palmach, 159
Polish Jewry: contacts with, 23, 24

Proceedings of Lenin Academy of
Agricultural Sciences of U.S.S.R.,
277 ff.

Rishon-le-Zion, 3, 4
Rothschild, Baron Edmond de, 6;
support of colonization, 47, 48,
80, 81
Ruthenberg, Pinchas, 32

science, role in Israel, 275 ff.
Shomer, 53
Sieff Institute, 284
Solel Boneh: constitution of, 167;
controversy over, 168 ff.; future
of, 183 ff.
Szold, Henrietta, 103

terrorists, 53, 71 ff.
The Gentleman and the Jew, 16
The God that Failed, 187
totalitarianism. and anti-Semitism,
245 ff.
transport co-operatives: achievements and failures, 175 ff.

Uganda, controversy over, 29, 30
Ussishkin, Menachem Mendel, 33

Warburg, Felix, 47, 81
Weizmann, Chaim: first meetings
with, 4, 8; renewed contact with,
22; personality, 5 ff., 225 ff., 300 ff.;
before United Nations Special
Committee, 70 ff.; his *Yiddishkeit*, 10, 11; as fusion of East and
West, 6 ff.; sense of form, 7, 45;
family background, 91 ff.; and
Achad Ha-Amism, 33, 34; controversy with Brandeis, 22, 25 ff.;
views on terrorism, 71 ff.; as fund-
raiser, 217 ff.; views on kibbutzim
and moshavim, 90 ff., 106; and
Kibbutz Galuyot, 65 ff.; on postwar immigration, 275 ff.; relation
to Jewish nationalism, 225 ff.; on
science and Israel, 275 ff.; on science and Zionism, 282 ff.; and
Technion, 284; on craftsmanship,
275 ff.; on Presidency, 75; last
sickness, 11 ff.; death, 292; obsequies, 295 ff.; world reaction to
his death, 296 ff.; place in Jewish
history, 293 ff.
Weizmann Institute of Science:
284 ff.
Wise, Stephen S., 7
workmanship, standards of, 188 ff.

Yad Weizmann, 303
Yelide Aretz, 206
Yiddish: views of Chalutzim on, 38, 39
You Gentiles, 16
Youth Aliyah, 103

Zangwill, Israel, 6, 33
Zionism: as represented by Weizmann, 5 ff.; first contacts with, 15,

Zionism *(continued)*
17; as renaissance movement, 19–21; as renaissance of world Jewry, 43, 44; versus inertia of Jewish masses, 49, 50; role of persecution in, 18; as refugee movement, 29, 30; and east European Jewry, 23–5; development in America, 214 ff.

A NOTE ON THE TYPE USED IN THIS BOOK

The text of this book has been set on the Linotype in a type-face called "Baskerville." The face is a facsimile reproduction of types cast from molds made for John Baskerville (1706–1775) from his designs. The punches for the revived Linotype Baskerville were cut under the supervision of the English printer George W. Jones.

John Baskerville's original face was one of the forerunners of the type-style known as "modern face" to printers: a "modern" of the period A.D. 1800.